HYDERABAD

Hyderabad

The Social Context of Industrialisation, 1875–1948

C.V. SUBBA RAO

Orient Longman

ORIENT LONGMAN PRIVATE LIMITED

Registered Office
3-6-752 Himayatnagar, Hyderabad 500 029 (A.P.), INDIA
e-mail: cogeneral@orientlongman.com

Other Offices
Bangalore, Bhopal, Bhubaneshwar, Chennai, Ernakulam, Guwahati, Hyderabad, Jaipur, Kolkata, Lucknow, Mumbai, New Delhi, Patna

First Published 2007

ISBN 13: 978 81 250 1565 9
ISBN 10: 81 250 1565 5

Typeset in 11/13 pt. Adobe Garamond

Typeset by
Scribe Consultants
New Delhi

Printed in India at
Chaman Enterprises
New Delhi

Published by
Orient Longman Private Limited
1/24 Asaf Ali Road
New Delhi 110 002
e-mail: delgeneral@orientlongman.com

Contents

List of Tables		vii
Preface		ix
Abbreviations		xii
A Note on the Author		xiii
Introduction		xv

Section I
State and Society: A Prelude

ONE	Social Framework	3
	1-A Indigenous Industry and Trade	
TWO	Salar Jung and the State	23

Section II
Industrialisation 1875–1948

THREE	Evolution	37
	3-A Statistical Tables	
	3-B The Industrial Base of Hyderabad	
FOUR	Capital	68
	4-A Capital: A Statistical Review	
FIVE	Labour	93
	5-A Labour: A Statistical Review	

SIX Appraisal 114
6-A Statistical Tables
6-B Industrial Growth: A Statistical Review

Section III
State and Society 1875–1950

SEVEN Social Framework 143
7-A Statistical Tables
7-B Commercialisation of Agriculture

EIGHT Crisis and Collapse 178

NINE Conclusion 187

Bibliography 190

Glossary 205

Index 211

List of Tables

3.1 Hyderabad in India: A Profile
3.2 Industry in 1947: India, Pakistan and Hyderabad
3.3 Loans to Small-Scale Industries: 1930–1945
3.4 Dispersal of Industries: District-wise Break-up, 1911–1949
4.1 Distribution of Corporate Capital: 1921–1945
4.2 Capital in the Corporate Sector: Index of Growth: 1921–1945
4.3 Changes in Corporate Capital: 1921–1945
4.4 State Aid to the Corporate Sector: 1929–50
5.1 Occupational Structure: 1901–1941
5.2 Growth of Labour Force in Organised Industry: 1930–45
5.3 Structure of Industrial Labour Force: 1930–45
5.4 Female Labour in Industry: 1901–1941
5.5 Labour Force in Organised Industry: Index of Growth, 1930–1945
6.1 External Trade: 1882–1950
6.2 Changing Composition of Trade: 1912–1951
6.3 Composition of Industries: 1900–1952
6.4 Growth of Labour Force: 1930–1948
6.5 Capital Intensity: Select Industries
6.6 Industrial Output
7.1 Patterns in Public Expenditure: 1900–1948
7.2 Patterns in Revenue Receipts: 1900–1948

7.3 Acreage by Crop: Index of Growth, 1925–1950
7.4 Cropping Pattern 1920–1950 (Percentages)
7.5 Index of Agricultural Output: 1925–1950
7.6 Prices, Acreage and Output: Select Commodities, 1926–1945
7.7 Index of Agricultural Prices: 1921–1944
7.8 Agricultural Prices: 1941–1948

Preface

Hyderabad City, like so many other feudal capitals. evokes images of charm and romance. Its grandeur and splendour woven with legend, continue to inspire contemporary folklore. Those who have lived there, at one time or another, like the present author, themselves perpetuate these images that survive even outside the elegantly printed brochures of the tourist department. But these images are part of a self-perpetuating mythology created by the literate. The romance of the city has now degenerated into disease and one has seen, in the words of a poet, 'even the messiah afflicted by it'. Now it is necessary to transcend the barriers created by inherited images to understand the dynamics of a disease-ridden society and its people. But any attempt to transcend these powerful romantic images that are being continuously remoulded by a not so romantic contemporary society, with as arid an account as economic history is bound to be limited in its effectiveness. The alternative of course, is to generate a country-mythology as Hyderabadi poets Maqdum Mohiuddin and Tilak did, with their haunting and enchanting verses. Nevertheless we feel it is worth taking a risk. Hence the present work and its explorative character.

This study is the result of a two-year project financed by the Indian Council for Social Science Research (ICSSR). Its Southern Regional Centre (SRC) gave me accommodation in Hyderabad. I was granted leave by Shri Guru Teg Bahadur Khalsa College (Eve.), Delhi University, where I teach. I am grateful to the staff and

Libraries of the Andhra Pradesh State Archives and its Interim Repository at the Secretariat, the State Central Library, Salar Jung Museum Library, Nizamat Jung Memorial Library, Osmania University Library—all in Hyderabad, the Nehru Memorial Museum and Library and National Archives, New Delhi and the libraries of Nagpur, Marathwada and Gulbarga Universities who all helped me.

It may not currently be in vogue to acknowledge the present that shapes one's view of the past. But I would like to say that my present is constituted by my association with the Revolutionary Writers Association (VIRASAN), the Andhra Pradesh Civil Liberties Committee and the People's Union for Democratic Rights, Delhi, which in their own special ways influence my outlook on the past and the future.

In a work of this kind the researcher accumulates a wide ranging variety of debts. I would like to acknowledge Venkatayya and Nageswara Rao (Centre for Economic and Social Studies, Hyderabad), Uday Bhaskar (then of A.P. Industrial Development Corporation), Yadagiri (SRD, ICSSR, Hyderabad) for help at the stage of collecting and processing material; Kavita Rao (Indian Statistical Institute, Calcutta), Harish Dhawan and Archana Agarwal (Jawaharlal Nehru University, New Delhi), Ashok Prasad (Delhi University) for statistical assistance; Prasanna Tripathi (Sambalpur University) for intermittent interaction; D. Narasimha Reddy (University of Hyderabad) for his intellectual and spiritual support; Sathyanarayana (Indira Gandhi National Open University) for his undiscriminating help to all of us who do research in Hyderabad; Sumanta Banerjee for protecting me from the hazards of writing in an alien language; Sumit Guha (St Stephen's College, Delhi) for his almost cold, but diligent way of pointing out logical inconsistencies; Amit Kumar Gupta for sharing the excitement of knowledge and undertaking some responsibility for its fruition; Kodandarami Reddy, Vasanta Laxmi, Jhumur Ray and Anuradha Ghandhy for small but crucial ways of support; my students at the University of Hyderabad for teaching me many things about methodology and communication; and Akkineni Kutumbarao and Rambabu for leading me out of the blind alleys of Hyderabad both literally and metaphorically. Ashok Prasad helped me in more ways than he knows. Venkata Ramana was there all through the stages of this work. His ability to sustain efficiency despite the demands being made on his patience deserves my amazed gratitude. Finally, I would like to acknowledge Dr R. Radhakrishna, Director of the project, for his subtle way of provoking other people to think in diverse directions. I do not have a wife to thank for 'domestic help and patience'. But I must confess that some of my friends suffered me the way many housewives suffer their scholastic husbands.

Professional research is always taken to be individual in its character, perhaps because the rewards are always to the individual. That obscures the collective character of research work. In any case, this study is a product of the collective efforts of the people named and unnamed, so I will not add that I alone am responsible for the work.

C.V. Subba Rao

Abbreviations

AS	Agricultural Statistics
B.G.Rs.	British Government Rupees
CID	Commerce and Industries Department
CIDAR	Commerce and Industries Department Annual Reports
CIDF	Commerce and Industries Department Files
F	*Fasli* year, from October to September. Christian year is given by the formula n+590 where n is the *Fasli* year.
FBIDAR	Factories and Boilers Inspection Department Annual Reports
GAR	General Administration Report
GOH	Government of Hyderabad
GOI	Government of India
HBECR	Hyderabad Banking Enquiry Committee Report
HCAAR	Hyderabad Companies Act Annual Reports
HGBEA	Hyderabad Government Bulletin of Economic Affairs
IS	Industrial Statistics
ITF	Industrial Trust Fund
O.S.Rs.	*Osmania Sicca* Rupees
SA	Statistical Abstracts
TS	Trade Statistics
WWI	World War I
WW II	World War II

A Note on the Author

It is indeed difficult to write a note on a book authored by Subba Rao who is no more with us. Chennapragada Venkata Subba Rao passed away suddenly after a cardiac arrest on 17 January 1994. Subba Rao was born in Rajahmundry in the East Godavari district of Andhra Pradesh on 17 November 1953. The tribal movements in the neighbouring district of Srikakulam in the 1960s, and a deep interest in literature, fired young Subba's imagination. He wrote his first poem dedicated to Gurujada Apparao – a nineteenth century poet (whose work *Kanyasulkam* is regarded as a milestone in Telugu literature) – when he was thirteen years old. Subsequently Subba Rao wrote stories, poems, essays in literary criticism, a play (*Thodimileni Puvullu*) and edited a collection of writings on literature (*Vibhata Sandhyalu*). He was also closely associated with *Srijana*, a Telugu literary periodical. His play (*Thodimileni Puvullu*) was included in a collection (*Sangdhigdha Sandarbham*: January, 1995) of all his unpublished writings, compiled and published by his friends and admirers as a tribute on his first death anniversary.

After finishing school, Subba Rao took up Physics as an undergraduate student in Vishakapatnam and participated in radical left politics. He was arrested for his activism during the 'Emergency'. He completed his M.A. in Economics in jail with a first class. To complete the degree, he had to take his *viva voce* and was produced for the examination in handcuffs and fetters. The examiner, Prof. J. Krishnamurty of the Delhi School of Economics, refused to conduct the examination till his shackles were removed.

Subba Rao was finally released when the Janata government came to power at the centre.

Soon after this he moved to Delhi and became involved with the activities of the People's Union of Democratic Rights. He also began teaching Economics at the Khalsa Evening College, University of Delhi. His research interests included developments in Maoist China, on which he did his M.Phil. He was also attracted to nationality movements in the north-east and feminist theories.

The present book was originally submitted by Subba Rao as a Report to the Indian Council for Social Science Research. A copy of this report was also in our possession and being convinced about the rigour with which its author had researched and written it, we thought of getting it published. This work explores the political economy of what was the erstwhile Hyderabad state. In this study Subba Rao situates Hyderabad's industrialisation within the broader context of colonialism, taking into account the social and agrarian systems of the region.

We would like to express our gratitude to Syamala—Subba Rao's sister—for helping us out at different stages related to the production of this book. We would also like to thank the publishers, Orient Longman, especially Hemlata, Nandini and Priti, for doing everything possible to get this work published.

AMIT KUMAR GUPTA
BISWAMOY PATI

New Delhi

Introduction

The former Hyderabad State, with over four per cent of the population of undivided India and five per cent of its area, was one of the largest princely states in the country. The Asaf Jah dynasty, which ruled the state for over two centuries, came to power in the early decades of the eighteenth century when the Mughal empire was disintegrating. The ruler was often referred to as the Nizam, after the original title of the Mughal representative in the Deccan, *nizam-ul-mulk* (regulator of the realm) and the state was also known as the Nizam state.

A series of treaties which culminated in the Subsidiary Alliance of the early nineteenth century, made the state a faithful ally of British colonialism. Till the end of the Raj, the state served as a crucial link of strategic importance for the continuation of colonial rule south of the Vindhyas, and in the process, claimed a special status. After the declaration of independence in 1947, the state opted to stay out of the Indian Union. Its conflict with the Indian Government ended with the entry of the Indian army in September, 1948, and Asafia rule came to an end, although formally the deposed Nizam, Mir Osman Ali Khan, was made the *rajpramukh* (governor) of the state.

The agrarian economy of Hyderabad was marked by strong feudal relations. The commercialisation of agriculture, especially in cotton and oilseeds, did not radically alter the precapitalist social organisation of the state. But the commercial crops, among other things, became the basis of colonial trade. The development of infrastructure that facilitated the growth of external trade also led to the development of industry. Rich in mineral resources, as part of the Deccan plateau, rich in forest resources as part of larger Gondwana and possessing extensive black cotton soil, the state was also a source of diverse industrial raw materials. The present study seeks to investigate the process of industrialisation in Hyderabad state during the period 1875–1948.

II

Studies on industrialisation in the princely states of India are few and far between,[1] but a number of studies have been conducted on industrialisation in British-administered India.

Chanunjay Gadgil's *Industrial Evolution of India in Recent Times, 1860–1939* first published in 1924 was not only the pioneering work among studies on industrialisation under the Raj, but also remains unique in many respects.[2] It covers the indigenous artisan sector and traces industrial evolution in relation to agriculture. Studies conducted during the later period have a relatively restricted scope, focusing more on large-scale industrial establishments.

However, the later studies are more analytically sophisticated. In particular, these studies, mostly undertaken during the postcolonial period, seek to analyse the nature of the constraints on industrial growth that caused industrial backwardness. One major school of research emphasises supply constraints on industrial growth. Scarcity of capital and entrepreneurial talent, technological inadequacies and shortage of skilled labour, it is suggested, have contributed to high factor prices. In turn this resulted in increasing demand for both fixed and working capital where it was in short supply, setting a limit to industrial growth.[3] In sharp contrast, the other major trend emphasises demand constraints on industrial development. Amiya Kumar Bagchi, with the help of systematic and extensive documentation, demonstrates the under-utilisation of factors of production in macroeconomic terms to counter the supply side thesis. He concludes that the constraints imposed by the limited size of the market were the primary cause of industrial backwardness. In particular, the limited size of the market is seen here as the product of the absence of appropriate government policies.[4] More recently, another study, in a self-conscious attempt to distinguish itself from both sides, rejects any macroeconomic generalisations, stating that constraints can only be assessed at the level of a specific industry at a given point in time. In particular, it assigns a crucial role to technological factors.[5]

For the purposes of this study, we can identify some of the important features that informed the entire paradigm of the debate over all these years. The debate has focused, more or less exclusively, on modern large-scale industry. In the context of these studies, modern large-scale industry means private industry. During the colonial period such industry developed in response to the stimulus provided by foreign capital and essentially sought to serve the external market. It is this restricted base of the studies that has led to a focus on the policies of the colonial government. Although scholars have noted the changes that took place in government policies during the last two decades of colonial rule, the absence of industrial policy *per se*, as distinct from suitable tariff and fiscal policies, was still considered a major factor in inhibiting the growth of industry. But it should be noted that almost all these studies were confined to British-administered provinces. The 'India' referred to in the works (and titles) of Gadgil, Morris, Bagchi, Ray and others excluded the Indian states that constituted one-third of India. Our study thus marks a departure from the focus of existing major studies.

This also leads to a departure from the other major feature of the debate, namely the focus on private industry. In many Indian states, such as Hyderabad, Mysore, Travancore, Baroda and others, the state provided not only some form of protection to indigenous capital but also provided a market and in some cases, finance. In Hyderabad in particular, the state established infrastructural facilities, owned or financed a substantial number of industrial enterprises, pursued a suitable technological policy and generally encouraged industrial development. The focus here shifts from constraints on large-scale industry to the role played by the state in industrialisation and its limitations.

It should be noted, however, that these two points of departure also inhibit us from making a more direct intervention into the wide debate on industrial development in a colonial context. But we hope that the implications of our study will nevertheless illuminate some aspects of the nature and constraints of industrialisation in India during the colonial period.

III

Studies on the economic history of Indian states have to encounter the relatively underdeveloped state of research, the paucity of data and the negative image of the states that informs much of the historiography of colonial India. These negative images originated as part of the political campaign of the nationalist movement against colonial rule. In essence these images were woven around the fact that these states served a strategic role in the perpetuation of the paramount power and in general, they denied civil and democratic rights to their subjects. The political context of the anti-colonial movement perhaps justifies the negative images. But now it can be suggested that the complexity and heterogeneity of the social processes in the Indian states and the contentious dimension of their relationship with the colonial power, makes it difficult to sustain any generalised image, yet these negative images persist and influence contemporary research.

The database of research on princely states is also imperfect. The governments of these states, given the inherited traditions of a largely oral culture, did not maintain systematic records. In a number of cases the data were either not collected or not published, and even when available, they lack consistency. The absence of reliable and regular data makes it difficult to profitably employ the standard variables in economic analysis. The limitations imposed by data and image have contributed to the relative lack of studies on the economic history of Indian states.[6]

The problems of research into sectors like industry are far more formidable. In some cases private enterprises simply faded into oblivion, in others, their records disappeared. Government publications with their inherent biases and imperfections, remain the major sources. Consequently we have had to make a number of approximations, as in the case of output data and we have very little to say on the rate of return of the enterprises. The resource constraints on our project have also compounded the problem.

It may be pointed out that part of the data limitation has to do with the nature of industrialisation in a colonial context. For instance, capital, when it penetrated Europe, first led to a Factories Act and then to a Companies Act, with consequential differences in the data generated by these legislations. But, when the history of capital is repeated in the colonial context, the Companies Act comes first followed by the Factories Act. In Hyderabad, for instance, the Companies Act came into force in 1910 while the Factories Act only came into force in 1930. Consequently, more detailed and systematic data on capital in registered companies is available from an earlier period than on the labour force in organised industry. Capital, it would seem, shaped the data in its own image although it could not do the same with the social organisation.

Despite all these limitations, it would still be worth undertaking a study of industrialisation in Hyderabad state, if only because it anticipated, ironically, many elements of the state with which the postcolonial Indian state has become identified. In critically examining the industrial evolution of the state, we will focus on the limitations imposed on it by a precapitalist social organisation. Hence this work is essentially a study of the social context of industrialisation in Hyderabad.

IV

Chapter 1 traces the evolution of Hyderabad State from the Qutub Shahi period. In the historic specificity of the eastern Deccan, it was not the colonial power but the native state that undertook the restructuring of the social organisation under the prime ministership of Salar Jung (Chapter 2). The relative autonomy that the state acquired during this period served as the source of strength for the industrial policy it pursued.

By focusing on state policy, we can trace the industrial evolution of Hyderabad in three distinct phases (Chapter 3). In the first phase, 1875–1919, infrastructure facilities were established on a firm base, in both the transport and energy sectors. In turn these facilities paved the way for the commercialisation of segments of the agrarian economy and the development of industry. In the second phase, 1919–1939, the state provided the institutional and financial support for the development of industry. In the third phase, 1939–1948, not only was an effort made to bring about a structural change in industry but it was undertaken with a perspective on planned economic development. In this long, often chequered, evolution of industry, state policy was helped by the resource base of industry in the state (Appendix 3-B).

The growth of capital in the industrial sector in such a context was primarily due to state finance (Chapter 4). An analysis of the differential growth of capital in different branches of the corporate sector reveals firstly, that the growth was not very significant in extent, and secondly, that within it there was a structural change by the late 1930s, from agro-based industries to metal and engineering, chemical and forest-based industries (Appendix 4-A). On the whole, private entrepreneurs never took enough initiative in investing and were dependent on state support. In such a context, an identifiable social group of capitalists never emerged in Hyderabad. Nevertheless, a working-class, conscious of its political role did emerge in the state (Chapter 5). The total labour force engaged in industry declined as a result of the general decline in artisan industry. But in organised industry, it grew in strength (Appendix 5-A). It was in some of these units that the working-class movement, which later became linked with the peasant movement, developed.

But one should note the marked limitations of state policies, not only in cottage and small-scale industries, but also in official efforts to finance the corporate sector (Chapter 6). The limited growth in almost all indicators of industrial development was a reflection of these limitations (Appendix 6-A). However, a more limiting factor was the precapitalist social organisation which constrained industrial growth, both on the supply side and on the demand side.

The precapitalist social structure essentially maintained the feudal aristocracy and its social power in the villages (Chapter 7). The commercialisation of agriculture only resulted in the intensification of feudal forms of exploitation (Appendix 7-B). The assiduously maintained relationship between the feudal aristocracy and the bureaucracy and the autocratic polity based on it, eventually faced a multi-faceted crisis from which it never recovered (Chapter 8). An armed peasant movement in Telangana, communal strife in Hyderabad city and Marathwada and nationalist pressure marked the last days of the regime. The state, till the end, defended the feudal social organisation and the autocracy based on it, with force of arms. An isolated intervention through industrial policy that remained external to the dynamics of the interrelations of power within society could not, in the end, make any significant difference to the industrial backwardness of the state.

Studies in economic history often remain incomprehensible to the general reader, a fate sometimes shared by fellow historians as well. This is perhaps unavoidable, given the tools used in economic analysis. But our study is a conscious attempt to address the lay reader and to generate his or her curiosity about little-known aspects of little-known regions. We have therefore, separated the statistical analysis from the main text and added it as appendices at the end of most chapters. In each case, the findings of the account and analysis in the appendix have been incorporated into the text while their statistical base is given in the appendix. To the extent possible, we have attempted to maintain a structural integration between the two, without resorting to repetition.

Finally, a word of caution on the connotations of the processes that we analysed. Industrial development, especially where the state plays a leading role, is often identified with social progress. Yet we do not intend to suggest that the state presided over by Mir Osman Ali Khan was a progressive state. It remained a feudal autocracy that was incapable of making any progress. If there is a paradox here, it is located not in social development itself but in the contemporary discourse on development.

Notes

1. Among the earliest was Balakrishna's study on Mysore (R.Balakrishna, *Industrial Development in Mysore*, Bangalore, 1940). Currently some work is in progress on industrialisation in Travancore at the Centre for Development Studies, Trivandrum. In Hyderabad, Madhava Rao in 1956, M.F. Jussawalla in 1961 and B.K. Narayan in 1962 did work on aspects related to industrialisation, to which we shall refer later.
2. Dhanunjay R. Gadgil, *The Industrial Evolution of India in Recent Times, 1860–1939* (Fifth Edition), Oxford University Press, Delhi, 1972.
3. The argument summarised is a rather simplified version of the supply-side thesis. See Morris O. Morris, 'Private Investment in Indian Sub-Continent 1900–1939: Some Methodological Considerations', *Modern Asian Studies*, Vol. 8, No. 4, October 1974. See also his essay on 'The Growth of Large Scale industry', in Dharma Kumar (ed.), *Cambridge Economic History of India*, Vol. 2, 1757–1970, Orient Longman, Delhi, 1982, pp.553–676.
4. For our present purposes only a simplified version of the thesis is presented. See Amiya Kumar Bagchi, *Private Investment in India: 1900–1939*, Orient Longman, New Delhi, 1980 (Reprint).
5. Rajat Kanta Ray, *Industrialisation in India: Growth and Conflict in the Private Corporate Sector, 1914–1947*, Oxford University Press, Delhi, 1982 (Second Edition).
6. On Hyderabad, for instance, there are no macro-level studies on economic history, except Anwar Iqbal Qureshi's *The Economic Development of Hyderabad State*, Vol. I, Rural Economy, Orient Longman, Bombay, 1947 and B.K. Narayan's *Agricultural Development in Hyderabad State, 1900–1956*, Kesav Prakashan, Secunderabad, 1960. The Telangana region however generated some economic history because the Communist movement attracted many scholars. The literature is referred to in detail elsewhere.

SECTION I

State and Society, A Prelude

CHAPTER ONE

Social Framework

The origins of what came to be known as Hyderabad State lie in the fall of the Bahmani kingdom. It was during the last years of Bahmani rule that Sultan Quli, *tarafdar* of the province of Telangana, acquired control over the region and declared formal independence in 1512, the date usually identified with the beginning of Qutub Shahi rule.[1]

The reign of Ibrahim Quli (1550–1580) marks the zenith of the Qutub Shahi dynasty. During his rule almost all the Telegu country including the east coast, became part of the kingdom. His son, Mohammad Quli (1580–1612), laid the foundations of Hyderabad city which remained the capital of successive regimes for over four centuries, right upto the present time.[2] Changes in the agrarian revenue system and the penetration of colonial traders began during Qutub Shahi times. But Qutub Shahi rule ended when the Mughal empire, under Aurangzeb, annexed the state in 1687. The last Qutub Shahi ruler, eighth in succession, died in Kala Mahal palace, his glorified prison in Daulatabad, in 1688, thus ending nearly one hundred and seventy five years of Qutub Shahi rule.[3]

After its conquest of Golconda in 1687, the Mughal empire administered the state for about thirty-five years[4] during a period when the empire was already disintegrating. This interlude introduced a number of changes but Mughal rule did not affect the economy and polity of the Deccan to the same extent as northern India. However, the social organisation assiduously built up by the Qutub Shahis became dysfunctional and disorderly during the Mughal administration. It was against such a background that

Qumareddin Chin Qlich Khan, the 'regulator of the realm' (*nizal-ul-mulk*) for the Mughal empire in the Deccan, acquired effective control over the state. Thus began the long reign of the Asaf Jahis, known after the title bestowed on them by the Mughal emperor. The present study covers the Asaf Jahi period.

The first Nizam, during the quarter-century he reigned (1724–1748), consolidated his power not only over the Telugu country but also over parts of Karnatic territory.[5] Meanwhile, the conflict between the French and English traders that was to ravage the state later, began in the Deccan. Qumareddin's death in 1748 resulted in uncertain conditions. The ensuing struggle for succession became a battle, by proxy, between the French and the English. Gradually the Asaf Jahi rulers lost administrative control over the region and began to lose territories. In 1762, Nizam Ali Khan, the first ruler to refer to himself as the Nizam of Hyderabad, came to power. The Northern Circars assigned to the French in 1752, were ceded to the English during his rule by the treaty of 1766. His reign signifies the consolidation of the English East India Company's hold over the region with the defeats of Tipu Sultan in Mysore and the Marathas. During the forty years that Nizam Ali ruled the English obliged Hyderabad to sign a series of five treaties.[6]

By the treaty of 1790, a representative of the Company, effectively the first Resident, settled in Hyderabad. Under the Subsidiary Alliance, British troops were stationed at what came to be known as Secunderabad. Until the end of colonial rule in India, Secunderabad remained a British-administered pocket in the vast expanse of a princely state. The unwitting and ironical implications of the distinctive character of this pocket for the working-class movement in twentieth century Hyderabad will be discussed later.[7] For the present we should note that in return for the troops, Nizam Ali ceded the Rayalseema region, later known as the ceded districts of Madras Presidency. The treaty of 1802, made after the defeat of Tipu Sultan and the Marathas, finally set up the framework for the Subsidiary Alliance that governed relations between the state and the British till the end of colonial rule.

In the ensuing period, as the pay of the contingent troops had fallen into arrears, a fresh treaty was concluded in 1853, by which some more territories were lost by the state. These included Osmanabad (Naldurg), Raichur Doab and Berar. But in return for the support given by Hyderabad during the 1857 disturbances, Osmanabad and Raichur were returned to the state. It was this territory, shaped by the vicissitudes of one empire, two local kingdoms and two colonial trading companies, that came to be known as Hyderabad State. In 1881 it covered an area of 82698 sq. miles with a population of 9.8 million.[9]

II

The area that eventually became Hyderabad state can be divided geologically and ethnologically into two large, almost equal parts. On the northern and western side is the trappean rock region where wheat, jawar, and paddy, were the principal crops. Later cotton became an important crop. It was essentially a Kannada and Marathi-speaking region. The south and east are the granite regions where jawar and paddy were the principal crops. Later oilseeds became an important crop. It was essentially a Telugu-speaking region and referred to as Telangana. Here, tank irrigation, facilitated by black and sandy soil, was a notable feature.[10]

By the early half of the nineteenth century, the agrarian economy consisted of remnants of three major attempts to introduce changes in tenurial relations, by the Qutub Shahis, by Malik Amber and by the Mughals. The Qutub Shahis, in forging alliances with local ruling groups, established *ijara*, the revenue farming system in which collection rights wee auctioned. Such assignments were called *muqasas*. *Muqasadars*, who held enormous judicial, administrative and social power, were the precursors of the *jagirdars* who remained an important centre of power till the end of Asaf Jahi rule. In addition there were also crownlands and *inam* lands which were assigned for the support of religious leaders and institutions. These grants, known as *madad-i-ma'ash* grants included those granted to the Muslim *ulema* and the Hindu *agraharams*. In almost all these lands there was an elaborate hierarchy of lessees and sub-lessees through whom revenue was collected. The struggle included *mirasidars* (those who held their right to collect revenue on a hereditary basis) and *watandars* (those who held hereditary rights under official tenure) who included *deshmukhs* and *deshpandes.* Some of the essential features of the Qutub Shahi revenue system remained, despite attempts at change, till the end of Asaf Jahi rule.[11]

Measures initiated by Malik Amber, the prime minister of the Nizam Shahi kingdom (1604–1626), can be considered the second major attempt to change the tenurial system.[12] The relevance of his attempts, for our purposes, is confined only to those areas that became part of Hyderabad State.[13] The system of *nazar-pahani* (glance survey) introduced by him, was in a rudimentary form, the first attempt at a systematic survey anywhere in the region.

A more thorough and systematic survey and reorganisation of the entire system, however, was undertaken during the Mughal administration,[14] which abolished *ijara* and appointed *manasabdars* as official collectors of revenue. As the revenue assignments were renamed *jagirs, jagirdars* replaced *muqasadars.* There were many types of *jagirs.* In addition crown and *inam* lands also continued. There were also *paibaqi* (unassigned) lands. Concomitant changes were also made at the village level where the hereditary rights of the *watandars* were curtailed. Records, prepared after a thorough survey, became the basis of land-revenue collection for the first time in the region.

But the changes were introduced at a time when the Mughal empire was disintegrating. Incessant wars with the Marathas and feuds for power between factions of the Mughal aristocracy marked the period. Although the system appears to have been more stable during the reign of the first Nizam, it again fell into disarray after his death.[15] While central authority could not establish its control in many territories, Maratha intrusions and Bidar raiders continued to plague the region. The high-revenue-yielding Northern Circars was lost to colonial traders. In addition to hereditary military *jagirs,* many soldiers and their chiefs were granted land in lieu of their salaries. The assignment of land for the maintenance of the household troops of the king originated during this period, leading to the emergence of *paigah* nobles who remained the most powerful group of aristocrats in Hyderabad society till the end. The practice of contracting the revenue rights to the highest bidder (*ta-hud* and *sarbasta*) reached its zenith during this period. Some of these *tahuddars* were also *taluqdars*, i.e., administrative chiefs of the area. *Taluqdars* in charge of revenue and police in directly administered (*diwani*) areas became an all-powerful group. Over time, as state finances dwindled, large sums of money were taken as loans from traders and bankers in lieu of which revenue collection rights were granted to them. Known as *tankahi mahalat jagirs*, these assignments became very prominent by the beginning of the nineteenth century.[16] In such a situation, at the village level, the landed gentry, consisting of former officials like *deshmukhs*, *deshpandes* and *mirasidars*, became very powerful. It was these myriad and bizarre, sometimes overlapping, tenurial arrangements that came to prevail by the early half of the nineteenth century. There were as many as six types of *jagirs*, including *samstanams*, crown lands now known as *sarf-e-khas*; lands auctioned off under *ta-hud* or *sarbasta paishkash* (tribute) and *inam* lands and the so-called *diwani* lands where *taluqdars* at the *paragana* level and the *naibs* and *watandars* at the village level dominated the scene. Thus what became the agrarian revenue system by the first half of the nineteenth century consisted of the remnants of the three earlier systems, of the Qutub Shahis, Malik Amber and the Mughals, as shaped by a century of anarchy.

The assorted set of landed aristocrats included *muqasadars*, *taluqdars*, *jagirdars*, *rajas* of *samstanams*, *paigah* nobles and bankers and traders. Most of them were located in Hyderabad city and some of them were closely aligned with the ruling family and also held *mansabs* and administrative posts at different levels of the state apparatus. At the village level, *naibs, mirasidars, deshmukhs, deshpandes* and *watandars* constituted the landed gentry. Their control over land, law, police and general administration was absolute. Propped up by the state and sanctified by custom, their social power was complete and final. Some of them were traditional gentry but a large number of outsiders joined them in the second half of the eighteenth century. One estimate indicates that by 1820 the proportion of outsiders from northern India, among the Hindu *jagirdars* and *inamdars*, was as high as 62 per cent.[17]

Revenue farming, the increasing amount of agrarian surplus and the finality with which social power was held by the dominant groups had three important implications for the economy and society. Firstly, absolute social power facilitated the institutionalisation of many forms of extra economic coercion. These became, over time, customary practices that even survived the commercialisation of agriculture in the twentieth century. Such practices left no incentive for the actual producers to improve the production organisation. The practice of *takdama* where the peasants were compelled to advance a portion of the revenue, made conditions especially oppressive for them. In fact, in some cases evidence suggests that the peasants, unable to bear the burden of revenue, left vast acres of land uncultivated,[18] especially during famines.[19] As for the gentry, it took no interest in production and production organisation. Instead, its only interest was to perpetuate the arbitrary system which became the source of its ever-increasing surplus. Thus the system led to stagnation in the agrarian economy. The most notable reflection of this was in the decline of tank irrigation.[20] Secondly, in a situation where a large number of assignments were made in lieu of services or credit, the state's own revenue declined significantly. State deficit perpetuated further public debt. Salar Jung described this system as one where 'both the subjects and the state suffered equally'.[21] Thirdly, the multiplicity of tenures also increased the number of people who had access to the ever- increasing agrarian surplus. In turn, this contributed to an increase, to some extent, in effective demand for non- agricultural products.

III

Hyderabad had a fairly well developed industrial sector dating from Qutub Shahi times. (See 'Indigenous Industry and Trade', Appendix 1-A). Rural artisans, engaged in localised commodity production and structurally integrated with the agrarian economy, were the base of this sector. But more importantly, outside this sector, a large number of industries flourished in Hyderabad. Increasing demand for industrial products, the phenomenal growth of urban centres during the Qutub Shahi period, and the military and administrative requirements of alien rulers were some of the factors that contributed to the development of industry. But these demand factors only partly explain the growth of industry. The widespread diffusion of technology should also be taken into consideration. The Bahmani conquest of the Deccan and later, the more direct Persian influence under the Qutub Shahis, led to the development of new products and new methods of production in the region. With the Mughal conquest the region also acquired many technologies and products that the Mughals had brought to other parts of India earlier. Artisan communities from Agra, Delhi, Ahmedabd and other areas came and settled in Hyderabad, Aurangabad, Daulatabad and other places during the Mughal period.

Industrial products can be broadly classified into three, somewhat overlapping, groups.[22] The first consisted of items related to statecraft, notably arms and armaments. Facilitated by the extensive availability of iron-ore, the manufacture of arms both for the state and for the numerous private armies of the nobility flourished in the state. During the earlier phase, arms were also exported. But over time, as the military strength of the state and the nobility declined directly in proportion to the rise of colonial military power, the arms industry suffered a decline. The second group of industries related primarily to exports which included certain specialised textile products, diamonds and shipbuilding for which Qutub Shahi Hyderabad was very famous. Diamonds in particular attracted colonial traders. The famous 'brightest jewel in the crown' of Queen Victoria, the Kohinoor, was a product of the Golconda mines.[23] But diamond production, along with shipbuilding, declined by the end of Qutub Shahi rule with the advent of colonial traders and their superiority in navigational instruments. In the case of diamonds, however, it appears that depletion of stones was the important cause of decline.[24] In any case, both these industries were located in the Northern Circars that was later ceded to the East India Company. The third group of industries consisted of luxury goods that served the domestic market and, to a lesser extent, the export market. They included textile products like silk, muslin, *mushroo, himroo*, gold and silver lace work, *khamkhwab*, metal products like bidriware and some wooden articles and timber. The manufacture of these products flourished till almost the mid-nineteenth century. But later, as the composition of external trade changed and manufactured goods gradually became the dominant part of imports, this group of industries declined. Thus, as elsewhere in India, the advent of colonial traders critically overshadowed industrial development during this period.

The Dutch were the first colonial traders to arrive in Hyderabad. They obtained a *farman* from Muhammad Quli Qutub Shah in 1606[25] and till the end of Qutb Shahi rule (1687), they were more dominant than the Portuguese on the Coromandel Coast and in Golconda. The textile industry received an impetus from their trading activities. They introduced *dadani*, the advance contract system among textile industry artisans. They were also the first to establish factories at Masulipatnam and later at Golconda. By the end of the seventeenth century, local merchants were completely subdued by the Dutch. But soon the English East India Company and later, the French, came to dominate the scene. The English entered Golconda in 1611. But their ascendancy began only after they had consolidated their hold over Madras in the 1670s. Their importance, both in strategic terms and in volume of trade, increased during the Mughal period. Around the same time, the French East India Company gained access to the Nizam's court. The end of stability in the region, with the death of the first Nizam, saw the rivalry between the two Companies coming to the fore. By the time Nizam Ali Khan came to power English traders had emerged victorious[26] and the series of treaties referred to earlier, consolidated their hold over Hyderabad.[27]

The actual volume of trade and its conduits were conditioned by the anarchic conditions in the state during this period. In particular, the *rahdari* (transit) duties imposed by *jagirdars* and other sections of the landed gentry inhibited the free flow of goods.

The Commercial Treaty of 1802 sought to eliminate these by explicitly prohibiting all kinds of transit duties. It included a clause to the effect that no article should pay duty more than once.[28] But given the absolute lack of control over the *jagirdars*, the Treaty could not achieve its goal. These transit duties were finally abolished much later, after Salar Jung undertook his extensive reforms. The Supplementary Treaty of 1860 formalised the abolition.

The rise of colonial traders also had an impact on the economy. Some industries, like armaments, declined while others like textiles, received an impetus from external trade, at least during the initial years. The marketing of a number of new products also developed in this period and the scale of production of old products increased. These developments led to an increasing division of labour, the introduction of new technology and the emergence, in a rudimentary form, of factory organisation. The composition of trade changed over time and with it the balance of trade, to the disadvantage of the state, leading to the subjugation of powerful native traders and trading groups. This facilitated the entry of new trading communities into the state, as sub-contractors for colonial traders. Parsis, Marwaris, Khojas, Maimoons and Bohras emerged as leading merchant groups in Hyderabad. From these communities arose the powerful bankers and traders who advanced loans to the state and in return gained control over land.

The emergence of arbitrary centres of power in the agrarian economy and the rise of new groups of traders in urban centres, coupled with the prevailing political anarchy, contributed to widespread social unrest. The abandoning of fields by peasants, referred to earlier, resulted in an acute food shortage leading to occasional disturbances in Hyderabad city.[29] Strife between soldiers of different communities serving different *jagirdars* became very common.[30] The Wahabi movement that had earlier rocked parts of India, also had its impact on Hyderabad in the 1830s. The ruler's brother himself was its leader in the state.[31] There were also tensions between *Shias* and *Sunnis*.

An even more serious reflection of social unrest was the series of insurrections by the tribal communities in the state. Throughout the first half of the nineteenth century practically every district in all the outlying areas of the state witnessed these revolts. Rebellions were led by Banjaras in Bhir, Hatkars in Nanded and Parbani, Bhils in Aurangabad, Mahadeopur and Sironcha and Gonds in Adilabad.

It was against this background that Salar Jung undertook his reforms. The space for his measures was created both by the infirmities of the local ruling groups and the constraints of the colonial power.

By the early half of the nineteenth century, the ruling elite of Hyderabad were incapable of taking any meaningful initiatives to counter the anarchy in both the economy and in polity. In all sectors of the economy, the traditional nobility were joined by powerful groups of outsiders. Together they contributed to the perpetuation of a system of arrangements where aggrandisement that brooked no rules came to prevail. For the economy in general and the state treasury in particular this spelt disaster. The ruling family was engrossed in palace intrigues. Bankers and traders, sometimes with the help of willing Residents, were able to indulge in what can only be described as plunder.[34] A section of the nobility, especially the all powerful chiefs of *daftar-i-mal* and *daftar-i-dewan*, lent their support to these bankers and traders.[35] As a result the system became even more oppressive for the ordinary people.

The colonial power in Hyderabad was primarily guided by its strategic requirements. Wars with the Marathas and Tipu Sultan of Mysore engaged its attention till almost the end of the eighteenth century, so Hyderabad became the operational headquarters for establishing its control in the Deccan and the south. Its position was consolidated by the Subsidiary Alliance. As the interests of a dithering native state coincided with the requirements of an expanding colonial power, both powers became 'one and the same in interest, policy, friendship and honour', as the treaty of 1800 described it.[36] Although trade remained important, it was the strategic considerations of establishing and consolidating its paramount power south of the Vindhyas that guided colonial policy towards Hyderabad. This aim was fulfilled half a century later in 1857, when Hyderabad served, in Lord Canning's often-quoted words, as 'the breakwater in the storm that would have swept us [the British] in one wave'.[37] The colonial power after taking over the higher-revenue-yielding coast and Berar, left the internal agrarian revenue system of Hyderabad to its rulers. Neither in agrarian economy nor in administration did the British undertake a restructuring of the old system, as they did in other parts of India. Measures initiated by Residents like Charles Metcalfe, for example, were not encouraged by the colonial power and were thwarted by the local ruling elite.[38] Such domination, control and interference as the Residents exercised in the affairs of the state were primarily related to matters of strategic importance.

Apart from its requirements, the colonial power in Hyderabad was conditioned by its relationship with the local ruling elite, who, unlike the elites many other Indian states, was not a creation of the colonial power. The pre-colonial structure was not disturbed as it was, for instance, in Mysore. The power and legitimacy of the elite were not located in Treaties but in their long and chequered evolution from Qutub Shahi times. Located historically in the structure of society, the ruling elite in Hyderabad state were far more autonomous from the colonial power than the elite in many other Indian states.

The space for the reforms undertaken by Salar Jung was thus located in the relative autonomy of Hyderabad State.

Notes

1. For a basic history of the Qutub Shahi period, see Haroon Khan Sherwani, *History of the Qutub Shahi Dynasty*, Munshiram Manoharlal, New Delhi, 1974.
2. For a brief period during 1740–1750, Aurangabad was the capital of the state.
3. The sharp contrast between the Qutub Shahis and the Asaf Jahis is striking in the evolution of the state. For the Qutub Shahis art, literature and culture were far more effective instruments for maintaining their hegemony than military power. Their court also patronised the *deshi* (native) tradition in Telugu literature. This

policy of forging a stable alliance with the local ruling groups was also reflected in their agrarian revenue system.

4. For a basic work on the Mughal interlude, see John Folsom Richards, *Mughal Administration in Golconda*, Oxford University Press, London, 1975.
5. Basic works on the Asaf Jahi period are: Yusuf Husain Khan, *The First Nizam; Life and Times of Nizamul Mulk Asaf Jahi*, Asia Publishing House, Bombay, 1963, P. Sethu Madhava Rao, *Eighteenth Century Deccan*, Popular Prakashan, Bombay, 1963, Sarojini Regani, *Nizam–British Relations; 1724–1857*, Book Lovers, Hyderabad, 1963 and Moulavi Syed Mehadi Ali, *Hyderabad Affairs*, (12 Vols.), Times of India Press, Bombay, 1886.
6. For the text of the treaties, see Henry George Briggs, *The Nizam, His History and Relations with the British Government*, Vol. I (1862) Reprint, Manas Publications, Delhi, 1985.
7. See Chapter 5; Labour, in Section II below.
8. The districts were Bellari, Anantapur, Cuddapah and Kurnool.
9. Census, 1881.
10. By the end of the nineteenth century, even after considerable decline, there were still as many as 370 large tanks, 11000 smaller ponds (*kuntas*) and about 124000 wells in the state, Mirza Mehadi Khan, 'Imperial Gazetteer of India', Provincial Series, Hyderabad State, Government of India Press, Calcutta, 1909, p. 347.
11. The description of the Qutub Shahi revenue system here is based on Sherwani, 1974, op. cit. (note 1), pp. 474–480. See also H. Fukazawa, 'Agrarian Relations and Land Revenue; Medieval Deccan and Maharashtra' in Tapan Raychaudari and Irfan Habib (ed.) *The Cambridge Economic History of India, Vol. 1, 1200–1750*, Orient Longmans, Delhi, 1984, pp. 249–260 and Richards, 1975, op. cit. (note 4), pp. 21–30.
12. See, Radhe Shyam, *Life and Times of Malik Amber*, Motilal Banarsi Das, Delhi, 1968.
13. The parts included what were later to become Adilabad in Telangana; Nanded, Parbhani and Aurangabad in Marathwada.
14. The account here is based on Richards, 1975, op. cit. (note 4) and M.A. Nayeem, *Mughal Administration of Deccan under Nizamul Mulk Asaf Jahi (1720–48)*, Jaico, Bombay, 1985.
15. The agrarian revenue system in Hyderabad went through violent changes during the period from the death of the first Nizam (1748) to the reforms undertaken by Salar Jung (1850s). But there is as yet

no systematic account of this century of upheaval. The account here is based on Moulavi Chirag Ali, *Hyderabad Under Salar Jung*, Vol. I, Bernard Quaritch, London, 1885; Regani, op. cit. (note 5), Nani Gopal Chowdary, *British Relations with Hyderabad* (*1798–1843*), University of Calcutta, Calcutta, 1964, pp. 154–158.

16. The infamous Palmer and Co. for instance was assigned a number of districts yielding a revenue of Rs 3 million per annum. Regani, op. cit. (note 5), p. 225.
17. The percentage in 1784 was around 45 per cent. See Karen Isaken Leonard, *Social History of An Indian Caste: The Kayasths of Hyderabad*, University of California Press, Berkeley, 1978, p. 29.
18. For some references see, Chirag Ali, 1885, op. cit. (note 15), p. 162 and Choudary, 1964, op. cit. (note 15), p. 156.
19. According to the 1891 Census, there were four major famines in the eighteenth century and twelve in the nineteenth century. Census, 1891, Hyderabad State, Part I, pp. 22–23.
20. On the decline of tank irrigation see Chirag Ali, 1885, op. cit. (note 15) Vol. III, pp. 161–62. Mehadi Khan, 1909, op. cit. (note 10), p. 347.
21. Quoted in Chirag Ali, 1885, op. cit. (note 15), vol. I, p. 25.
22. For sources of the account here, see Appendix 1-A.
23. For details on Golconda diamond mining, see Sherwani, 1974, op. cit. (note 1), pp. 471–75.
24. Syed Hossain Bilgrami and Charles Willmott, *Historical and Descriptive Sketch of His Highness the Nizam's Dominions*, Vol. I, Times of India Press, Bombay, 1883, pp. 234–35.
25. On Dutch traders in Golconda see Tapan Raychaudari, *Jan Company in Coromandel, 1605–1690: A Study in the Inter-Relations of European Commerce and Traditional Economies*,. S. Grave, The Hague, 1962.
26. The French dominance in Hyderabad was essentially during the period of Salabat Jung (1751–1762) whom they helped to acquire power. On the rivalry between French and English traders in the state, see, Regani, 1963, op. cit. (note 5).
27. See Briggs, 1861, op. cit. (note 6).
28. For the text of the treaty, see ibid., pp. 292–95.
29. Two notable instances of such disturbances were reported in 1750 and later in 1833. See, *The Chronology of Modern Hyderabad, 1720–1890*, Central Records Office, GOH, Hyderabad, 1954, pp. 6 and 207.
30. *The Chronology of Modern Hyderabad*, cited above, records a number

of such instances between Arabs and Sikhs (p. 192 and 199), between Arabs and Rohillas (p. 120) and between Arabs and Pathans (p. 264).

31. *Freedom Struggle in Hyderabad*, Vol. I (1800–1857), Hyderabad State Committee for the Compilation of the History of Freedom Movement in Hyderabad, Hyderabad, 1956. Chapter XII, pp. 125–80.
32. Thirteen people were killed in 1847 during a riot that took place following the assassination of a Shia *darogah* of Mecca Masjid. *Chronology of Modern Hyderabad*, 1954, op. cit. (note 29), p. 223.
33. *Freedom Struggle in Hyderabad*, Vol. I, cited above (note 31) gives an account of a number of such rebellions. See in particular Chapters VIII, IX, XIII and XIV, pp. 87–115, 181–86 and 211–18.
34. The activities of the infamous William Palmer and Company were illustrative of the state of affairs. Members of the Company included a British financial expert, a Hindu banker, a surgeon of the Residency and as it was discovered later, the Resident himself. With the connivance of the *daftardar*, Maharaja Chandulal, the Company systematically looted the treasury. Regani, 1963, op. cit. (note 5).
35. See 'The Rise of *daftardars*', in Karen Leonard, 1978, op. cit. (note 17), pp. 61–64.
36. From the text of the treaty, Briggs, 1861, op. cit. (note 6), p. 280.
37. Lord Canning quoted in the 'White Paper on Indian States', GOI, Delhi, 1952, p. 12.
38. For Charles Metcalfe's aborted reforms in Hyderabad, see John William Kaye, *Life of Charles Metcalfe*, Vol. I, Smith and Elder, London, 1858, pp. 340–454. See also Regani, 1963, op. cit. (note 5). See also, Zubaida Yazdani, *Hyderabad During the Residency of Henry Russel, 1811–1820: A Case Study of the Subsidiary Alliance System*, University Press, Oxford, London, 1976, pp. 97–129.

APPENDIX 1-A

Indigenous Industry and Trade

At the base of industry in Hyderabad was the village-based artisan sector. By and large, this sector served the specific needs of the subsistence village economy. But the functions of traditional *balutedars,* which included *pottadars* (money changers) and *chaudaries* (head of traders), indicates that commodity relations with the market outside had developed to a considerable extent during the Qutub Shahi period.[1] A wide range of artisans was spread all over the state. Later, the census of 1881 identified five weaving castes, five castes of food-preparers, seven castes engaged in gold, silver, iron, brass, copper and other metal work, and two castes each in carpentry, pottery, and stone work. In 1881, these castes taken altogether, constituted about 10 per cent of the population.[2] Beyond the village-based artisan sector, the industrial sector was well developed from Qutub Shahi times. The diffusion of technology from Persia and later the spread of new products following the Mughal conquest, apart from demand conditions, seem to have helped this growth. We shall briefly review the growth of indigenous industry prior to the Salar Jung period.[3]

As elsewhere in India the textile industry was highly developed in the region. It included coarse and fine varieties of cotton cloth and a variety of silk stuff. *Tasar* obtained from the forests in the southern and eastern parts of the state served as the source of very highly developed *tasar* silk products and *mashru.* In addition carpet and rug manufacture also flourished. Later, Persian immigrants brought the skills of making the Persian carpets that constituted a major portion of exports. Embroidery with gold and silver thread was also very well-known. The following list indicates the range of products and their location in Hyderabad. Cotton weaving has been left out of the list because it was found at every one of these major centres and other places.

Location of Textile and Allied Industries

1. Silk Stuff including *tasar* silk	Charlapalii, Pangal, Armur, Mahadeopur, Elgandal, Jagityal, Sangareddy, Siddipet, Yadgir, Matwada, Parkala, Hasanparthy, Warangal, Chinnur and Narayanpet—Telangana
2. Muslin and *Mashru*	Gadwal and Hyderabad—Telangana
3. *Himroo,* Gold, Silver and Silk thread, embroidery and lace work	Armur, Hyderabad, Jagityal and Hanamkonda—Telangana Vaitapur Paithan and Aurangabad—Marathwada
4. *Khamkhwab*	Paithan and Aurangabad—Marathwada
5. Dyeing and Printing	Vijaypur, Khuldabad and Deogaon—Marathwada Medak and Elgandal—Telangana Raichur—Carnatic.
6. Woollen and Silk Carpets Carpets and rugs	Warangal—Telangana

Source: Mirza Mehadi Khan, *Imperial Gazetteer: Hyderabad State,* Government Press, Calcutta, 1909.

In volume, the mining industry ranked second in Hyderabad. Diamond mining were very famous during the Qutub Shahi period,[4] but it appears to have declined by the early eighteenth century, primarily due to the depletion of stones. In any case, most of these mines were located in areas that were ceded to the English. A major attempt was made in the mid-eighteenth century by the Hyderabad Deccan Company to mine some of the areas within the state, but it ended in complete failure.[5] Iron ore mining and steel based on it, was a major industry in the state. A simple and primitive process of mining was common. It was the basis of the armament industry. The manufacture of swords, blades, guns and inferior smooth-bore muskets for the use of the regular and irregular troops of the Nizam and the private armies of the *jagirdars* was a flourishing industry. Cast steel was manufacturered and exported to Persia. But with the establishment of British troops and the gradual disbanding of all kinds of irregular troops during the post-Salar Jung period, the armament industry faced severe demand constraints. Later, Sardar Dilar Jung prepared a scheme for the revival of iron ore mining on a large scale, but the scheme was never pursued.[6] Copper mines and gold mines were also worked but they were not significant. Notable among the metal-based industries was bidriware from Bidar.

Industries based on the valuable teak and timber from the forests of northern Telangana also developed to some extent with Nirmal as a major centre. The availability of timber, along with iron, led to the development of the shipbuilding industry during the Qutub Shahi period, but this industry declined with the advent of colonial traders. The coast, where the ships were built, also ceased to be part of the state. Among other industries were oilpressing, manufacture of shoes and boots, silverware, fine filigree and wire work and paper of different kinds, etc. An exhaustive list of different industries and their location is given below:

List of Industries and Their Location

1. Diamond Mines	Kolluru—Northern Circars
2. Shipbuilding	Narasarao Pet—Northern Circars
3. Iron-Ore Mining	Nirmal, Jagityal, Yellendu and Warangal—Telangana
4. Iron-Ore Smelting	Indurti, Nizamabad, Warangal, Konosamudram, Anantagiri and Lingampalli—Telangana
5. Steel	Konasamudram, Ibrahimpatnam, Konapur, Chintalpet and Gudalore—Telangana
6. Armaments	Indalwal, Wanaparty, Gadwal, Nirmal, Hyderabad and Hanamkonda—Telangana
7. Gold Mines	Gudalore, Lingasagar, Manvi and Deodurg—Carnatic

8. Copper Mines	Ramghir—Carnatic
9. Limestone Mines	Devalapalli—Telangana
10. Brass and Copper Ware	Lingampet, Ramayam Pet, Pebarthi and Siddipet—Telangana
11. Bidriware	Bidar—Carnatic
12. Silverware	Jagityal, Hanamkonda and Elgandal—Telangana Aurangabad—Marathwara
13. Filigree and Wire Work	Elgandal—Telangana Aurangabad—Marathwada
14. *Shatranz*	Gulbarga—Carnatic Parkal—Telangana Nanded—Marathwada
15. Wooden articles and Timber	Nirmal—Telangana
16. Paper	Korutla, Surampet and Kolikonda—Telangana
17: Building Stones	Shadnagar—Telangana
18. Earthen Vessels	Bhongir—Telangana
19. Glass Bangles	Manikonda, Gajulapeta and Koyalkonda—Telangana
20. Leather Goods	Nirmal, Narayanpet, Sivanagar and Jogipet—Telangana

Source: S.H. Bilgrami and C. Willmott, *Historical and Descriptive Sketch of His Highness the Nizam's Dominions*, Times of India Press, Bombay, 1883 and Mirza Mehadi Khan, *Imperial Gazetteer of India, Hyderabad State*, Government Press, Calcutta, 1909.

The list of major centres identified here and earlier, indicates that about twenty places developed as some sort of industrial centres in the state. Most were located in the Telangana region.

The development of industry contributed to the growth of trade. The urbanisation that marks the long reign of the Qutub Shahis facilitated industrial growth and provided the infrastructural arrangement for the conduct of trade. Hyderabad city was the pivotal trading point because it was located on the land route that connects Masulipatnam on the east coast and Goa and Surat on the west. During the initial period, traders seems to have been exempted from the paying *zakat*, the tax on merchandise.[9] The commodity markets in the city included those for grain, textiles, timber, spices, oilseeds and other products. In artisan industry, the *chaudariyan* (headmen) operated as links between urban-based trade and industry located in similar centres. As the two lists given above indicate, there were at least twenty such centres in the state. In particular, regional centres like Aurangabad, Gulbarga, Narayan Pet and Nirmal served as the links in the network. Independent merchant groups closely aligned with industry thus emerged both in these regional centres and in Hyderabad city.

At the apex of the trade network were big merchants. They were primarily engaged in the diamond and armaments trade. Some of them also belonged to the all-powerful landed gentry. They were also close to the state and played a role in succession battles both during the Qutub Shahi period and later.[10] These big monopolistic merchants, at least in the initial years, gave stiff resistance to colonial traders, but over time, indigenous trade and indigenous industry were both overshadowed by colonial trade.

Notes

1. Haroon Khan Sherwani, *The History of Qutub Shahi Dynasty*, Munshiram Manoharlal, New Delhi, 1974. His account of *balutedars* was some what different from that given in Yusuf Hussain Khan (ed.), *Farmans and Sanads of Deccan Sultans* (*1408–1687*), State Archives, GOAP, Hyderabad, 1980.
2. Census, 1881.
3. The following review is based on Mirza Mehadi Khan, *Imperial Gazetteer of India, Provincial Series, Hyderabad*, Government Press, Calcutta, 1909; Claude A. Campbell, *Glimpses of the Nizam's Dominions*, C.B. Burrow, London, 1898; Syed Hussain Bilgrami and Charles Willmott, *Historical and Descriptive Sketch of His Highness the Nizam's Dominions*, Vol. I, Times of India Press, Bombay, 1883, pp. 371–433; Ghulam Yazdani, *Bidar: Its History and Monuments*, Oxford University Press, London, 1947; and, Sherwani, 1974, op. cit. (note 1).

4. Based on the travel accounts of Tavernier a diamond merchant and those of Thavenot in the seventeenth century, Sherwani gives a detailed account of diamond mining in Golconda. Sherwani, 1974, op. cit. (note 1), pp. 471–75.
5. See Bilgrami and Willmott, 1883, op. cit. (note 3), pp. 234–35 and Campbell, 1883, op. cit. (note 3), pp. 138–39.
6. See Campbell, cited above, pp. 140–47. See also IS, pp. 318–24.
7. The impressions on trade mechanisms given here are based on Kambhampati Satyanarayana, *Andhrula Samskruti Charitra—II* (Telugu), Hyderabad Book Trust, Hyderabad, 1982, pp. 322–46; Sherwani, 1974, op. cit. (note 1) and Sarojini Regani, *Nizam–British Relations 1724–1857*, Book Lovers, Hyderabad, 1963.
8. The city structure, at the time of its foundation, was reported to have had provision for 14,000 shops. Mohini Rajan and Harriet Ronken Lyton, *The Days of the Beloved: Life and Times of Mahbub Ali Pasha*, University of California Press, Berkeley, 1974, p. 12.
9. Yusuf Hussain Khan, 1980, op. cit. (note 1), p. 25.
10. Satyanarayana, 1982, op. cit. (note 7).

CHAPTER TWO

Salar Jung and the State

The changes in the social organisation of Hyderabad initiated by the State are associated with the Prime Ministership of Mir Turab Ali Khan, popularly known by his title, Salar Jung (1829–1883).[1] Earlier, during the prime ministership of his uncle Sirajul Mulk, he served as the *taluqdar* of some districts in Telangana. Later, after the death of Sirajul Mulk, he became the prime minister (*diwan*) in 1853, during the reign of Asaf Jah IV (1829–1857). He continued in this post upto his death in 1853, serving three rulers. In 1869, when the sixth Nizam, Mahboob Ali Khan, was still a minor, Salar Jung also become a co-regent and during the last two years, he was the sole regent. Thus Salar Jung was effectively at the helm of affairs in Hyderabad State for the three decades from 1853 to 1883.

Salar Jung, himself a leading *jagirdar*, belonged to a *Shia* family that originally migrated from Bijapur Deccan. His gradual control over the entire state apparatus became a source of tension with the *Sunni* aristocracy, especially the *paigah* nobles. A number of his initiatives were constrained by the manoeuvers of the *paigah* nobles. In fact, after the death of the co-regent in 1877, he bitterly opposed the appointment of a *paigah* noble to the post, but he had to yield to pressure from the British. Similarly, there was serious tension between him and the traditional bureaucracy, especially the *daftardars*.[2]

His relations with the two Nizams whom he directly served, Asaf Jah IV and Asaf Jah V, were also marked with contradictions. During the initial years, every major initiative he took encountered suspicion from the ruler as he was perceived as an agent of the British. On at least four occasions, he was on the verge of losing his position, but the British intervened in his favour.[3]

His relationship with the British was also marked by extremes. He was honoured with the title of Knight Commander of the Star of India (KCSI) by the Queen, but on one occasion he as threatened with deportation to Madras Presidency. To a certain extent the subjective element in the personal relations between him and the seven Residents during his prime ministership determined the nature of the relationship between the two powers. But more fundamentally, the relationship was governed by the unity or conflict of interest between the colonial rulers and the native government. Initially his support to the British during the 1857 disturbances endeared him to them.[4] Later his measures to provide the infrastructure of a modern society received the support of the colonial masters when it suited their interests, but on other issues where the British perceived a threat to their power, he was opposed by the Residents. Notable among the contentious issues were the restoration of the cotton-surplus Berar to Hyderabad,[5] the attempt to modernise the armed forces including plans to introduce machinery in the state workshops[6] and efforts to raise, independent of the British Government in India, capital for the state railway in the money markets of London.

Thus, Salar Jung's relationship with all three centres of power—the Nizam, the aristocracy and the Residency, were marked by ambiguities and contradictions. In all, during the thirty years of his prime ministership, he was threatened twice with dismissal and once with deportation. He submitted his resignation four times, but always withdrew it. He survived two assassination attempts. His sudden death at the age of 53, officially ascribed to cholera, remained under a cloud. Long after his death, a financial scandal, of which he was later cleared, haunted his credibility.

In a sense, the ambiguities and controversies that coloured the personality of Salar Jung were part of the unique role he played in nineteenth century India. The unity and conflict between the colonial rulers and the native ruling elite, the tension between tradition and modernity, between religious revivalism and secular liberalism mark social, cultural and religious life during the period. They also serve as the background for the rise of a number of eminent personalities in diverse fields during the latter half of the nineteenth century. But for Salar Jung, unlike his other illustrious contemporaries, the instrument for ensuring continuity and change was the state apparatus. This makes his role in nineteenth century India unique. An evaluation of his personality falls outside the scope of the present study, but it serves as a backdrop for the changes in social organisation initiated by the state under his leadership.

I

The extensive restructuring of the social organisation that Salar Jung undertook is often analysed under the rubric of administrative reforms, but the framework of administrative reforms is an inadequate tool for grasping the significance of his initiatives. The agrarian revenue system, trade and manufacture, development of public works and infrastructural facilities and the overhauling of the fiscal system were all integrated parts of these initiatives. We shall, however, focus on the central features of these measures in order to trace the elements of transition.

In the agrarian revenue system, the primary focus of these measures was restoring administrative control over the system and increasing land revenue.[8] The area under direct government administration, *diwani* territories, increased from 26,000 sq. miles in 1853 to about 71,589 sq. miles in 1889.[9] Excluding the 10,000 sq. mile area of Raichur Doab, Sholapur and Naldurg districts which were restored in 1860, the percentage increase was a phenomenal 136 per cent. Consequently the proportion of area under *diwani* territories became about 86.56 per cent, in sharp contrast to the 4.84 per cent of *jagir* areas, in 1881.[10] The *tankahi mahalat jagirs* were completely abolished. Similarly in *diwani* territories, systems of contract like *sarbasta* and *ta-ah-hud* were abolished. The basis of revenue was also shifted from the village to the individual, with differential rates based on the quality of the land. Simultaneously, a new revenue administration system was set up whereby hereditary collectors of revenue were replaced by salaried officers. All there measures contributed to land revenue increasing by over 163 per cent during the period 1853–1862.[11]

Changes in the agrarian revenue system were accompanied by changes in the trade mechanism. The drastic reduction in *jagir* territories coupled with the curtailment of the powers of contractors in *diwani* territories enabled the government to eventually abolish pervasive private *rahdari* duties. The levying and collection of transit duties became a monopoly of the government for which an administrative apparatus, including customs houses on the frontiers, was created. The measures led to an increase both in the volume of trade and in customs revenue but reliable estimates are not available. One source estimates the increase in customs revenue during 1863–1864 at 700 per cent.[12] But a different estimate for part of this period, 1861–1864, indicates that the increase was only 54 per cent.[13]

It was primarily the increase in land revenue and customs revenue that enabled the government to establish its fiscal system on a sound footing. The increase in these two major traditional sources, among other things, led to an increase in the total revenue of the state. Total public revenue was reported to be around Rs 0.8 million in 1853,[14] but by 1883 it became about Rs 35.0 million.[15] The increase in revenue was accompanied by a reduction in public expenditure. The burden due to the Hyderabad contingent of the British Army was reduced as a result of the assignment of Berar to the British. It also earned a sizable surplus for the government. Salaries of troops, especially for the maintenance of irregular troops (*fauz-e-baiquda*), allowances, assignments and *mansabs* were reduced. One source indicates that the fall in public expenditure in 1853–1877 was 47 per cent.[16] The reduction in expenditure coupled with the increase in revenue eventually enabled the government to reduce its enormous public debt to a nominal amount. The public debt according to one source, was around Rs 35.0 million in 1848[17] but it was reduced, according to another source, to Rs 4.1 million in 1882.[18] It was this drastic reduction in public debt that enabled the government to abolish *tankahi mahalat jagirs* and the system of contracting in *diwani* areas. The improvement in the fiscal position was accompanied by the establishment of the central treasury, replacement of officiating private bankers with state treasuries in the districts and taluks and the introduction of a formal budget system. Private mints owned and financed by *jagirdars* were abolished. A state monopoly in minting was established with the introduction of a uniform system of coinage based on the *hali Sicca* Rupee.[19]

II

The improvement in the budgetary position of the government enabled it to launch what is now called development programmes for investment in social overhead capital. Offering Berar surplus as a security, the government was able to raise loans that financed the establishment of railways in the state.[20] The first line between Secunderabad and Wadi was opened to traffic in 1874. But the returns from the railways remained very low as the line served British strategic interest more than the Hyderabad economy. The government consequently took the initiative in establishing another line to connect the capital to coal fields and the cotton-producing districts. But the proposal was not encouraged by the colonial Indian government. In particular, the efforts of the Hyderabad government to independently raise capital in London money markets was strongly resisted.[21] But eventually the state was able to convince the Home office. Thus with the help of the National Provincial Bank of England, the government floated 'His Highness The Nizam's guaranteed State Railway Company Limited'. The lines to the coal fields and the cotton districts however only materialised more than a decade after Salar Jung's death. It was also during this period that initial surveys and negotiations with the colonial government were undertaken to start coal mining in the state. Eventually in 1887, the Hyderabad (Deccan) Mining Company, with two thirds of its capital provided by the state government, began its operations.[22]

Other measures taken by the state government included the pioneering work undertaken by the Public Works Department

(PWD) in the repair and maintenance of irrigation works, road building and establishing a civil engineering workshop.[23] The creation of a separate forest department facilitated the systematic exploitation of forest products for industrial purposes.[24]

In the field of education, the first institution established by the state government was a civil engineering college, under the Public Works Department, in 1868. The college, a unique experiment, trained engineers who were obliged to serve the department. It was later closed down. But the school attached to the college became the precursor of the first arts college in the state with affiliation to Madras University. The education department, created in 1869, was able to establish government schools in almost all *talukas* and districts. In 1884, there were 162 such schools in the state.[25]

All these measures were initiated in the context of wide-ranging administrative reforms.[26] The distinctive features of these reforms included the administrative redivision of the state with corresponding revenue divisions, the appointment of salaried government officials in place of hereditary occupants in positions ranging from the village level to the state secretariat; and the establishment of separate departments of revenue, judiciary, police, finance, public works, forests, customs, education, health, military and political affairs. The most significant measures in this regard relate to the police and the judiciary. Revenue and police functions were separated at all levels. A separate police force, with a vertical administrative structure corresponding to that of administrative divisions was set up. An attempt was also made to separate quasi-judicial functions from the police. In the judicial structure, civil and criminal jurisdictions were separated. The criminal courts of judicature (*adalat-e-fauzdari*) formed the base of the new system with a high court at the apex.

III

The initiative taken by the state under the prime ministership of Salar Jung fundamentally altered the social organisation of Hyderabad. In the agrarian revenue system, it brought in a hitherto absent degree of uniformity. Leaving aside the crown lands (*sarf-e-khas*), almost the entire state was brought under the direct or indirect administration of the revenue department. In fact, for the first time, areas falling under the former Gondwana on the northern frontiers where a more egalitarian tribal revenue system prevailed, were brought within the purview of government administration.[28] More importantly, the measures eliminated the centres of arbitrary power that had come into prominence from about the middle of the eighteenth century, in the feudal social base of the regime. In particular, the abolition of *tankahi mahalat jagirs, sarbasta* and *ta-ah-hud* systems of contract re-established the state's administrative control over the agrarian revenue system. The consequent reduction in the absolute power of the landed elite also enabled the state to initiate the restructuring of the trade, fiscal and monetary systems. In the process, the power of the traditional aristocracy from the level of *paigah* nobles and *jagirdars* located in the city to that of *deshmukhs* and *deshpandes* in the villages received juridicial sanction. This juridicial sanction, backed by a new modern state apparatus, reinforced their customary social power. It can perhaps, be suggested that the process of strengthening of the social power of the elites was responsible, ultimately, for the defeat of attempts by the state to curtail their role as arbitrators of justice and administration at the village level.

But the restructuring of feudal social relations enabled the state to take initiatives in other directions. Restrictions on the power of *jagirdars* and other landed elites, among other things, led to an improvement in trade mechanisms. The interference of *jagirdars*, in trade conduits, had earlier reduced the commercial treaties with the colonial power to a state of atrophy. In fact, this had become a source of friction between the two governments. The measures taken to establish state control over customs duties led to a growth in the volume of trade. In turn, this strengthened the bonds between the colonial power and the state government.

The improvement in fiscal and monetary administration enabled the state to develop infrastructural facilities. Hyderabad state became the first native state to finance and eventually own road and rail transport, coal mines and later, power generation. The distinctive development of large-scale industry, where the state played the most important role later, was facilitated by the base established during this period.

The development of infrastructural facilities, the improvement of trade mechanisms and the restructuring of feudal social relations, especially the shift in the basis of revenue from the village to the individual—all in the immediate content of the late nineteenth century—paved the way for the commercialisation of segments of the agrarian economy. The growth, initially, of cotton in Marathwada and later, of oilseeds in Telangana and the social processes generated by them were primarily the result of the initiative taken by the state during this period.

The development of the administrative apparatus led to significant changes in polity. Initially the reforms required men trained in British India. This introduced an entirely new element, north Indian elites, mostly alumni of Aligarh Muslim University, into the state apparatus replacing to a certain extent, the traditional occupants from elite native families. Over time, this new element emerged as a powerful social category, the non-*mulkis*. The conflict between *mulkis* and non-*mulkis* influenced state policy in a number of ways.

IV

The measures taken by the state under the prime ministership of Salar Jung laid the basis of industrialisation in Hyderabad. The state undertook these measures under conditions of relative autonomy. The space for such an autonomous initiative was facilitated by the specific conditions of nineteenth century Hyderabad.

The traditional feudal aristocracy was, by then, completely incapable of taking any meaningful initiative. The anarchy that came to prevail in the economy and in polity led to the emergence of new and arbitrary centres of power in all sectors of the economy, which in turn perpetuated the anarchy. This vicious circle necessitated and facilitated the intervention by Salar Jung. He was able to placate the traditional aristocracy such as *paigah* nobles and a section of *jagirdars* even while systematically and ruthlessly eliminating the recently-emerged arbitrary centres of power. It was this tactful manoeuvring that enabled him to re-establish central authority in the agrarian revenue system where even areas hitherto outside the feudal social organisation were brought within its fold. The frequent ups and downs in policy matters, especially in the years preceding the minority regime of Mahabub Ali Pasha, in a sense, indicates the limited space for such manoeuvring. But eventually Salar Jung survived and succeeded.

The most important factor contributing to his success was the support he received from the colonial power whose strategic constraints in Hyderabad forced them to patronise the forces which would undertake a restructuring of the social organisation in a way that would serve their interests. But later, after the economy had regained strength and stability, some of the measures only aroused resistance by the colonial power. More direct challenges to its power such as attempts to strengthen the army, legitimate attempts to repossess the commercially profitable areas like Berar and independent assertion of control over larger economic processes like the Godavari Valley railway line, all faced resistance and hostility from the colonial power. Here, in sharp contrast to his earlier efforts, Salar Jung's manoeuvring was marked by much less success. The army was never allowed to be modernised and in the end it collapsed without resistance in its first and only attempt at war. Berar remained with the British till the end. The only exception was the Godavari Valley railway line which, significantly, also eventually served colonial trade. In fact, social and administrative reorganisation facilitated colonial penetration of the economy.

The restructuring of feudal social relations thus eventually strengthened the political and social base of the colonial power. Later one can see, while analysing state and society in the twentieth century, the ultimate limitations of Salar Jung's measures, but for the present we should note that they provided the strength and autonomy to the state in which one can locate the origins of the industrial evolution of Hyderabad.

Notes

1. For basic works on the life and times of Salar Jung, see Moulavi Chirag Ali, *Hyderabad Under Salar Jung*, (3 vols.), Bernard Quaritch, London, 1885, and Vasant Kumar Bawa, *The Nizam Between Mughals and British, Hyderabad Under Salar Jung I*, S. Chand, New Delhi, 1986.
2. See, 'Salar Jung and the Mughalai Officials', Karen Isaken Leonard, *Social History of Indian Caste, The Kayasths of Hyderabad*, University of California Press, Berkeley, 1978, pp. 65–68.
3. Sarojini Regani, 'The Appointment of *Diwans* in Hyderabad State (1803–1387)', *Andhra Historical Research Society Journal*, Vol. XXV, pp. 11–18, 1960, and Ajit Neogy, 'British Role in the Selection of Nizam's *Diwan* in Nineteenth Century', *Quarterly Review of Historical Studies*, Vol. XI, No. 3, 1972.
4. Govindraja Chari, 'Role of the State of Hyderabad in the Uprising of 1857', Unpublished Doctoral Dissertation, Department of History, Andhra University Waltair, 1972.
5. Bharati Ray, 'Salar Jung, Berar and the British', *Calcutta Historical Journal*, 2, July–December 1977, pp. 102–13.
6. Bawa, 1986, op. cit. (note 1), pp. 129–137.
7. Bharati Ray, 'The Genesis of Railway Development in Hyderabad State: A Case Study of Nineteenth Century British Imperialism', *Indian Economic and Social Historical Review*, Vol. XXI, No. 1, 1984, pp. 45–69.
8. The basic work on reforms in the agrarian revenue system still remains Chirag Ali, 1885, op. cit. (note 1), Vol. I.
9. Ibid., Vol. I, p. 14.
10. Based on the table given in Chirag Ali, ibid., p. 71.
11. Based on the figures given in GAR, 1294 F., p. 343.
12. Ibid., p. 207.
13. Based on the figures given in Richard Temple, *Report of the Administration of the Government of His Highness the Nizam in Deccan*, GoH, Hyderabad, 1868, pp. 112–18.
14. GAR, 1294 F. see also B.K. Narayan, *Finances and Fiscal Policy of Hyderabad State (1900–1956)*, GOAP, Hyderabad, 1973, p. 15. The incredibly low figure could be an underestimate.
15. GAR, 1294 F.
16. Based on the figure given in Bawa, 1986, op. cit. (note 1).

17. The estimates of the Resident, Colonel J. Low (1853), quoted in Bawa, cited above, p. 235.
18. William Digby, 'India for Indians and for England', included in Moulavi Syed Mehadi Ali, *Hyderabad Affairs*, Vol. III, Times of India Press, Bombay, 1886, p. 14.
19. The standardisation of coinage was introduced in 1857. The value of the *Hali Sicca Rupee* was approximately 15 per cent less than the British Indian Government Rupee.
20. For details see, James Adair Crawford, *Precis of Correspondence Regarding Railways in Native States*, Foreign Department Press, GOI, Calcutta, 1884, Chapter II.
21. Bawa, 1986, op. cit. (note 1), pp. 117–29 and Bharati Ray, 1984, op. cit. (note 7).
22. For the genesis of coal mines in the state, see GAR, 1294 F. pp. 239–41.
23. See, George Palmer, *Report on the Operations of His Highness the Nizam's Public Works and Allied Department (1277–1293 F)*, GOH, Hyderabad, 1885.
24. For details of the development of the Development of Forests in early years see, GAR, 1294 F. pp. 238–39.
25. Bawa, 1986, op. cit. (note 1), p. 86, see also Syed Hossain Bilgrami, *History of the Operations of His Highness the Nizam's Education Department of the Last Thirty Years Together with a Detailed Report and Returns for 1883–84–85*, GOH, Hyderabad, 1886.
26. On administrative reforms under Salar Jung see, Muhammad Fathulla Khan, *A History of Administrative Reforms in Hyderabad State*, New Hyderabad Press, Secunderabad, 1935.
27. Mohammad Abdul Muttalib, 'The Administration of Justice Under the Nizams, 1724–1947', Unpublished Doctoral Dissertation, Department of Political Science, Osmania University, Hyderabad, 1957.
28. On the revenue system in the Gondwana areas see Christof von Furer Haimendorf, *Raj Gonds of Adilabad*, Oxford University Press, London, 1980.

Section II

Industrialisation: 1875–1948

CHAPTER THREE

Evolution

The 1870s can be considered the period which marks the beginnings of modern industrialisation in Hyderabad state. In 1870, a Central Public Works Department workshop which pioneered engineering works, was established. In 1871, large deposits of coal were discovered. In 1872, construction work began on the first railway line in the state. In 1874, the first textile mill was established in Hyderabad city.

Almost seventy-five years later, when Hyderabad state was integrated into the Indian Union in 1948, a wide range of industrial goods was being produced in the state. By that time, the state, with a population of about four per cent of the total Indian population, had three per cent of India's factory labour, seven per cent of its factories and about six per cent of the paid-up value of capital in the corporate sector. The share of the state in the output was four per cent or more in cotton, matches, sugar, liquor, coal and other goods (See Tables 3.1 and 3.2, Appendix 3-A). The considerable growth in industry was made possible by the distinctive role played by the state in industrial development. In Hyderabad the state played a pioneering role in ownership and financing of industries, in taking diverse technological initiatives and evolving a conception of planned development. The present chapter traces the evolution of industry with the focus on state policy.

The industrial evolution of Hyderabad state had three distinct phases.[1] The first phase, starting roughly from the 1870s ended with the end of World War I (WW I). The second phase was the inter-war years, 1919–1939. The third phase was from the beginning of World War II (WW II) in 1939 to the end of the Nizam's regime in 1948. The division of industrial development into these three phases is fairly common to all studies on industrialisation in India. But our division in the case of Hyderabad is based on the role of the state in industrial development.

The first phase, beginning with the last days of Salar Jung's prime ministership, was marked by the reorganisation of the economy and polity which created an environment necessary for the development of modern industry. It was during this period that a firm base for infrastructure was laid. In the second phase, 1919–1939, the state took the initiative in providing institutional support to industry. Financial and technological aid to industries helped in the development of local industry, both in the small-scale and large-scale sectors. The third phase, 1939–48, marks a decisive attempt by the state to initiate structural changes in industry from agro-based industries to metal and engineering, chemical-based and forest-based industries. The structural changes were sought to be effected within the wider perspective of planned economic development.

While taking the state as the basis for dividing industrial development into three distinct phases, two considerations should be kept in mind. Firstly, like any other chronological division of economic and social processes, the demarcating points should not be taken as watertight divisions. As we shall see later, the process of industrialisation in Hyderabad, by its very nature, defies such time-based compartmentalisation. Secondly, the evolution of state policy was a non-linear process where a clear policy outline sometimes emerged long after the measures inherent in it had actually been enforced. Except perhaps since the 1930s, no well-defined policy framework preceded the actual initiatives taken by the state. Very often the measures were marked by faltering steps that indicate a lack of conceptual clarity. It is possible to suggest that no account of actual economic processes is free from such a zigzag course and that a unilinear course of development is only theoretically possible in development theory or in a development model. But in Hyderabad specific historical factors contributed to the course of development. The state first took the initiative for industrial development in response to the demands of the colonial power. But in the gradual evolution of its industrial policy the state was conditioned by the contradictions with that very colonial power. On the other hand, despite its autonomous initiatives in the field of industry, the state was obliged to defend the interests of the feudal aristocracy from whom it derived its political power and economic strength. The historical factors which conditioned the existence and conduct of the state thus contributed to the chequered evolution of its industrial policy. Any attempt to outline the path of this transition, with its focus more or less exclusively, on industry, cannot always reflect these contradictions. The following account is no exception as it has the advantage of hindsight.

II

First Phase: 1870–1919

The wide-ranging measures initiated by Salar Jung laid a firm base for infrastructure in the state. Salar Jung's prime ministership coincided with a period when such developments were also taking place elsewhere in India. The construction of railways in India began in 1851. A decade later, in 1861, a proposal was mooted, for the first time, to connect Hyderabad by rail. Hyderabad had already been connected by electric telegraph in 1857. By 1872 there was a regular postal network between Hyderabad city and district centres.

The controversial Hyderabad Godavari Valley Railway line, a 386-mile route connecting Manmad, Aurangabad, Parbhani, Nanded and Secunderabad, was opened to traffic in 1899. The line boosted economic activity in the region and also helped the Nizam Guaranteed State Railway Company (NGSRC) recover its strength. By the end of WW I three broadgauge lines (352 miles) and three meter gauge lines (620 miles) connected Hyderabad city with different parts of the state.[2] The new lines also connected the collieries with the rest of the state.

Meanwhile, the Hyderabad Deccan Mining Company, a London-based concern with seventy five per cent of its capital held by the Hyderabad government, began extracting coal at the Singareni coal fields in Warangal district. The management and control of the company was initially in the hands of the government. Later in 1920, a new company, Singareni Collieries Company (SCC) financed by the government took over the coalfields. With the opening of other pits at Sasti and Paoni, Adilabad, there was a considerable increase in coal production. The average annual output which was around 296000 tonnes in 1892–95, increased to around 652000 tonnes by 1916–1919.[3] Meanwhile power generation was also started in the state.

Of the other developments in the economy around this time, the major one which had far-reaching implications for industrial development, was the gradual expansion of the area under commercial crop cultivation. Cotton was already a major commercial crop in the state. The Godavari Valley Railway Line, given the increasing demand all over India, helped in a phenomenal increase in cotton cultivation. It was also during this period that oilseed cultivation began in the Telangana districts. The efforts by the Public Works Department (PWD) to reorganise irrigation also helped the process.

It was in this context that industrial establishments emerged in the state. The first cotton mill was established in Hyderabad city in 1874, and two more mills were added by the end of the century. In all the cotton-producing districts, cotton ginning and pressing mills developed in large numbers.[4] Several rice and flour mills also came up during this phase. In other groups, the state-owned railway, the mint and the general engineering workshop (*Sanat-e-Hind*) were the notable units.

In 1901, according to the general Administration Report there were 68 large industrial establishments, employing average daily labour of ten or more. By the end of WW I in 1920 their number had risen to just above 330[5] with an overwhelming majority being units in agro-based products.[6] According to the 1921 industrial census, the labour force engaged in organised industry numbered about 35000. In addition, there were about 23000 workers employed in railways and coal mines.

Second Phase: 1919–1939

During this phase the state actively provided institutional support to industry. In fact such measures had already been initiated in the last years of the first phase.

Throughout the initial years, industries were under the revenue department. As their number increased, the government enacted a Factories and Boilers Inspection Act (1319 F) in 1909, to regulate the working of the burgeoning cotton ginning and pressing mills. As the need for developing other industries was brought home by WW I, a committee was appointed to go into the question.

The committee's report recommended the establishment of a separate department for industry.[8] A year later, in 1918, *Sanat-o-Hirafat*, Commerce and Industries Department (CID) was formed. A nine member Board of Advisors, which included five non-official members, was set up to guide industrial activity in the state. In 1921, this department was transferred to the wider Department of Development, but later, in 1927, it again became a full-fledged department. It was this department of the government that played the leading role in industrial development. For a number of years the department was headed by Englishmen, who were either retired or serving members of the Indian Civil Service or the military. But otherwise it was run by officials of the Hyderabad civil service. Later, the Industrial Trust Fund (ITF) handled some of the functions of the department. Even though the ITF was formally part of the department, it enjoyed considerable autonomy.

The department took initiatives in a number of directions. Initially an effort was made to encourage the development of cottage and small-scale industries. Later, with the help of an Industrial Laboratory, set up in 1917, the department undertook research and development work in a wide range of areas. On the basis of the experiments carried out by the laboratory, the department was able to start what were called pioneering industries. Around the same time some initiatives were also taken to finance large-scale undertakings, but the measures taken by the department during its first decade were marked by their ad-hoc nature. A number of measures initiated were not pursued. For instance, the grant of Rs 50,000 for assistance to small-scale industries remained unspent for over two years.[9] On the other hand, the large-scale Deccan Glass Works suffered from inadequate finance.[10] A soap factory, pioneered by the department, was handed over to a private owner much too early for it to survive, and the department had to take it over again.[11] The Power Alcohol Factory also had a chequered career during this period.[12] To a certain extent, the department was constrained by its budgetary resources; its average annual expenditure, in 1918–1929, was about Rs 1.45 lakhs.[13] Eventually this period of flux came to an end with the formation of the Industrial Trust Fund (ITF) in 1929.

The ITF was unique among institutions of its kind in colonial India. It corpus of about Rs 10 million was invested in a number of large industrial establishments in the form of shares, debentures and loans. The income from these investments was used to develop cottage and small-scale industries, initiate many types of research, provide training scholarships to students and businessmen and sponsor industrial and economic inquires. The ITF also acted as a managing agent for a number of companies in the state.[14]

The government's efforts to provide small-scale industries with financial assistance began with prolonged negotiations with Tata's Industrial Bank. The Bank established a branch in Hyderabad city in 1918 with the help of the government. The government deposited Rs 20 lakhs in the Bank, at a low interest rate. The department proposed that the Bank should give loans to small-scale industries. Initially the bank was not in favour of the proposal but later, under pressure, it agreed to provide loans to small-scale industries at 12 per cent per annum interest and demanded government security for the loans. The government, which opposed both the high rate of interest and the security clause, argued that since it was already a major depositor in bank there was no further need for additional security. Eventually negotiations broke down.[15] The department launched its own scheme in 1920. A total of Rs 2.06 lakhs was granted to about 90 parties in 1920–1930.[16] Since a number of problems beset the scheme, the ITF took over the job in 1929. Subsequently, a number of small-scale units in different groups of industries developed. Our estimates, based on the department's annual reports, show that oil mills, expellers, and rice mills in the agro-based industries, chemical-based factories and animal-based industries, followed by engineering units received the highest proportion of the loans (see Table 3.3, Appendix 3-A).

In cottage industries, the major initiative of the department in the initial years was in handlooms. An attempt was made to improve technology with the help of the Demonstration Weaving Factory established in 1920. Later a number of district demonstration weaving Parties were set up, and their number eventually went up to nine. Basing themselves at select district centres, which changed from time to time, the Parties toured the villages in the district. The primary objective of these demonstration Parties was to introduce fly looms and to train artisans in the use of the improved looms.[17] In addition, the Parties also supplied yarn to the weavers on credit. The centre at their district headquarters also trained young persons selected from the weaving community. An extension of this scheme was the establishment of the Cottage Industries Institute (CII), in Hyderabad city in 1930. The Institute offered training in weaving, dyeing, printing silk, woollen goods and in later years, bidriware, Nirmal toys and leather goods. The Institute seems to have only selected people from the respective artisan communities for training in improved methods and also in new variations in the product.[18] In addition the department also set up a similar institute for jacquard weaving at Paithan, Aurangabad. With financial assistance from the ITF, a state-owned carpet factory was set up at Warangal. For leather goods, a number of model tanneries were set up in different parts of the state to train tanners in improved methods and to introduce the making of new varieties of leather goods.

These measures to improve the technological base of artisan industry were backed by financial support. Both flylooms and yarn were supplied at subsidised prices. The students at various institutes also received scholarships. In addition, small-scale units, usually set up by the students of these institutes, were given financial aid as part of the scheme to develop small-scale industries, but the major initiative was to introduce cooperatives among the artisans.

Cooperatives were introduced in the state in 1914 through the Hyderabad Cooperation Act, II of 1323F. Initially they were confined to agriculture. But from 1920, Industrial Cooperatives came up initially among weavers. Towards the end of the 1930s, there were about 130 such industrial cooperatives.[19] They included weavers, tanners, and silver and brass makers.

Along with technological and financial assistance the government also attempted to provide market facilities to artisan industries. The first attempt was to conduct or participate in industrial exhibitions to promote the sale of these products. In Hyderabad this tradition dates back to the mid-nineteenth century during the early years of Salar Jung's prime ministership. Thereafter the government participated in a number of such exhibitions held in India and abroad. From 1930, a permanent industrial exhibition was set up in Hyderabad city. The Osmania University Graduates Association which organised this exhibition with the assistance of the state, also published a journal, *Mulki Industries*. In later years, the Cottage Industries Institute organised its own sales depot. The Depot acted as a middleman between village artisans and urban consumers.

In the field of technology, the major achievement was the establishment of the Industrial Laboratory in 1917. The routine work of the Laboratory was the analysis of samples sent to it by different departments of the government and by private parties. More importantly, the Laboratory conducted experiments in manufacturing products from local material. Among the notable experiments were manufacturing sugar from date palms, power alcohol (which is a substitute for petrol) from mahua flowers, boot polish from locally-made methylated spirit, soap making, paper from the bamboos of the Adilabad forests, salt and katha from the backwaters of Raichur and Gulbarga, and various products from oilseeds.[20] The Laboratory also trained young men in the manufacture of some of the products. In later years, the work of the Laboratory was supplemented by the Laboratory of Osmania University. The research undertaken by the department was backed by the extensive economic and industrial surveys sponsored by the ITF. Altogether the ITF sponsored 42 industrial or economic surveys.[21] A number of industries, like soap-making, power alcohol, paper matches and others came up as a result of these efforts.

The department also provided other kinds of technical support. The Industrial Engineering Section was set up in 1926. This division undertook preparation of blue prints for new factories, erection of machinery and providing of technical advice to a number of industries. The government also took initiatives to impart technical training. Besides three major technical training institutes, industrial schools were set up at a number of places. Vocational courses were introduced in many schools, including primary schools.[22] The ITF spent about Rs 6.17 lakhs on scholarships to *mulki* students for industrial training in 1929–1949.[23]

In addition, a major attempt was made to create industrial areas in the state. A committee of experts which included the well-known prime minister of Mysore state, M. Visweswarayya, was set up to examine the feasibility of the proposal. On the basis of the recommendations of the committee, the Mushirabad- Azamgarh area of Hyderabad city was selected as an area reserved for industry in 1930.[24] Two hundred acres of land were selected in the area. Some existing factories like Vazir Sultan Tobacco, shifted to the new area. Factories set up in the area were given concessions in land, power and water facilities.

The most significant initiative taken by the state was providing financial aid to the corporate sector. The first company to receive such aid was the Shahbad Cement Company of the Tatas, set up in 1925. Later the till-fated Deccan Glass Works also received aid. After the establishment of the ITF, a number of companies received large and liberal financial aid from the government. In 1929–1950, as many as 43 out of the total 85 companies in the manufacturing and mining sectors received financial aid of about Rs 76.26 million.[25] Both in the corporate sector and in the small-scale industrial sector it should be noted that financial aid was granted largely to *mulkis*, the domiciles of the state.[26]

These diverse initiatives were backed by a suitable fiscal policy. The new budgetary system, introduced in 1922, provided fiscal strength to the state and enabled it to increase public expenditure to a significant extent.[27] The purchase policy of the government gives some idea of the effect of increasing public expenditure on industrial development. In general, the government appeared to have followed a policy of preference to local products, where available. Under the guidlines of the general *mulki*-oriented policy, government departments were directed to buy products from local manufacturers.[28]It is difficult to estimate the extent of its impact, but considering the nature of the requirements of the state, we can conclude that it could not have been significant and that a large proportion of public expenditure did leak out.[29]

The government exempted the income earned by these industries from any form of taxation. Income tax and supertax which were already being collected in British India, were not introduced in the state. In fact, a proposal to levy corporate tax on a federal basis by the government of India was opposed by the Hyderabad Government.[30] Excise duties on industrial products, other than alcohol, were introduced in the late 1930s, first on matches, cigarettes and sugar and later on other products, but they do not appear to have been significant.[31] Sales tax was only introduced in 1948, just before the fall of the regime.

The tariff policies followed by the government generally exempted all industrial raw materials from import duties. Similar exemptions were also made in case of export duties on all industrial exports. The growing list of goods exempted from import and export duties provided in the statistical Abstracts every year covers a wide range, but it appears that the government exercised discretionary powers in the actual levying of duties. For instance, import duties on raw materials required for leather goods and exemption of export duties on leather goods followed in 1933.[32] Similarly in 1932, when depression hit oilseed production in the state, the export duty on oilseed products was abolished resulting in an increase in the number of oil mills. Four years later when the industry stabilised, the duties were reintroduced.[33] Other examples can be found in the Annual Reports of the Department.

The significance of this tariff policy for actual industrial growth cannot be estimated in the absence of more detailed data,[34] but some features can be noted. In imports, machinery required for industrial development was a major component and in general, the government followed a liberal policy towards such imports.[35] Among industrial products, cement and coal essentially served the export market.[36] Among other notable products that served the internal market were cigarettes, glassware and power.[37]

Although the tariff policy remained a source of tension between the two governments, the Hyderabad government made attempts to co-ordinate with the British in Industrial Policy matters. Its efforts to persuade the colonial government to involve native governments in its annual conference of directors of industries failed. Then the state government took the initiative and sponsored a parallel conference of directors of industries departments of Indian states.[38] Except Baroda, almost all major states including Mysore, Travancore, Nabha, Holkar and Patiala responded positively. Eventually one such conference was held at Indore, but it did not become an annual event.

It was within this kind of wider framework that industries developed during the second phase. Among infrastructure, the railway company became a completely state-owned undertaking. The Nizam State Railway Company (NRSC) as it now came to be known, also started a Road Mechanical Transport Service Department (RMTS) in 1932. Taking over the monopoly of select trunk routes, the RMTS became the first state-owned road transport undertaking in India. Similarly civil aviation was also initially started under the NSRC. Hydro-electric generation from the Nizam Sagar Canal started in the 1930s.[39] Coal production increased from an annual average of 0.65 million tons in 1916–1919, to over one million tons in 1936–1939.[40]

Large industrial establishments increased from about 354 in 1920 to 879 in 1939.[41] Oil, rice, and flour mills, small-scale motor and engineering workshops, button factories, match factories and tanneries increased substantially. In the corporate sector, three more textile mills, two cigarette factories, two glass factories and a sugar factory came up. The labour force in organised industry increased from 23,000 in 1930 to over 47,000 in 1939.[42] In addition, there were another 30,000 workers engaged in railways, mining and other infrastructural industries.[43]

IV

The Third Phase: 1939–1948

Almost all activities initiated by the state during the second phase continued into the third phase, but this phase was marked by two notably distinctive features. Firstly, a concerted effort was made to effect a structural change from agro-based industries to others. Secondly, the conception of an integrated plan for economic development emerged and was sought to be put into practice.

It must be noted that the first five years of this phase were war years. In this period the increase in demand due to WW II gave an impetus to industry all over India. In Hyderabad it also had its effect.[44] This was also the period when, along with other well-established industries, machine factories, chemicals, paper mills and other forest-based industries developed in India.

It was within this national context that the Hyderabad government took initiatives to make structural changes in industry. Earlier the focus had been on agro-based industries, but the government attempted to shift it to other industries with the help of the ITF. As with cement during the earlier phase, the government followed the policy of encouraging industrial products based on the pattern of a single unit with a large capacity. These included sugar and starch in agro-based industries, metal works, machine tools and wire products in metallurgical and engineering industries, pharmaceuticals, fertilizers, heavy chemicals, plastics and synthetic products among chemical industries. All these factories, needing heavy capital investment, were financed by the state. In many cases the plant capacity of these factories was one of the largest in that industry in India. This structural change was reflected in the proportion of each group of industries among the total number of factories.[45] In fact it reflected more sharply in capital concentration. Cotton textiles and allied companies whose paid-up value of capital in the total manufacturing and mining sector of corporate capital was about 42 per cent in 1935–36, declined to 22 per cent by 1944–45. But the proportion increased to become about 7 per cent in the case of metallurgical and engineering industries and 14 per cent in chemicals.[46] While changing demand conditions since WW II gave an impetus to the development of these industries here as elsewhere in India, the state policy on capital and technology helped this process in Hyderabad.

A more significant development during the third phase was the emergence of the idea of state-planned economic development. It should however be noted that by this time the emergence of the idea of planning was not unique to Hyderabad. Since the 1930s it had become central to Indian nationalist economic thought.[47] Recent studies have also pointed out that even the colonial government experimented with the idea of planning,[48] but what distinguishes the idea of planning in Hyderabad from others, was that it was rooted firmly in years of practice.

Elements of planning were ingrained in the budgetary system introduced by Akbar Hydari in 1922.[49] Hydari had, around the time of the formation of the ITF, mooted the idea of planning in the state. Later others also joined him.[50] In fact the ITF had a number of features that later became part of the postcolonial planning process.

More directly, a post-war Planning Department with an initial budget of Rs 30 million, was formed in 1943.[51] During the last years of WW II, an ambitious 'Godavari Industrial and Agricultural Development Plan' was prepared. This massive scheme, at an estimated cost of Rs 240 million, envisaged an industrial township on the south bank of the river Godavari in Karimnagar district with a number of industries including heavy industries.[52] The formalities for starting the project began by the end of WW II. Meanwhile, a blueprint for a steel factory in the valley was also prepared.[53] Proposals were also submitted to the Authority for setting up chemical, glass, cement, rayon and other industries.[54] This project eventually became part of the first Five Year Plan prepared by the government of Hyderabad.

The concept of planning and the role assigned to the state in planned development were best reflected in some of the publications of the Industries Department. Arguing the need for a 'third body' that could give 'assurance to capitalists and employ technical men available', the Director of the Commerce and

Industries Department emphatically stated that 'it is the government and government alone that can take the place of this third body'.[55] In particular, the role of the state in heavy industries was emphasized. Quoting from Vladimir Illiych Lenin, described as 'a Russian social reformer', the Director argued that 'heavy industries needs state subsidies. If we are not able to find them, we as a civilised state will perish'.[56] Leaving aside the irony of an official of the Nizam's government approvingly quoting Lenin in 1946 when the state was already facing an armed peasant movement led by the communists, what should be noted is that this approach was part of a state policy that was clear in its conception. As the First Five Year plan adopted by the government stated: 'the state and only the state can create conditions in which productivity and the standard of living will continuously rise, has come to be accepted to an ever increasing degree'.[57]

The First Five Year Plan document of the Hyderabad government was a product of the deliberations of fifteen committees. The plan envisaged 108 projects, including those covered by the Godavari Valley Project. The proposed initial investment was about Rs 2500 million.[58] To raise the required finance the plan also proposed the levy, for the first time in the state, of incometax, surcharge, corporation tax and in fact practically every conceivable tax other than agricultural incometax.[59] Concomitantly, it was also proposed that a separate economic civil service should be created in the state.[60]

Some of the projects were taken up for active consideration, but many were not, because soon the regime faced a social and political crisis from which it never recovered. In 1948 the regime collapsed with the Indian army intervention.

V

The nature of industrialisation in Hyderabad was different from that in British administered provinces. In the British India of this period 'modern industry…meant…private industry'.[61] The colonial government did not have any cogent framework that can be described as an industrial policy. Its hostility towards native capital and industrialisation in India was reflected in its fiscal, tariff and monetary policies. It is here that the distinctive features of industrialization in an Indian state lie. Far from being hostile, native governments evolved a positive industrial policy in states such as Baroda, Mysore, Travancore and Hyderabad. Their political separateness partly explains this distinction.[62]

In Hyderabad in particular, the industrial policy of the state was rooted in the autonomous initiatives taken by it in social reorganisation during the Salar Jung period. The establishment of an infrastructure, especially the more or less complete state monopoly in the transport and energy sectors, facilitated the industrial development of the state. The infrastructural development was backed, during the later period, by the necessary institutional support.

A notable feature of state policy was a flexible technological policy. Firstly, the government took steps to develop the manufacture of new products based on local resources. These included soap, power alcohol, mill-made paper, paints and varnishes and glass. In all these cases, years of experimentation with local raw materials by the Industrial Laboratory preceded manufacture on a commercial scale. Secondly, the diffusion of new technology was preferred and popularised in other cases like handmade paper, carpets, and tanneries. Simultaneously the state also preferred outright purchase of imported technology, as for instance in metals and machinery, heavy chemicals, fertilizers and pharmaceuticals or entered into technical collaboration with external agencies as in the case of rayons and machine tools. In a few cases, outside agencies were assisted by the state to introduce new technology or products as in case of cement and hume pipes.

This flexible technology mix was backed by a suitable capital policy. Except textiles to a certain extent, almost all major industries received state finance in some form. The policy of preference for *mulkis* informed all these initiatives taken by the state. From the early 1930s state policy reflected a conscious effort with a clear conception of planned economic development emerging by the end.

It should however be noted that the evolution of industry in

Hyderabad closely followed that in British India. The policy measures that the Hyderabad government undertook were similar in many respects to those of the colonial government, but perhaps the impetus was not the same.

In the first phase prior to WW I, the colonial government pursued a policy of *laissez faire* which all but inhibited the growth of Indian industry. The fiscal policy, acknowledged later as 'ill-judged parsimony' by the Viceroy, Lord Chelmsford,[63] led to inadequate investments in social overhead capital. In any case it had no direct correlation with the requirements of industrialisation. The Hyderabad government's distinction lies in that, within the space available for maneuvering, it attempted to develop infrastructure and did so in response to the needs of industrial development. The contentious Godavari Valley Railway line was a case in point. The government not only developed industrial infrastructure but also eventually controlled the process of its development, despite recurring tension with the colonial government. The cotton textile industry, already under the guidance of the government grew out of these developments during the first phase. In a sense the Subsidiary Alliance, that took care of Hyderabad's defence, became a blessing in disguise, because it enabled the government to respond to the needs of industry instead of the requirements of strategic defence, while developing social overhead capital.

The similarities and dissimilarities between the policies of the two governments were more striking in the second phase—the inter-war years. The outbreak of WW I made the British government realise the weakness and rudimentary nature of the nature of the industrial infrastructure. The Industrial Commission set up in 1916 was a direct response to this. The report of the Commission suggested a major role for the government in industrialisation including, among other things, investment in social overhead capital, promotion of technical education and research and supply of direct financial assistance to private industry.[64]

But after the war, the recommendations of the Commission did not result in any identifiable industrial policy. Industries Departments were formally established at the central and provincial levels. Their activities were confined to gathering industrial intelligence, running some state factories and providing perfunctory assistance to small-scale and cottage industries. The formal measures to provide state aid to industry did not actually make any significant contribution to industrial development. Instead of an industrial policy what emerged was a more favourable tariff policy where discriminatory protection on a select basis replaced the free trade policies of the earlier era. This policy did of course provide some impetus towards import substitution in manufactured goods, especially consumer goods. But every concession granted in tariff protection was gained due to the prolonged battle waged by the nationalists. Even when tariff policies became somewhat more favourable to Indian industry, monetary policies remained a source of tension between the colonial government and the nationalists.

Again, within the larger framework, we can note some of the distinctive features of the industrial evolution of Hyderabad during the second phase. In monetary policy, it had no option but to accept the official exchange rate between the *Osmania Sicca* Rupee and the British Government Rupee. Nor did it have any control over the forces that determined the real exchange rates as we shall see later. In tariff policy, the Hyderabad government extended the policy of discriminatory protection to local industry. But both in developing technical education and research and finance to industry, the Hyderabad government's policies were distinctive. The growth and diversification of industry in the inter-war years was common to both Hyderabad and British India, but in Hyderabad it was the state that assumed the leadership of the process.

The third phase, after 1939, was a peculiar phase for Hyderabad in comparison with British India. The structural change, away from agro-based industries, was common to both. In the absence of substantial evidence, it is difficult to arrive at accurate assessments, but it can be suggested that industry in Hyderabad was relatively more geared to the civilian economy than industry in British India. But the crisis that engulfed the state in the immediate aftermath of WW II adversely affected industry in Hyderabad. The growth of industry in the third phase was substantially lower in Hyderabad than in British India. Many of the initiatives taken by the government were lost in the political and social crisis that overtook the regime.

In summing up, it can be concluded that the industrial policy of Hyderabad even while confined within the larger imperial framework, did maintain its own distinctive features. It is in this sense that the political separateness of a princely state and the particular autonomy of Hyderabad state become important explanatory variables in any analysis of industrial development in Hyderabad.

But no actual economic process can be judged solely by the policy measures of the government. We shall presently focus on some aspects of growth and the limitations of industrialisation in Hyderabad. Later we will analyse the limitations imposed by a feudal social order and the autocratic polity based on it, which the state resolutely defended to the last.

Notes

1. The account of industrial evolution outlined here is based on General Administration Reports (GAR), Commerce and Industries Department Annual Reports (CIDAR) and the reports of the ITF sponsored surveys on various industries. See the detailed 'Note on Sources', Bibliography.
2. In 1930, the government became the sole owner of the whole railway system, excluding 58 miles under British Railways. The total route mileage under its operation was about 1238 miles SA, 1343 F.
3. GAR, relevant years. See also output tables in the Appendix 6-A, Chapter 6: An Appraisal.
4. By 1905 the increase was already alarming enough for the owners to request the government to stop further issue of licenses. But the government refused to intervene. GAR, 1313–1315 F., p. 126.
5. Annual administration reports in this phase give the number of units, but not the number of workers engaged in them. The figures given here are from GAR, relevant years.
6. Elsewhere, in Appendix 6-B, Chapter 6, we have analysed the changing composition of industry in each phase.
7. Census, 1921. The definition of large industrial establishments in the 1921 Industrial Census, unlike in the 1911 Census, was more or less

the same as that of the Hyderabad government i.e. those employing an average daily labour of ten or more. This changed in 1945 when those employing less than twenty were excluded.

8. G.E. Wakefield, *A Note on the Industrial Potentialities of Hyderabad*, GOH, Hyderabad, 1917.
9. See, 'Allotment of Rs 50,000 for Advancement of Small Industries', CIDF 418/1328 F.
10. CIDAR, 1340 F., p. 15.
11. CIDAR, 1328 F., p. 24 and CIDAR, 1342 F., p. 10.
12. The proposal for the manufacture of Power alcohol was mooted in 1918, with an initial investment of Rs 8 lakhs (GAR 1328 F., p. 23). The factory had technical and managerial problems for a number of years in its initial phase (GAR, 1335 F., p. 30). But it got stabilised after waste molasses from the Nizam Sugar Factory began supplementing mahua flowers, the original raw material. The production was reported to have augmented petrol supplies by 25 per cent during the War period, D.K. Brahma, 'Sugar production in Hyderabad'; *HGBEA*, June–July 1951, p. 470.
13. 'Financial Statistics, 1301–1359 F', GOH, Hyderabad, 1951, Table 38, p. 172.
14. See, among others 'Industrial Trust Fund Secretariat 1929–1949', GOH, Hyderabad, 1950.
15. See, 'Granting Loans to Factories', CIDF 8/257/1329 F.
16. Computed from the data given in CIDAR, relevant years. See also GAR, relevant years.
17. The proportion of fly looms among the total looms increased from 26 per cent in 1921 to 56 per cent in 1941, IS, p. 52.
18. See 'Prospectus of Cottage Industries Institute', GOH, 1938. Also see IS, p. 126.
19. 'Annual Report of the Working of Co-operatives, 1340 F', GOH, Hyderabad, 1930.
20. See Khwaja Habib Hasan, *Report on the Working of Industrial Laboratory*, CID, GOH, Hyderabad, 1923 and C.V. Raman et. al., *Report on the Working of Industrial Laboratory*, CID, GOH, Hyderabad, 1934.
21. They include the famous Rural Economic Inquiries conducted by Prof. Kesav Iyengar. For a complete list of the surveys see 'ITF Secretariat 1929–1949', op. cit. (note 14) and IS, p. 71.
22. In 1933, there were about five industrial schools and vocational courses were offered in more than 50 schools (SA, 1343 F,

pp. 156–58). The number of exclusively industrial schools and institutes increased to about 25 in 1945, (SA, 1351–1354 F, pp. 1136–37). For a complete list of Industrial Institutions and the expenditure on them, see, IS, pp. 112–13.

23. 'ITF Secretariat', op. cit. (note 14), p. 5.
24. M. Visweswarayya et. al., *City Improvement Schemes*, CID, GOH, Hyderabad, 1930.
25. These figures are estimated from information given in diverse sources. See, 'State Aid to Industry' in Appendix 4-A, Chapter 4: Capital.
26. In 'The Rules for the grant of Loans', clause 14 ('Qualifications of a borrower') specifies that 'An applicant must be a subject of the State. Although the government did retain the right to permit a *gair mulki* to introduce a new industry', it was seldom exercised. For the text of the Rules see, 'Rules Regarding Granting Loans to Factories' CIDF 257/1329 F. No pagination.
27. For the new system and its impact, see B.K. Narayan, *Financial and Fiscal Policy of Hyderabad State (1900–1956)*, GOAP, Hyderabad, 1973, Chapter IV, pp. 21–28. See also S. Kesav Iyengar, *A Review of Hyderabad Finance*, GOH, Hyderabad, 1951. We have referred, in somewhat more detail, to fiscal policy in our Section III. See Chapter 7: Social Framework.
28. Some instances of this policy were given in 'Protection to Mulki Industries', CIDF 188/12/1355 F.
29. One indicator of this is the increase in the volume of imports. Except for a brief period, 1925–35, the volume of imports steadily increased from 1882 to 1950. The proportion of manufactured goods also substantially increased. For data and details see, Chapter 6.
30. 'Papers Pertaining to the Proposal of the Federal Finance Committee', GOH, Hyderabad, 1932, p. 10.
31. See B.K. Narayan, 1973, op. cit. (note 27), pp. 66–67.
32. Raw materials were a specifically complex problem in the Hyderabad leather industry. See Anwar Iqbal Qureshi, *Economic Development of Hyderabad State*, Vol. I (Rural Economy), Orient Longman, Bombay, 1948, pp. 83–84. See the detailed report on the ITF-sponsored survey, A. Guthrie, *Report on the Hides and Leather Industry Survey in Hyderabad State*. CID, GOH, 1931. It was this report which recommended the abolition of duties.
33. GAR, 1344 F.
34. As a matter of fact this forms part of a larger study on the commercial relations between the British Indian Government and

Indian states. There seem to be no major studies in this area. Our observations are taken from scattered sources.

35. Apart from references to it in the Annual Reports of the Department, see IS, pp. 625–26. In value terms the proportion of general machinery in the total volume of imports was about 1.84 per cent in 1938–40, 2.25 per cent in 1940–45 and 4.72 per cent in 1945–50. (Computed from TS, relevant years. See also SA, 1952–53, p. 72 and IS, p. 625).
36. The proportion of coal outturn exported was over 55 per cent in 1935–40 and over 68 per cent in 1940–45 IS, p. 307. In case of cement, it was over 80 per cent in both periods, IS, p. 400.
37. The proportion of exports of cigarettes was above 34 per cent (IS, pp. 431–33) and was about 36 per cent in the case of glassware (IS, p. 404) in 1935–40. In 1940–45, the proportion for glassware was 39 per cent (IS, p. 404) and above 42 per cent for paper. (IS, p. 262). In sharp contrast, the proportion of cloth that was exported was never more than 30 per cent (IS, p. 172).
38. See, 'Conference of Directors of Industries of Native State', CIDF 259/1329 F.
39. By 1938–39 about 20 million KWH was being generated in the state, SA, relevant year.
40. GAR, relevant years. See output tables in the Appendix 6-B, Chapter 6: An Appraisal.
41. GAR, relevant years.
42. SA, relevant years.
43. Ibid.
44. The government created separate cells in both the Industries Department and the Defence Department to meet wartime demands. In the first three years of the war, products worth Rs 28.57 million were supplied to the colonial government. IS, p. 128.
45. Agro-based industries, which constituted more than 90 per cent earlier, declined to 70–80 per cent during this phase: See the analysis of changes in the composition of industries in Appendix to Chapter 6.
46. See Appendix 6-B, Chapter 6.
47. The best reflection of the trend was the National Planning Committee sponsored by the Indian National Congress, in 1938. A representative of the Hyderabad government also attended the meeting. See 'Notes', in *Mulki Industries*, Vol. V, No. 1, January 1939, p. 10.

48. See Raghabendra Chattopadhay, 'An Early British Government Initiative in the Genesis of Indian Planning', *Economic and Political Weekly*, Vol. XXII, No. 5, January 31, 1987, pp. 19–29.
49. See note 27, above.
50. On the genesis of planning in Hyderabad see, *Mulki Industries*, Vol. IV, No. 7, July 1938 and Vol. V, No. 1, January 1939.
51. S.K. Iyengar, *Review of Hyderabad Finance*, GOH, Hyderabad, 1951, p. 307. See also 'Implementation of Post-war Schemes', CIDF 148/F 22/1355 F.
52. E.W. Slaughter, *Godavari Industrial and Agricultural Development Plan*, GOH, Hyderabad, 1944. See also, 'Development of Industries in Godavari Valley', CIDF 142, F/14/1335 F.
53. Ahsan Yar Jung Bahadur, *Manufacture of Steel in H.H. The Nizam's Dominions by the Direct Process.* Nizam Silver Jubilee Press, Hyderabad, 1943. The proposal was backed by the Hyderabad Construction Company.
54. See CIDF 142 F/14/1355 F op. cit. (note 52) and 'Starting of a Group of Industries in Godavari Valley Development Project', CIDF, 15-726/1355 F.
55. IS, p. 29.
56. IS, p. 5.
57. 'Five Year Plan', GOH, Hyderabad, 1945, p. XIV.
58. Ibid. See also the first draft of the plan in 'Post-war Planning Incorporating the First Five Year Plan (First Draft)', GOH, Hyderabad, 1944.
59. Ibid.
60. Gulam Mohammad, *Report on Economic Civil Service*, GOH, Hyderabad, 1946.
61. Amiya Kumar Bagchi, *Private Investment in India, 1900–1939*, Orient Longmans, New Delhi, 1972, p. 4.
62. In a perceptive comment, Bagchi noted that 'the political separateness of the native states in British India was more important for industrial growth than the semi-feudal structure of administration within many of these states, given the discrimination practiced against Indian businessmen under the imperial system', ibid., p. 215.
63. Lord Chelmsford in a report to George V, quoted in B.R. Tomlinson, *The Political Economy of the Raj, 1914–1947: The Economics of Decolonisation in India*, Macmillan, London, 1979, p. 58.
64. Ibid., pp. 58–59.

APPENDIX 3-A

Statistical Tables

Table 3.1
Hyderabad in India: A Profile

	As Percentage of all-India Total
1. Population	4.20
2. Area	5.25
3. Working Population	4.50
4. Factory Labour	3.00
5. No. of Registered Factories	7.00
6. No. of Jt. Stock Cos.	6.00
7. Paid-up Value of Capital	5.50
8. Railway Goods Traffic	4.00
9. Railway Passengers	2.00
10. Power generation	1.67
Output	
1. Cotton Bales Pressed	8.50
2. Cotton Yarn Spun	2.00
3. Total Woven Goods (Cotton)	1.90
4. Woollen Goods	4.00
5. Matches	4.00
6. Cement	12.00
7. Liquor	4.00
8. Sugar	4.00
9. Coal	5.00
10. Total Mineral Production	2.00

Note: The area and population percentages relate to the 1941 Census. All other figures are based on five yearly averages in 1940–45.
Source: IS.

Table 3.2
Industry in 1947: India, Pakistan and Hyderabad
(No. of Factories)

	India	*Pakistan*	*Hyderabad*
1. Cotton Mills	671	9	6
2. Iron and Steel Factories	17	—	—
3. Engineering Workshops	369	45	38
4. Sugar Factories	149	—	1
5. Paper Mills	66	2	5
6. Match Factories	80	5	14
7. Chemical Factories	29	2	4
8. Glass Factories	71	2	3
9. Soap Factories	16	1	6
10. Cement Factories	10	3	1

Source: TS, 1359 F. (1949–50).

Table 3.3
Loans to Small-Scale Industries: 1930–1945

Name of Industry	*Amount Advanced (O.S. Rs)*	*Percentage of the Total Loans Advanced*
1. Weaving	12,200	2.37
2. Knitting and Garments	7,084	1.37
3. Ginning and Pressing	18,500	3.59
4. *Himroo*	7,000	1.36
Agro-based Industries-I Sub-total	44,784	8.69
5. Rice Mills	52,400	10.16
6. Oil Mills	91,740	17.79
7. Others	35,430	6.87
Agro-based Industries-II Sub-total	179,570	34.82
8. Engineering Industries	35,817	6.95
9. Buttons	8,667	1.68
10. Bidri-ware	13,005	2.52
Metal and Engg. Industries Sub-total	57,489	11.15

(*contd.*)

Table 3.3 (*Contd.*)

11. Chemicals	59,652	11.57
12. Animal-based Industries	55,000	10.67
13. Forest-based Industries	10,000	1.94
14. Glass	22,000	4.27
15. Others	87,115	16.90
GRAND TOTAL	5,15,610	100.00

Note: The data is computed from the detailed list of the names of the borrower, purpose for which money was borrowed and the amount that was given in some of the annual reports. It excludes aid to cottage industries and other grants made by the ITF. Amounts for which details are not available have been excluded.
Source: GAR and CIDAR, 1340–1354 F.

Table 3.4
Dispersal of Industries
District-wise Break-up: 1911–1949
(Percentage)

District	*1911*	*1931–32*	*1948–49*
Aurangabad	9.92	13.93	11.25
Parbhani	9.09	19.41	9.68
Gulbarga	15.71	8.71	7.19
Nanded	7.44	11.94	6.15
Raichur	7.44	9.21	9.15
Osmanabad	4.14	3.49	2.10
Bhir	0.83	3.98	2.88
Bidar	0.00	0.75	0.95
Marathawada and Karnatic Sub-total	56.20	71.40	49.29
Warangal	13.23	9.21	9.15
Nizamabad	5.79	4.98	5.62
Karimnagar	1.66	1.75	2.62
Adilabad	0.83	2.74	2.23
Medak	1.66	2.24	4.71
Nalgonda	0.83	1.50	3.40

(*contd.*)

Table 3.4 (*Contd.*)

Mehbubnagar	0.00	1.25	4.97
Hyderabad City	21.49	4.98	18.04
Telangana Sub-total	43.81	28.61	50.74

Note: Data relates only to large industrial establishments.
Source: 1911: Census
1931–32: SA, relevant year
1948–49: GAR, relevant year.

APPENDIX 3-B

The Industrial Base of Hyderabad

Hyderabad, the largest of the Indian states, was rich in industrial raw materials. As part of the Deccan plateau it was rich in mineral resources and as part of larger Gondwana, it had vast forest resources. It also possessed extensive tracts of black cotton soil. In this note and throughout the text we have divided industries into ten broad groups. Except in the case of infrastructural industries, the classification is based on the input base of the industry.

The first group, infrastructural industries, includes railways, road and other transport, power and communications. Initially, the railways were managed by the British-owned Great Indian Peninsular Railway (GIPR). Later an autonomous company, in which the Hyderabad government held a controlling interest, the Nizam's Guaranteed State Railway Company Ltd. (NGSRC) owned and operated the railways. Eventually in 1930, the company became a completely state-owned enterprise, the Nizam State Railway (NSR). Road transport was in the hands of private companies till the 1930s, but in 1932 a Road Mechanical Transport Service (RMTC), under the management of the railways, was established. Coordinated with railway service, it had taken over specific routes under the monopoly, and operated both passenger and cargo services. In power, Hyderabad, along with Mysore and Kashmir, was one of the few states or provinces in the country where generation and supply was completely state-owned. In addition to thermal power plants, the state also had one major hydro-electric plant on the river Manjira.

The second group consists of minerals. Coal was the major mineral of the state with deposits in the Gondwana series of geological strata towards the eastern parts of the state in the Godavari and Pranahita river valleys. These areas are in the Adilabad, Karimnagar and Warangal (presently Khammam) districts of the state. Here the lease was initially given to a foreign company in which the government held controlling shares. Later in 1920, the old company was replaced by the state-financed Singareni Collieries Company which, in 1944, became a wholly state-owned company. Among other minerals, limestone was found in the Krishna and Bhima river basins. The Bhima series, also known as Shahbad stones, fall in the Karnataka region of the state. Regular extraction was started only in the 1920s. Garnets were found in different parts of Palwancha and Yellendu taluqs of Warangal (presently Khammam) district but actual extraction took place only in 1910–1930. Marble was found in Yellendu taluq. In 1930, a state-financed company, Deccan Marble and Mining Company, undertook the extraction. A number of problems contributed to the irregular outturn by the company. Systematic extraction took place only for a brief period, 1935–40. Gold was found in the Dharwar series of rocks, mostly in Raichur district. A private mining company was engaged in mining in 1901–1924. Later a new company, Hutti Gold Mines Company, financed by the state, attempted to revive production. Its limited success was confined to the period 1948–1950, after the fall of the regime. Among other metals, iron ore of a low grade was available to a considerable extent, but no major attempt was made to extract the ore.

The third group consists of agro-based industries which occupied the top position in the state in terms of number of units, capital invested and labour force. As Hyderabad had an essentially agrarian economy, it was the agro-based industries that constituted a large part of the industries in the state. For the sake of convenience, we have divided agro-based industries into two groups: cotton and other textiles (Agro-based Industries-I) and all other agro-based Industries (Agro-based Industries-II).

Agro-based Industries-I consists of cotton, cotton textiles and other textiles like silk and wool. Cotton was a major commercial crop in the state. Despite the disputed transfer of the cotton-rich Berar provinces to British India, the state had about 14 per cent of all India cotton acreage. Most of these areas lie in the Marathwada districts of Aurangabad, Nanded, Parbhani and to a lesser extent in Adilabad, Telangana and Gulbarga, in the Karnatic region. As elsewhere in India, the state had both handloom and mill sectors.

Of the total cotton piece goods consumed in the state both these sectors supplied an almost equal proportion of 30 per cent each. The remaining 40 per cent came from imports. Of the six major cotton textile mills three were state-financed. Cotton ginning and pressing mills constituted a large portion of the industrial units in this group. Most of these mills were located in the Marathwada districts. In addition, silk, woollen and certain specialised products like *khamkhwab, himroo*, and carpets are also included in this group.

Agro-based Industries-II includes all other agro-based products such as oilseed products, rice, pulse and flour mills, alcohol, sugar, food products and cigarettes. Oilseeds occupied an important position in the agrarian economy of Hyderabad. Nalgonda, Warangal and Mahbubnagar in Telangana, Gulbarga and Raichur in the Karnatic area and Aurangabad in Marathwada, were the oilseed cultivating districts in the state. Rice mills flourished in the paddy-cultivating Telangana districts. Among food products, biscuit manufacturing in Hyderabad city was the most notable in the state. Sugarcane cultivation was confined to less than one per cent of the total cultivated area but a modern large-scale sugar factory was set up with the help of the state in 1939, so sugar production was high in the state. The brewing and distilling of liquor was based on the abundant supply of mahua flowers available in the forest districts of Telangana. The production of power alcohol for industrial purposes was a distinctive part of alcohol production in the state. Most of the alcohol distilleries were state-owned undertakings. Tobacco suited for cigarettes was not cultivated in the state, but cigarettee manufacturing was one of the major industries of the state. Raw tobacco was one of the major industries of the state. Raw tobacco was imported from Guntur in Madras Presidency and other provinces. Similarly, tea was imported for processing, blending and packing in the state. One large-scale tea unit was established in Ghatkesar, Hyderabad during the last years of the regime.

Metal and engineering industries occupied a prominent position both in terms of number of people employed and the amount of capital. The traditional sector in this group included blacksmithies and other iron works, brass, copper, silver and gold ware and bidriware. The manufacture of knives, *gund* and other arms was also a traditional occupation in the state. In the modern sector, a general engineering workshop established by the government in 1870 was a pioneering effort. Later, there was a state-owned railway as well as mint workshops. In later years a number of small-scale motor and engineering workshops came up, especially in Hyderabad city. Among the small and medium-scale units, button manufacturing of metallic buttons was prominent in the state. In the last decade of the period a variety of large-scale factories came up in this group. They included machine and machine tool manufacturing factories. Most of the industries in this group were concentrated in Hyderabad city.

Forest-based industries came next in order of importance. Hyderabad had about 12 per cent of its land area under forest. Most of this was in the eastern half of the Telangana districts. The forests were essentially deciduous forests. With an average rainfall of more than 40 inches per annum, the forests had a number of products useful for industry including teak, nallamaddi, sandal and bamboo. But the use of forest products was very limited in the state till the last years of WW II. The traditional sector in this group included handmade paper and wooden articles. In the modern small and medium-sector, beedi and matches were prominent. Towards the end, one large-scale state-financed paper mill was set up in Adilabad. Allied products like cardboard also came up during the period, as did a rayon factory.

The Ceramic group of industries includes cement, glass bricks, tiles, pottery, pipes, stone dressing and quarrying, enamel and porcelain industries. Both glass and pottery were traditional industries which engaged a significant section of the work force. Silica from sand and quartz in the state, especially from around Hyderabad city, was the base of the glass industry. In cement there was only one company located in the limestone belt of Shahbad. Owned by the Tatas and partly financed by the state, this company was one of the largest in India, contributing over 12 per cent of all-India production. A British-Indian concern ran a hume pipe company with three branches. The hume pipe industry developed due to the availability of quartz sand and cement. There were also a few large-scale glass factories and a number of medium-scale brick and tile-making units.

Among chemical-based industries, the manufacture of indigenous medicine was the only significant product in the traditional sector. Later, the manufacture of aerated water, soap, paints and varnishes, scents and disinfectants, and gun powder also came up especially in medium-scale units. In the last decade, large-scale companies manufacturing pharmaceuticals, fertilizers, drugs and synthetics were established with the support of state finance.

Animal-based industries include dairy products, tanneries, shoes, boots, sandals and other leather goods. Tanneries were the major manufacturing units in the traditional sector. During the last years of the regime, a few large-scale leather goods industries were established.

'Others' is a group which includes miscellaneous industries that do not fit into any of the above categories. Prominent among these were printing and allied industries.

Throughout this book we have adopted this classification and consequently reclassified all available data into these ten groups.

[This note is prepared on the basis of Industrial Statistics (IS) cited earlier and Leonard Munn, *The Geology and Economic Minerals of H.H. the Nizam's Dominions*, GOH, Hyderabad, B.N. Chaturvedi, *Descriptive Atlas of Hyderabad State*, Indian press, Allahabad, 1956, S.A. Hameed, 'Industrial Pattern of Telangana: A Geographical Analysis', *The Indian Geographical Journal* Vol. XXXVI, No. 2, April–June 1962, pp. 45–54 and Khurshid Mirza, *A Brief outline of the Geographical History of Hyderabad State with Special Reference to It's Mineral Resources*, GOH, Hyderabad, 1943.]

CHAPTER FOUR

Capital

In Hyderabad, unlike in British India, there were no well-organised bodies of industrialists, nor were there any big business houses who bequeathed records, along with property, to their descendants. In fact, a large number of companies closed down after the fall of the regime, and small-scale units vanished into oblivion. This kind of track that leaves few traces, which is perhaps inherent in the nature of industrialisation in the state, makes it difficult to draw analytical inferences on industrial capital, with any finality.

We have divided industry into two sectors; corporate and non-corporate.[1] The former consists of companies registered under the Companies Act that came into force in 1910. The latter are essentially small-scale and to a lesser extent, medium-scale industries. There is no worthwhile quantitative information on capital in the non-corporate sector, but we should recall the role played by the state in financing small-scale industries.

In the corporate sector, we have excluded departmental undertakings of the government such as railways, part of road transport, electricity, general engineering and railway workshops among the large-scale units, and the carpet factory, Warangal and the power alcohol factory, Kamareddy among the medium-scale. However, Singareni Collieries, eventually taken over by the state, was a registered company.

In 1921, there were eleven joint-stock companies with paid-up capital of Rs 10.50 million.[2] By the end of the period, in 1947–48, there were 200 companies with capital of about Rs 104 million.[3] But the total corporate sector also included banking, transport, trade and other services. Leaving out the mining and manufacturing industries, there were 10 companies with a capital of Rs 10.40 million in 1921. This number increased to 84 companies with a capital of Rs 50.60 million in 1945.[4] Behind this impressive growth lie some interesting features.

Capital in agro-based industries which constituted almost 17 per cent of the total corporate capital in the initial years, reached a peak of almost 48 per cent by the mid-1930s and then declined to about 30 per cent by the end of WW II. Capital in the mining sector which was about 68 per cent initially declined to just about 15 per cent by the end of the war. But this decline is only proportionate; in absolute terms the capital remained fairly constant, between Rs 7 to 7.5 million. Capital in metal and engineering and ceramic and chemical-based industries which had rather violent fluctuations, eventually constituted 25 per cent. Thus a noticeable structural change in industry was a striking feature of the corporate sector during the inter-war period. This shift away from agro-based industries was facilitated by the concentration of capital in some of the modern industries. Even in agro-based industries it was the second group which included cigarettes, sugar and food products, that had a consistently high growth rate. (The figures and observations here are based on a more detailed statistical analysis included in the Appendix).

What is more interesting are the sources of finance for industrial capital. Firstly, it must noted that commercial banks played a relatively minor role in financing industry. Although the banking sector had made spectacular progress, it had very little do with the demand for industrial capital (see the note on banking in the Appendix). As the Banking Inquiry Committee Report put it 'the local banks…do not encourage industry to deal with them on any account except that on cash basis e.g. releasing of railway receipts for imported articles on the payment of price'.[5] Even on short term loans, the interest rate was 9–12 per cent per annum.[6] The real rate of interest was much higher than the nominal rate due to intricate exchange transactions between British government Rupees and *Osmania Sicca* Rupees.[7] Thus, till at least the early 1940s, banks played a very small role in industrial finance.[8] Eventually the

Hyderabad State Bank (HSB) established in 1942, helped the flow of funds from the banking sector to industry. Assuming that a third of the total loans, cash-credits and overdrafts advanced by the HSB were to industry, Jussawala worked out the amount as Rs 34.88 million in 1942–48.[9] But this estimate was based on policy statements and not on actual figures and could be an overestimate.

Internal financing of companies also does not appear to have been significant, despite the fact that there were no direct taxes. If accumulated reserves are to be taken as an indicator of the potential of such a source, then there were, during and after WW II, not more than eight companies which held such reserves.[10] It should be noted that most of them received enormous loans from the ITF.

In fact it was state financing through the ITF that can be identified as the single largest source of finance to industry. The ITF advanced finance in the form of shares, debentures and loans, mostly loans at an interest rate of 5 per cent per annum. Disbursements from the ITF, which began in 1930, were at their peak during the WW II period, when sugar mills, machinetool factories, paper mills, chemicals, fertilizers and synthetics etc. were set up with ITF finance, resulting in a kind of structural change in the corporate capital referred to earlier. Of the total sum of Rs 76.27 million that was disbursed in 1930–1950, mining, metal and engineering and forest-based industries received higher proportions, (see Appendix). Except in the case of companies in agro-based industries, especially group-I, almost all major companies in all other groups received state finance in some form. Our estimates, gathered from diverse sources, show that more than 40 registered companies out of a total of about 84 companies received state aid (see Appendix). But these companies were the large-scale companies in which a far larger proportion of capital was concentrated. The real significance of the singularly striking role played by the state in financing industries lies beyond mere finance. We shall return to that topic later.

We will now focus on the role played by private investment. In British India, foreign capital played a significant role, but in Hyderabad it was not much in evidence. Except in railway and mining companies during the earlier phases as in the case of British

India, foreign capital did not play any notable role. Later railways became a completely state-owned and managed enterprise. Singareni Collieries also became a completely state-owned enterprise, but foreign concerns (Best and Company, etc.) remained as its Managing Agents for some time. This was the case with the Hathi Gold Mines (John Taylor & Co.) and Deccan Mining and Marble Companies. This management by foreign concerns of companies that were otherwise owned or dominated by the state can be found in the case of Laminated Products (Bakelite London), Sirsilk Ltd. and others. To a certain extent the need for technical collaboration, especially in the case of new products like rayon, machine tools and laminated products, seems to have determined this arrangement. Otherwise, the only case of foreign capital investing in a Hyderabad company was the famous Vazir Sultan Tobacco in which the ITF also held substantial shares, as did the Imperial Tobacco Company. Brook Bond also opened a branch on its own towards the end of the regime in 1947. Thus in terms of finance, the role of foreign capital in Hyderabad was marginal. The policy of encouraging a single unit in any industry, the control of the state over all major companies and the preferential policy towards domiciles (*mulkis*) explain the inhibitions of foreign capital in Hyderabad. These factors also contributed to the shyness of capital from British India.

It must however be noted that in the late nineteenth century, it was capital from British India that pioneered modern large-scale industries in Hyderabad. The first three textile mills in Hyderabad were all established by Bombay industrialists.[11] Cotton ginning and pressing mills seem to have been the major attraction for merchants and industrialists from Bombay Presidency.[12] The Tatas, with the help of the Hyderabad Government established a cement factory at Shahabad that was eventually merged with their Associated Cement Company. The Tatas seem to have developed manifold relations with the Nizam, but there is very little evidence of their industrial investment in Hyderabad.[13] Among other notable companies was Indian Hume Pipes which had three branches in the state. But in general the preferential policy towards *mulkis* seems to have restricted the expansion of British Indian capital. This factor, however, could also be due to lack of quantitative evidence of British Indian capital, because, such capital could have flowed surreptitiously through a *mulki* concern. Inter-marriage between *mulkis* and non-*mulkis* among the elites could have facilitated such a flow.

Within Hyderabad, the flow of agrarian surplus into industry is a particularly problematic question. Both in the cotton ginning and pressing units in Marathawada and the oil, rice and flour mills in Telangana, the agrarian rich seem to have played some role.[15] But it would be difficult to assess this role as some sort of entrepreneurship on the part of the landlords. What appears to have happened was that a growing volume of trade in these commodities facilitated such units. Some of the landlords who were themselves money lenders and merchants or were aligned with such people, could possibly have invested in these units. But it would be difficult to describe such investment as a flow of agrarian surplus to industry. *Mahajans* or *Sahukars* who were involved in external trade of agrarian commodities either financed or owned some of the cotton-ginning and pressing mills.[16] However, these seasonal agro-processing units, large in number but small in scale fall outside the corporate sector.

In the corporate sector, private investment was from merchants, *jagirdars* and *deshmukhs*, most of whom were based in Hyderabad city or other leading urban centres. It was this amorphous group that seems to have been the source of funds for shares and debentures. Public subscription was not, however, a major source of industrial finance in Hyderabad. Although some kind of brokers associations had been functioning since the late 1930s, the stock exchange itself was only established in 1941. The issue of ordinary shares was the most common form, since preferential shares and debentures were not very popular.[17] Public subscription however seems to have declined after WW II due to the anarchy in the economy prior to the fall of the regime.[18]

Indigenous bankers and merchants were in some cases, also the owners of industrial concerns,[19] and there were quite a few members of the aristocracy who controlled a number of industries. Instances of *paigah* nobles, *jagirdars* and others taking an interest in industry are Sirpur Paper Mills, Osman Shahi Mills (textiles), a sugar factory and a host of other concerns[20] but almost all these concerns were essentially, state-financed companies. In the details available regarding 35 companies in which these merchants or *jagirdars* were directors, there was not a single company that had not received state finance.[21] The significance of the investments by the ITF, referred to earlier, lies here because whatever private investment was raised was largely a product of the initiative taken by the ITF. It was the ITF's initiative that mobilised private investment from merchants and *jagirdars*.

The initiative taken by the state also explains a particularly notable feature of these *jagirdars*, who held an interest in industrial concerns. They were all aligned somehow or other with the state bureaucracy. It would not be incorrect to characterise these people as civil servants, serving or retired, holding interests in industrial concerns, rather than as *jagirdars*. The assiduously maintained relationship between the aristocracy and the bureaucracy shows that this was true of almost all leading industrialists. Laik Ali, who controlled more than 20 companies through his Hyderabad Construction Company or independently, was, among other things, the last Prime Minister of the Nizam. He was also the President of the Chamber of Commerce and Industry.[22] His brother-in-law, Moin Nawaz Jung, a former minister, held an interest in HCC and in other companies like the Sugar Factory. Salar Jung (III) who was director of eighteen companies, was a former Prime Minister.[23] Pingali Venkata Rama Reddy served as a judge, as chief of Police and also as a minister.[24] Comar Tayabjee was the son-in-law of Sir Akbar Hydari, the visionary credited with the creation of the ITF.[25] Akbar Hydari's son was secretary of the State Bank of Hyderabad. Both Babu Khan and Alladdin also seem to have been related to powerful civil servants.[26] Ashan Yar Jung Bahadur who owned a pipe factory and the Hyderabad Steel and Wire Products Limited and also prepared the blue print for a steel factory in the Godavari Valley was the Chief Engineer and Secretary of the Public Works Department.[27] Joshi, an industrialist at Jalna, was Commerce Minister in Laik Ali's cabinet.[28] Even the well-known *jagirdars* of Malwala estate whose interest in industry was mentioned earlier, it appears, were connected with the bureaucracy.[29] Among others were Gulam Ahmed and Zahid Hussain, both former Finance Secretaries.

This phenomenon of civil servants or persons related to them controlling most of the industries, also explains the peculiar role of managing agents in Hyderabad. Their actual contribution to finance was very little.[30] They did not have any particular technical or organisational expertise, in fact, some of these managing agencies like Hyderabad Construction Company and United Commercial corporation, were financed by the ITF. In most cases, they were appointed managing agents not by the companies but by the ITF in its capacity as leading shareholder. The agencies received a fixed allowance and a commission or a percentage of net profits. Their remuneration had no relation to their contribution.[31] In reality, these managing agents were none other than powerful civil servants or those connected with them.

The role of civil servants or members of their families suggests some element of corruption and nepotism which become particularly notable features of industrialisation whenever the state plays an important role as is also evident in contemporary India. In Hyderabad, the role of managing agents indicates that a number of these powerful civil servants were merely using the state for personal gain. Such allegations, especially about Laik Ali, were common in Hyderabad.[32] But corruption could not be (and cannot be) the *raison d'etre* of any state policy. As noted in the previous chapter, the financing of industry was part of a larger framework of industrial policy.

From this record of private investment some inferences can perhaps be made about the social composition of industrialists. We must first note that a number of observers during the last days of the Nizam's regime argued that industry in Hyderabad was dominated by Muslims.[33] This belief is also part of communal folklore in contemporary Hyderabad and Aurangabad. But our evidence indicates that there was no particular reason for reaching this conclusion. Among the *jagirdar*-civil servant industrialists there were Muslims as well as Hindus. In organised industry as a whole, Hindus owned about 60 per cent of the units while Muslims owned only 19 per cent.

A review of private investment in Hyderabad shows the absence of any identifiable group of private capitalists. The industrial evolution of Hyderabad was essentially a product of the autonomous initiative taken by the state. Such private investment as was raised was not the basis of the industrial policy of the state, but it was state policy which mobilised private investment. The role of civil servants can also only be explained in this context. Private industrialists essentially consisted of local merchants at lower levels and well-placed *jagirdars* at higher levels, and neither had any autonomy. In the corporate sector this small coterie did not, to any significant extent, invest in industry nor was it known for technical or organisational expertise. Its members were essentially a group of speculators interested in quick and high returns and propped up by the state.

At a different level of abstraction, we can conclude that a class of capitalists never emerged in Hyderabad. In any colonial country subjugated by an imperialist economy perhaps such a class of capitalists would not emerge. But what is often not acknowledged is the congenital infirmities of this class in any industrial development in which the state controls the production process. In Hyderabad in particular state control of ownership, finance and technology overshadowed any possibility of such a capitalist class emerging. The articulation of the interests of a class in social and political fields, the emergence of what is referred to as class-for-itself, was conspicuously absent in the state. Towards the end when the political crisis plunged the state into anarchy, the so-called industrialists could not stand united and could not take any meaningful and coherent stand on any issue. As a small coterie of speculators, who could not emerge as a class, they collapsed as the regime collapsed.

Notes

1. The normal division of small, medium and large scale into those with a capital of Rs 5,000 or below Rs 5,000–50,000 and Rs 50,000 or above respectively (IS, p. 4) is not of much use since the data was neither available nor amenable to such divisions. These divisions do not directly correspond with the corporate and non-corporate sectors, except that usually there were no small-scale industries in the corporate sector.
2. GAR, 1331 F.

3. SA, 1952–53.
4. GAR, relevant years and HCAAR, relevant years.
5. HBECR, p. 71. See also IS, p. 31.
6. M.F. Jussawala, 'Industrial Finance in the Former Hyderabad State, 1941–1956', unpublished Doctoral Dissertation, Department of Economics, Osmania University, Hyderabad, 1961, p. 89.
7. For details of these transactions and their relationship with exchange rates see Appendix to this chapter.
8. IS, pp. 30–32 and p. 40.
9. Jussawala, op. cit. (note 6).
10. The companies included Singareni Collieries, Alwynn Metals, Vazir Sultan Tobacco, Praga Tools, Nizam Sugar Factory and three textile mills. See Jussawala, 1960, op. cit. (note 6). See also, 'Industries in Hyderabad', All India Industrial Exhibition Society, Hyderabad, 1950, pp. 34–35.
11. The famous Currimbhoy family, for instance, established the textile mills at Aurangabad, Gulbarga and Nanded.
12. A few other instances relate to Bombay merchants setting up oil (or combined) mills. Bhikaji Dadabhoy established four such mills in Warangal. (V. Ramakrishna Reddy, *Economic History of Hyderabad States, Warangal Suba, 1911–1950*, Giani Publishing House, New Delhi, 1987, p. 592). Similarly a Bombay merchant set up an oil mill in Jadcherla, Mehbubnagar (Penesetti Madhav Rao, 'Industrial Development of Hyderabad', unpublished Doctoral Dissertation, Nagpur University, Nagpur, 1956, p. 23).
13. We have earlier referred to negotiations between the Tatas and the Hyderabad Government about the bank. The Central Bank of India had seven branches in the state. It also appears that the ITF invested in some of Tata concerns in British India, including in addition to the Cement Company, Tata Chemicals Ltd., and Tata Hydro Electric Power Company (IS, pp. 32–33). The Tata's Empress Mills set up Ginning and Pressing Factories at Nirmal, Adilabad. (V. Ramakrishna Reddy, 1987, op. cit. (note 12), p. 602).
14. The famous Tayabji family, to which the leading industrialist Comar Tayabji belonged, was a case in point. The references to these intermarriages can be found in biographical literature or novels. See, Zeenuth Futrehally, *Zora*, Bombay, 1951, a novel based an social life in Hyderabad, Badruddin Tayabji, *Memoirs of an Egotist* (Vol. I, 1907–1956), Roli Books, New Delhi, 1988, G. Mohammad Abdur Rahman Khan, *My Life and Experiences*, Hyderabad, 1951, and

Bilkees Latif, *Her India: The Fragrance of Forgotten Years*, Arnold-Heinemann, Delhi, 1984. See also Karen Leonard, 'Hyderabad, The *mulki*, non-*mulki* Conflict' in Robin Jeffrey (ed.), *People, Princes and Paramount Power: Society and Politics in Indian Princely States*, Oxford University Press, Delhi, 1978, p. 81.

15. There was one notable instance of the Pingali family, from Waddepalli, Warangal investing in these units. Ramakrishna Reddy, 1987, op. cit. (note 12), p. 592. The family was also connected with the bureaucracy.
16. HBECR, p. 71.
17. Among the notable exceptions were the Nizam Sugar Factory (preferential shares worth Rs 1.2 million in 1942) and textile mills (debentures worth Rs 1.6 million in 1942). 'Industries in Hyderabad', 1950, op. cit. (note 10), pp. 21–22.
18. This decline was reflected in the drastic fall of share prices, with some companies even disappearing from the list. For details of the period October 1946 to September 1947, see 'Trade Statistics 1356 F', GOH, Hyderabad, 1947, pp. 6–7.
19. For instance, Raja Pannalal Pitti who controlled a number of Industrial concerns, was also the President of the Committee of Sahukaran and Vyapara (Anwar Iqbal Qureshi, *Economic Development of Hyderabad Vol. I, Rural Economy*, Orient Longman, Bombay, 1947, p. 321). But then he was also a *raja*, a *jagirdar*.
20. The original application for the establishment of the sugar factory carried the names of 25 noblemen and *jagirdars*, 27 bankers and businessmen and 22 landlords among others. Mr M. Laxmi Wadiyar, 'The Impact of Nizam Sugar Factory on Bodhan Taluq', unpublished M.A. Thesis, Department of Economics, Osmania University, Hyderabad, 1963, pp. 5–6. Eventually, however, none of them invested and the factory became a largely state-financed company. Similarly one *paigah* noble was reported to have invested, among others, in Osmanshahi Mills (All India State Peoples Conference. File No. 65 Nehru Memorial Museum and Library). Based on contemporary newspaper accounts, Ramakrishna Reddy indicates that Sirpur Paper Mills directors included *jagirdars* and rich local merchants. (V. Ramakrishna Reddy, 1987, op. cit. (note 12), p. 488), Pingali Vankatarama Reddy, a landlord from Warangal, was the director of five companies, Salar Jung III was director of eighteen companies, Naoshar Chinoy, an advocate from a well-known aristocratic family of *jagirdars* was director of seven companies. (See *The Hyderabad Problem: The Next Step*, Hyderabad Struggle Committee, Socialist

Party, Bombay, 1948, Appendix II). The Chinoys were originally settled in Jalna but later shifted to Hyderabad. All the leading industrialists like Laik Ali, Moin Nawaj Jung, Babu Khan, Khan Bahadur Ahmed Alladdin and Comar Tyabji were *jagirdars*. Raja Ram Karan Bahadur from Malwala Estate also owned some industries. (IS, p. 290, see also Raja Ram Karan Bahadur, *Industries in Malwala Estate* GOH, Hyderabad, 1941). Wanaparty rajas also held some industrial interests. Members of Goswami Raja families had a long tradition of investing in business and industry beginning with railways in the nineteenth century. One of them, Raja Dhanrajgir was the initiator of the proposal for the sugar factory. For some reference to these families see Bilkees Latif, 1984, op. cit. (note 14), pp. 108–115.

21. See 'The Hyderabad Problem', 1948, cited above, Appendix II.
22. On Laik Ali and Moin Nawaj, apart from the above reference see K.M. Munshi, *End of An Era*, Bharatiya Vidya Bhavan, Bombay, 1957, p. 211, Qureshi, 1947, op. cit. (note 19), p. 321. See also Rajendra Prasad, *The Asaf Jahis of Hyderabad: Their Rise and Decline*, Vikas, New Delhi, 1984, pp. 297–98.
23. For the list of Salar Jung's directorships see, 'The Hyderabad Problem', op. cit. (note 20, Appendix II). It appears Salar Jung II, also a prime minister, owned some companies too. Zahir Ahmed, *Life's Yesterdays: Glimpses of Sir Nizamat Jung and His Times*, Thacker, Bombay, 1945, p. 165.
24. On Pingali Venkatarama Reddy, see note 15 above. For the list of companies of which he was director, see 'The Hyderabad Problem' 1948, op. cit. (note 20) Appendix II.
25. Ibid., p. 30 and Appendix II.
26. We do not have much information on the background of Khan Bahadur Ahmed Alladdin also known as Nawab Ahmad Nawaz Jung Bahadur, who was director of about fifteen companies. But the CIF files include a letter from the Chief Registrar's Office, GOI, Indicating that he was blacklisted by the Government of India (for what ?) in 1946. The Hyderabad government replied in his defence. 'Supply of Information Regarding K.B. Alladdin and Co.', CIDF 98/1355 F.
27. See IS, p. 394 and 'ITF Secretariat, 1929–1950', GOH, Hyderabad, 1950, p. 4.
28. Munshi, 1957, op. cit. (note 22), p. 178.
29. Raja Mahbub Karan Mathur for instance, was personal secretary to the Prince of Berar, the Nizam's son. Karen Leonard, *Social History of an Indian Caste: The Kayasths of Hyderabad*, University of California Press, Berkeley, 1978, p. 29.

30. Jussawala gives the amounts contributed by managing agents in about 30 companies which were also financed by the ITF. In all these companies their contribution works out at 7.5 per cent of the paid-up value of capital (Jussawala 1961, op. cit. (note 6), pp. 97–103.) See also 'Industries in Hyderabad', 1950, op. cit. (note 10), pp. 18–19.
31. See, 'Industries in Hyderabad', op. cit., pp. 53–59 and Madhav Rao, 1956, op. cit. (note 12), p. 331.
32. For such allegations of corruption in the case of Laik Ali see some of the references cited in note 22 above.
33. See for instance, 'They Hyderabad Problem', 1948, op. cit. (note 20), pp. 29–30.
34. In the detailed list of industries in the Statistical Abstracts, referred to earlier, the names of the factories were given. Presuming that a Hindu name indicates a Hindu owner and a Muslim name indicates a Muslim Owner and so on, we have arrived at the following table. All others, which include those owned by other communities, owned by the state and those companies named in a secular fashion ('Hyderabad' or 'Deccan', being the most common) have been included in the category 'Others'. The data is based on the average for the period 1935–45.

Composition of Ownership (religion-wise)
(Percentage)

	Hindus	*Muslims*	*Parsis*	*Others*
1. Agro-based Industries-I	64	15	7	14
2. Agro-based Industries-II	73	12	3	12
3. Metal and Engineering Industries	27	38	—	35
4. Forest-based Industries	25	55	—	20
5. Ceramics	28	33	6	33
6. Chemical-based Industries	22	44	—	34
7. Animal-based Industries	30	35	—	35
8. Others	35	29	—	36
9. Total	60	19	3	18

Notes: 1. Data relates only to large industrial establishments.
2. It is based on the average for the period 1935–45.
Source: Estimated from the factory-wise list given in SDA, relevant years.

APPENDIX 4-A

Capital: A Statistical Review

Information concerning corporate capital is available in the Annual Reports on the working of the Hyderabad Companies Act (HCAAR). Although the Act came into force in 1910, the reports were only published from 1920. These reports also form the basis of information provided in Statistical Abstracts (SA) and the Government of India's 'Report on the Joint Stock Companies in British India and the Indian States'. But we have not taken the latter into account as we found that inexplicably Hyderabad was not regularly included in these reports.[1] In some cases we have found that the data in the source is also not complete.[2] It appears that there are also problems related to conversion between the two currencies. Hence we have not made much use of the data given in Government of India reports. Our analysis ends in 1944–45 since our sources dry up after that year. The data, in Government of India Reports: 1945–48 was also not used.

The Registrar of Companies in Hyderabad adopted the standard pattern of dividing all companies into six broad divisions. Based on the detailed company-wise data in the source, we have reported trade and manufacture and reclassified all companies into the input-based divisions that we have adopted. Where data on specific companies was not available, we were able to fill in the gaps from other sources and make approximations based on the data of previous and following years. But gaps still remain for some groups of industries for the period 1942–45.

At the outset we must note the absence of two groups; forest-based industries and animal-based industries. One paper mill (Sirpur Paper Mill) was registered in 1939. All the other companies in these two groups only started towards the end in 1943–46. They include four companies in forest-based industries with a paid-up capital of Rs 1.64 million and two companies with a paid-up capital of Rs 1 million in animal-based industries. All these companies are included in the category 'others'.

Structure of Capital

The following table gives the changes in the distribution of corporate capital over time by taking selected years in the period 1920–1945.

Table 4.1
Distribution of Corporate Capital: 1921–1945
(Percentage)

	1921 1922	*1925 1926*	*1930 1931*	*1935 1936*	*1939 1940*	*1944 1945*
Agro-based Industries-I	16.86	34.18	33.83	41.86	39.12	22.06
Agro-based Industries-II	0.00	0.00	6.14	6.02	28.96	18.78
Metal and Engineering Industries	0.28	0.18	0.22	0.05	0.73	6.50
Ceramics	11.32	18.95	21.53	18.16	0.81	5.10
Chemicals	3.82	2.42	0.04	0.00	0.00	14.34
Others	0.00	0.00	0.00	0.57	1.42	18.27
Mining	67.72	44.26	38.29	33.26	28.95	14.95
	100.00	100.00	100.00	100.00	100.00	100.00
Mining and Manufacturing Companies	98.50	96.75	95.00	91.80	91.70	85.90
Banking, Trade and Other Services	1.50	3.25	5.00	9.20	9.30	14.10

Notes: 1. Data relates to paid-up capital in registered companies.
2. All values in B.G. Rs are converted to *O.S.* Rs where necessary.
Source: Computed from the actual figures given in HCAAR, relevant years and SA, relevant years.

The table shows that although the share of mining and manufacturing industries remained predominant, it declined from 98.50 per cent to about 86 per cent. Its place was taken, essentially, by banking companies. The banks were intricately linked with agrarian trade and had very little to do with industrial development. Within the mining and manufacture sector, the proportion of mining declined sharply. In fact, the actual value remained fairly constant throughout the period (Rs 7 to 7.5 million), but its proportion declined due to the increase in total corporate capital. The proportion of agro-based industries initially increased but declined by the end of WW II as other groups attracted more capital. The category 'others' included companies from forest and animal-based industries in the later period, so it showed an increase.

Metal and engineering, ceramic and chemical-based industries show some peculiar fluctuations. Initially there were only a few companies in these groups. Later on, state policy encouraged the pattern of single-unit-based industry. As a result, the fate of one or two companies determined the proportions of these groups. In metal and engineering industries there was only a single engineering company in the earlier period till it was liquidated in 1934. It was only during WW II that a number of companies were set up and the capital in the group steadily increased. In ceramics, one earlier company, Deccan Glass Works, was liquidated in 1930, while another company, Shahabad Cement, consequent to its merger with the British India-based Associated Cement Company in 1938, was dissolved as a Hyderabadi company. In chemicals, the sole indigenous medicine-manufacturing company was liquidated in 1931, but in this group a number of new companies were set up during the war period. The ups and downs of the ill-fated companies thus determined the violent fluctuations in these groups of industries. However, by the end of the war all of them stabilised and together constituted more than 25 per cent of industrial capital, indicating a structural change in industry.

It must however be noted that our analysis both here and subsequently, is based on the nominal value of paid-up capital. Even in nominal value we have converted, where necessary, the amount given in British government Rupees to *Osmania Sicca* Rupees, at the official exchange rate. But the official exchange rate, as we shall see later, was not a true indicator of the real exchange rate, and the nominal value of paid-up capital was not a true indicator of the actual assets of the company, given the violent fluctuations in the price level. The usual method of adjusting the nominal value by using the Wholesale Price Index (WPI) as a deflator is also beset with problems. A reliable WPI for the entire period is not available and in any case, the basket on the basis of which WPI is constructed in Hyderabad has very little meaning to components of industrial capital. Since our inferences are broadly related to inter-group comparisons, we believe our statistical analysis will be useful.

Growth of Capital

Table 4.2 gives indices of growth for corporate capital in different groups of industries for the period 1921–45. We have chosen the base year as 1939–40. In our view, taking the base year from the early phase of development of the corporate sector would give an exaggerated account of its growth. In particular, problems specific to metals and engineering, ceramics and chemicals mentioned earlier, would assume unrealistic dimensions. The actual changes that took place in these groups of industries could not have been reflected if the base year had been from an earlier phase.

The table shows that the mining and manufacturing sector did not maintain as high a growth rate as banking, transport, trade and other services, where the most striking was the growth in banking capital. The growth rate of mining capital was more or less steady throughout the period since for all practical purposes the Singareni Collieries Company was the sole company in this group. In agro-based industries, growth was steady and modest. The group 'Others' shows a sudden jump by the end of WW II for reasons mentioned earlier. As for the problematic three remaining groups, the actual change began only in the late 1930s and they had a spectacular growth rate by the end of the war.

We have done regression analysis on the basis of the index. The linear trends are fitted to respective time series data. The results are presented in the following table.

Table 4.2
Capital in the Corporate Sector: Index of Growth: 1921–1945
(Base 1939–40 = 100)

Year	Agro-based Industries-I	Agro-based Industries-II	Metal and Engi-neering	Ceramics	Chemicals	Others	Mining	Mining & Manu-facturing	Banking	Trans-port	Trade & Other Services	Banking TPT. Trade & O. Services
1921–22	17	0	16	553	39800	0	93	40	2	25	5	7
1922–23	45	0	16	1441	40000	0	93	59	23	25	13	17
1923–24	45	0	16	1517	40100	0	98	60	31	25	14	20
1924–25	56	0	16	1512	40100	0	97	64	29	25	14	20
1925–26	56	0	16	1484	40300	0	97	64	38	40	14	24
1926–27	57	0.5	16	1606	14800	0	97	64	37	57	14	26
1927- 28	58	0.5	16	1948	14800	0	97	68	42	57	14	27
1928–29	69	1	16	1969	400	0	97	72	45	40	14	26
1929–30	69	5	22	1970	400	0	98	73	54	73	37	46
1930–31	64	16	23	1970	800	0	98	74	29	77	45	45
1931–32	65	18	23	1970	0	2	99	76	28	100	47	49
1932–33	79	18	6	1923	0	2	99	80	32	100	91	77
1933–34	89	18	6	1923	0	3	98	84	36	125	95	83

(*contd.*)

Table 4.2: (*Contd.*)

Year	*Agro-based Industries-I*	*Agro-based Industries-II*	*Metal and Engineering*	*Ceramics*	*Chemicals*	*Others*	*Mining*	*Mining & Manufacturing*	*Banking*	*Transport*	*Trade & Other Services*	*Banking TPT. Trade & O. Services*
1934–35	92	18	6	1923	0	37	99	86	36	125	99	86
1935–36	92	18	6	1923	0	35	99	86	36	125	97	78
1936–37	88	46	7	1923	0	43	99	93	47	100	98	85
1937–38	90	100	69	92	0	90	99	95	66	100	101	92
1938–39	90	100	69	208	0	90	99	96	69	100	101	92
1939–40	100	100	100	100	100	100	100	100	100	100	100	100
1940–41	100	100	55	108	100	101	100	100	115	100	98	103
1941–42	101	N.A.	N.A.	N.A.	N.A.	N.A.	100	N.A.	360	100	N.A.	N.A.
1942–43	105	N.A.	N.A.	N.A.	N.A.	N.A.	100	N.A.	848	100	N.A.	N.A.
1943–44	106	N.A.	N.A.	N.A.	N.A.	N.A.	100	N.A.	1003	100	N.A.	N.A.
1944–45	109	125	1718	1212	7258	2486	100	193	1026	100	119	356

Notes: 1. Data related to nominal value of paid-up capital.
2. All values are in B.G. Rs converted to *O.S.* Rs wherever necessary.
Source: HCAAR, relevant years, SA, relevant years.

Table 4.3
Changes in Corporate Capital: 1921–1945
(Base: 1930–40 = 100)

	b	R^2	*t*
Agro-based Industries-I	3.37	0.90	13.40
Agro-based Industries-II	5.85	0.77	7.94
Metal and Engineering Industries	*	*	*
Ceramics	*	*	*
Chemical-based Industries	*	*	*
Others	42.02	0.26	2.55
Mining	0.22	0.73	7.06
Mining and Manufacturing Total	3.89	0.71	6.87
Banking	17.70	0.28	2.73
Transport	4.58	0.69	6.55
Trade and Services	6.00	0.88	11.57
Banking, Transport, Trade and Other Services Total	8.91	0.62	5.60
Grand Total	4.91	0.75	8.18

* Statistically not significant.
Source: Table 4.2 given above.

The slope quotient in total corporate capital was around 4.91, but much of it was the contribution of banking, transport, trade and services. In particular, the growth in banking, practically the highest (leaving aside 'Others') among all groups, was the source of increases and was primarily related to the commercialisation of the agrarian economy, increase in trade transactions and violent price fluctuations in the period after WW I. Significantly, time as an explanatory variable (R^2) for the change is among the lowest in banking (again alongwith the group 'Others').

Within the mining and manufacturing sector slope quotients in metal and engineering, ceramics and chemical-based industries were not statistically significant, for reasons given earlier. Similarly, the high growth rate in the group 'Others' also has no analytical significance. Mining, by its very nature, had very low average annual changes. Agro-based Industries-II, which included cigarettes, sugar, food products, oil and flour mills, shows a higher level of average annual change than the mining and manufacturing industry total.

State Aid to the Corporate Sector: The Industrial Trust Fund (ITF) was almost the only channel of state aid to the corporate sector. Its constitution initially stipulated that preference would be given to debentures rather than to shares.[3] But eventually it was loans that became most prominent. In 1929 the proportion of disbursement was 24 per cent in shares, 58 per cent in debentures and 0.84 per cent in loans. A decade later in 1939, the proportions were 35, 17 and 26 per cent respectively. But towards the end in 1948, loans became 71 per cent and shares 21 per cent while debentures dwindled to 0.09 per cent.[4]

In addition to aid to the corporate sector, the ITF also disbursed funds for other activities in the state as well as for investments in British India.[5] The total amount of funds disbursed decreased from Rs 1.40 million in 1930–35 to Rs 0.93 million in 1935–40, but rose again to Rs 2.23 million in 1940–45 and was Rs 1.91 million in 1945–50.[6] The highest amount was disbursed during the war period when major metal and engineering, chemical and forest-based industries were set up.

The actual amount given annually, company wise, in the form of shares, debentures or loans, could not be ascertained as the balance sheets of the ITF are not available for all the years. We have assembled the following data from diverse sources. Although some of the data included refers to the position as on March 1950, we have only included those companies which were registered before the fall of the regime. There is no evidence to suggest that disbursement was made, to any significant extent, by the military administration in 1948–50. The data excludes the ITF's investments in British India but includes its investments in the British Indian-based company that operated in Hyderabad, the cement factory at Shahbad. It also includes the amounts sunk as in the case of the Deccan Glass Works. The total amount given here could be an underestimate.

Table 4.4
State Aid to the Corporate Sector: 1929–50

	No. of Companies	*Amount*	*Percentage of Total Aid*
1. Agro-based Industries-I	8	8.480	11.12
2. Agro-based Industries-II	7	7.295	9.56
3. Metal and Engineering Industries	6	15.671	20.55
4. Forest-based Industries	4	12.573	16.49
5. Ceramics	6	6.557	8.60
6. Chemical-based Industries	6	3.769	4.94
7. Animal-based Industries	1	0.300	0.39
8. Others	2	0.058	0.08
9. Mining	3	21.565	28.28
10. Grand Total	43	76.268	100.00

Note: B.G. Rs Converted to *O.S.* Rs where necessary.
Sources: (a) Balance sheets of the ITF, given in CIDAR, 1340 F, GAR, 1343 and I.S. pp. 32–33.
(b) GAR, 1333–1339 F, 1346 F and 1349 F
(c) CIDAR 1350 F.
(d) ITF Secretariat, 1929–1950, GOH, Hyderabad, 1952.
(e) Confidential Records of ITF, M.F. Jussawala, 'Industrial Finance in the Former Hyderabad State 1941–1956', unpublished Doctoral Dissertation, Department of Economics Osmania University, Hyderabad, 1961, pp. 97–103.
(f) S. Kesav Iyengar, *A Review of Hyderabad Finance* GOH, Hyderabad, 1951, pp. 367–370.

The table indicates that the highest proportion of aid was given to the mining sector, where all the three companies set up received state aid. Next were metal and engineering and forest- based industries. These two groups alongwith ceramics and chemicals received almost 50 per cent of the aid. Almost every major company in these groups received aid in some form. Agro-based industries received about 21 per cent of the aid. Not only were the amounts and proportions lower, but some major companies did not receive any form of aid, especially in group I.

The absence of more detailed information makes it difficult to estimate the extent of state finance in the corporate sector. In any case such an exercise carries some inherent limitations. The changing value of paid-up capital, real or monetary, makes it difficult to quantify the proportion, and there is no year to year data. Loans constituted the single largest segment. This compounds the problem further since loans could (and perhaps did) include loans for working capital. But some idea of the significance of the extent of state aid to the corporate sector can be gauged from the fact that the amounts in each case were equivalent to about sixty per cent of the paid-up capital in these companies which numbered 43 out of a total of 84 companies in the mining and manufacturing sector representing more than 50 per cent of the total number of companies. In their respective groups, these were also the major companies in which about 75 to 80 per cent of the capital was concentrated. In any case most companies, whatever the extent of state finance received by them, only came into existence because of the availability of such aid in the first place.

Banking

In 1868, the Bank of Bengal opened a branch in Hyderabad. Later, in 1927, it became the Imperial Bank of India, and served as the government bank till the establishment of the Hyderabad State Bank in 1942. It had six branches towards the end of the period. In 1918, Tata's Bank opened a branch in Hyderabad and later became the Central Bank of India. It eventually opened seven branches in the state. The Andhra bank had two branches. All these three banks were registered in British India. All of them were essentially deposit-receiving and exchange banks. According to the Banking Inquiry Committee Report of 1930, the percentage of loans on all accounts to the deposits of all kinds, in at least the Imperial Bank and the Central Bank, was never more then 20–30 per cent.

Besides these outside banking agencies, there were local joint-stock commercial banks. We have already noted their phenomenal growth, especially since the 1930s. According to the indices cited in Table 4.2, the total nominal value of paid-up capital in these banks increased by about 27 per cent in 1921–31 and by about 86 per cent in 1931–41. But it increased phenomenally during the WW II period 1941–45 by about 900 per cent. All these commercial banks were confined to exchange operations, and short-term lending for trade. They usually financed the storage of products and assisted in the movement of crops from the market centres to the consuming centres and from the distributing centres to the port towns by purchasing demand drafts against produce dispatched. Direct finance to the cultivators was very marginal. The banks usually charged 9–12 per cent interest per annum. But here the real rate of interest was more than the nominal rate of interest because advances were made during the busy season in British Government Rupees (B.G. Rs) when the value of B.G.Rs. in terms of *Osmania Sicca* Rs. (*O.S.*Rs.) rose and paid back during the slack season when the reverse was true. More on this exchange later.

The Hyderabad government established its own Hyderabad State Bank (HSB) in 1942. The bank not only served as the government bank but also advanced money for purposes other than trade. In addition, there were the Co-operative Bank and Post Office Savings Banks. The former was the open bank for providing financial support to cooperatives and helping them with their activities.

After commercial banks there were indigenous bankers or big *mahajans*, most whom were Marwaris who borrowed money from commercial banks. Some of them owned or controlled cotton ginning and pressing mills. In addition to running mills, and engaging in trading and exchange operations, the indigenous bankers were also the financing agents for *sahukars* or moneylenders in the district centres.

Moneylenders in district centres borrowed money not only from indigenous bankers but also, in some cases, from the rich landed gentry. They were also engaged in trade and exchange operations and in turn also financed village traders or moneylenders. The moneylenders were mostly Marwaris in the Marathwada districts and Komatis in the Telangana districts. Arabs and Pathans were the other notable moneylenders. According to the census note on moneylending in the 1931 census, about 70 per cent of the professional moneylenders were concentrated in the Marathwada districts. Trade in cotton in Marathwada, oilseeds in Telangana and grain in general was their primary concern. Peasants bore the brunt of their operations.

From the brief outline of the hierarchy of banking institutions given above, it can be seen that there was a regular flow of cash from one to the other. But generally there was no credit dependency. As commercialisation of agriculture spread, trade in agricultural commodities became the base of banking operations in the state.

It was exchange transactions that sucked in all creditor institutions from the Imperial Bank to district level moneylenders, and this was a feature specific to the state. Hyderabad State was just about the only state with its own currency in colonial India. Most of the exports of crops from Hyderabad took place immediately after the monsoon season. At this time merchants and agents coming from British India required *O.S.*Rs. to purchase the crops. So the value of *O.S.*Rs. rose against B.G.Rs. Just before the monsoon every year B.G.Rs. were converted into *O.S.*Rs. in large amounts. The regular conversion from one currency to the other from one season to the next made it necessary for all banking institutions to keep savings in cash. The magnitude of such idle cash hoarded was subject to the volume of trade and the supply of *O.S.* currency from the state government. In 1930, when the volume of trade was relatively low due to the depression, the Banking Inquiry Committee Report estimated that the shortage of *O.S.* currency during the season was Rs 3 crores.[10] In later decades, exports increased almost tenfold. To stabilise the exchange, the government began to build a huge *Osmania Sicca* Stabilisation Reserve.[11] But in the face of the increasing volume of trade, and rising price level, the government's efforts did not seem to have made any significant impact. In the last year of the regime a single member committee appointed by the government recommended that a Reserve Bank of Hyderabad should be established.[12] Among other things the Bank was to have exclusive control of all exchange transactions.

Before the recommendations could be actively taken up for consideration, the regime fell and one of the first acts of the military administration was the abolition of the *Osmania Sicca* Currency.

Notes

1. 'Report on the Joint Stock Companies in British India and Indian States', GOI, Delhi.
2. For instance, in 1945–46 in this source as many as 10 companies listed in Hyderabad reports were not included.
3. Firman-e-mubarak, 27 March 1920 and 'Industrial Trust Fund Secretariat, 1920–1949', GOH, Hyderabad, 1952, pp. 1–2.
4. All figures are from the confidential Records of ITF, quoted in M.F. Jussawala, 'Industrial Finance in the former Hyderabad State, 1941–56', unpublished Doctoral Dissertation, Department of Economics, Osmania University, Hyderabad 1961, p. 210. See also Penesetti Madhavarao, 'Industrial Development of Hyderabad', unpublished Doctoral Dissertation, Nagpur University, Nagpur, 1956, p. 362.
5. Notable investments by the ITF in British India included Tata Chemicals, Tata Power and Hydro-electric Power, Eastern Federal Insurance, Investment Corporation of India, Frontier Sugar Mills and the famous film producing company, Bombay Talkies. In 1942, according to one available estimate, the total investments in these companies was about *O.S.* Rs 3.9 million. IS, pp. 32–33.
6. All figures from 'Financial Statistics: 1301–1359 F', GOH, Hyderabad, 1950, Table 50, p. 74.
7. HBECR, pp. 22–23.
8. Ibid., p. 72.
9. On the establishment of the Hyderabad State Bank, see S. Keshav Iyengar, 'Central Banking in Hyderabad', *Economic Journal*, 53, 1945, pp. 274–80.
10. HBECR, p. 91.
11. B.K. Narayan, *Finances and Fiscal Policy of Hyderabad State 1900–1956*, GOAP, Hyderabad, 1973, pp. 10–14.
12. Khan Bahadur Taraporevala, 'Report on the proposed Establishment of Central Bank of Hyderabad (Confidential)', GOH, Hyderabad, 1947.

CHAPTER FIVE

Labour

Any analysis of labour unlike that of capital and output, is beset with the problem of bias. This bias is part of an ideology of development in which there is hardly any account of the labour force outside organised industry, except census data. The bias is political to the extent that organised struggles of labour were left out of the available records, and also patriarchal in that there was a consistent underplaying of the role of female labour in industrial development. Our analysis of the industrial labour force in Hyderabad is limited by this bias of the data base.

Census data on industrial labour as an indicator of long-term changes in the structure of the industrial labour force is inadequate, if not misleading.[1] But it is the only source that includes, on a systematic basis, the labour force in artisan industry. Hence we shall first consider the data on occupational structure given in the census. In 1901, the total population engaged in industry, minerals and infrastructure in Hyderabad was about 1.43 million but declined to about 1.18 million by 1941.[2] This decline of about 18 per cent was in sharp contrast with the increase, by about 47 per cent, of the population during the same period. The trend was also reflected in the proportion of industrial labour among the total working population in the state. However, the decline was not uniform in all groups of industries. Our detailed analysis of the census data (see, 'Occupational Structure', Appendix) shows that minerals and infrastructural industries were an exception to this trend. To a lesser extent this was also true in the case of ceramics and agro-based industries-II.

The decline in the total labour force was largely a reflection of the decline in artisan industry, but in organised industry, the labour force increased. According to the census reports, the labour force in large industrial establishments was about 24,000 in 1911, 35,000 in 1921, 64,500 in 1931 and was about 100,000 in 1941.[3] Similarly, the labour force employed in factories covered by the Factories Act increased from about 25,500 in 1930 when the Act came into force to almost 60,000 in 1947 towards the end of the regime.[4] The definition of a large industrial establishment changed in that initially it included all units which engaged an average daily labour of ten or more but later, in 1945, those establishments with an average daily labour of less than twenty were excluded. Yet the labour force engaged in large industrial establishments increased from about 29,000 in 1930 to 76,500 in 1945.[5] Excluding the units in prisons and schools, the labour force in manufacturing industry proper rose from 22,780 to 65,000 in the same period.[6] Thus all sources show that the labour force in organised industry grew by almost 200 per cent (see 'The Labour Force in Organised Industry', Appendix).

The results of our statistical analysis of annual increases in the industrial labour force show some significant changes in the structure of the industrial labour force. (see, Table 5.2, Appendix). The annual increase in the labour force, in 1930–45, was substantially higher in chemicals and metal and engineering industries, followed by agro-based industries-II and forest-based industries. In agro-based industries-I and ceramics, however, the growth rates were lower than the industrial average. The annual increase in the labour force engaged in manufacturing industry proper was considerably higher than that in the grand total of industry, mining and infrastructure. The most significant conclusion that emerges from our regression analysis is that the labour force in modern industries increased at a higher rate than in others, in tune with the structural changes in industry referred to earlier.

It must, however, be noted that despite these changes, the two major characteristics of the industrial labour force remained as they were. Firstly, the proportion of labour within organised industry remained limited, never having been more than seven per cent (see, 'Occupational Structure', Appendix). Secondly, agro-based industries, despite some decline, retained their primacy. Even at the end of WW II, the labour force in these industries was about 54 per cent of the total industrial labour force.

In organised industry, units that engaged labour on a seasonal basis were preponderant. They included agro-processing industries, beedi manufacture in forest-based industries, brick- making and quarry work in ceramics, aerated water in chemicals and other such seasonal factories.[7] The implication of this kind of industrialisation for the composition of the industrial labour force was that it was pre-dominantly seasonal in nature. Invariably it was composed of small peasants and agricultural labour who were attracted to these factories during the lean season. The wages in these factories it appears, were higher than the prevailing wage-rates in agriculture.[8] The prevalence of seasonal labour can also be noted in the mining sector. Reporting almost half a century after mining started, the 1931 census observed that a significant section of miners were 'usually small cultivators or agricultural labourers resorting to the mines during slack agricultural season'.[9]

The labour force, both skilled and unskilled, included what in Hyderabad was described as *gair mulki* labour, i.e., persons from outside.[10] According to the industrial census, the proportion of outsiders in managerial, clerical and skilled jobs was about 70 per cent in 1911 and 30 per cent in 1921. Among unskilled labour, the proportion was 10 and seven respectively.[11] Emigration caused by famines, the increasing demand for labour in the adjoining districts of Bombay Presidency and the unwillingness of local labour to engage in new industrial activity were some of the factors that explain the presence of outside labour in the initial years. Later their proportion seems to have declined, except in some stray instances.[12]

The status of women among the industrial labour force, shows some particular features specific to their gender (see, 'Female Labour', Appendix). The proportion of female labour among industrial labour declined sharply from 12 per cent in 1901 to five per cent in 1941.[13] The degree of decline seems to have been determined by the degree of change in the technological base and product mix. Even in organised industry, where the labour force otherwise increased, the proportion of women declined. Among labour covered by the Factories Act, for instance, the proportion of the women declined from 37 per cent in 1930 to 22 per cent in 1947.[14] In other words, both the general decline in the total industrial labour force and the specific increase of the labour force in organised industry, by its very nature, had adversely affected women.

The permanent labour force, employed on a regular basis and deriving their sustenance more or less exclusively from industry were, in the end, confined to a small segment of industry. Many of them were employed in large-scale units. These included textile mills, cigarette and sugar-manufacturing units in agro-based industries; machines, machine tools and small-scale button-making units and engineering workshops; cement and glass factories among ceramics; paper and match-making units in forest-based industries; pharmaceuticals and fertilizers among chemical industries; and, mining and railways.

Although government-appointed commissions and surveys conducted investigations from time to time, there is very little information concerning the wages and working conditions of industrial labour. Attempts to pass a Factory Act that could have regulated working conditions were thwarted in the initial years on the ground that such an act would inhibit industrial growth.[15] A commission appointed to examine the question also concurred with this view in 1911.[16] But following major strikes in the textile mills at Aurangabad and Gulbarga, a Factory Commission was appointed in 1920.[17] Its recommendations eventually resulted in the Factories Act that came into force in 1930. The Act sought to regulate, among other things, working hours for men and women and the employment of child labour. In addition, a number of legislations came into force from time to time.[18] The enforcement mechanisms however were left in the hands of *taluqdars* and *tehsildars*, except in the case of Hyderabad city. In the absence of any notable effort at enforcement, the measures had no effect on actual conditions in factories.

So working conditions remained as oppressive as was common during the early phase of industrialisation. The system of recruiting labour through contractors was prevalent in coal mines and to some extent, in the railways. In one instance, it was noted that the contractor's commission was five annas per head while labourers received seven annas per head.[19] In some cases the contractors were also moneylenders to whom the labourers were bonded.[20] Wages, as indicated by the Rege Committee appointed shortly after the fall of the regime, seem to have been very low in a large number of industries. Out of the seventeen industries or factories the committee investigated, only five were paying more than a rupee a day, only nine were paying Dearness Allowance and only five paid bonus in that year.[21] The few non-official accounts available also confirm the abysmally low level of wages.[22]

It was the struggle over wages that served as the immediate cause of the spontaneous outbursts of strikes in the state. The first recorded strike took place in the Aurangabad Textile Mill.[23] Later strikes were reported in textile mills in Aurangabad (1919) and Gulbarga (1920), railways (1927) and other industries. Officially 25 strikes were reported in 1931–45.[24] But official figures obscure the primary factor that facilitated the struggle of workers, viz., the development of trade unions.

The first major trade union formed in Hyderabad State was the Calendar Workers Union in 1927. Around the same time a strike in the Lalaguda railway workshop led to the formation of the Railway Workers Union.[25] Significantly both these unions were located in the British-administered pocket of Secunderabad where British Indian laws were applicable. A Trade Union Act came into force in British India in 1926 while in Hyderabad it came only in 1945. In both these unions, the leader was Congress trade union leader Varahagiri Venkata Giri who later became the President of India.[26] The second major development was the textile trade union, Girni Kamgar Union, formed in Aurangabad in 1935, under the influence of Mumbai Girni Kamgar Union. Earlier, Aurangabad was also the venue of the first state-level trade union conference in 1930. During WW II trade unions emerged in almost all units which had a permanent labour force. These included all the textile mills, Vazir Sultan Tobacco, Allwyn Metal, medium-scale button factories in the old city, cement and sugar factories and the Singareni Collieries. Among the high points of the trade union struggles were the forty five-day strike in the railways in 1942 and the strike in the button factories in the old city. By 1946, the state Congress leadership organised the first state conference of its Mazdoor Sevak Sangh in Aurangabad. In 1947, the Communist-led All Hyderabad Trade Union Congress (AHTUC) held its first conference. The Communist trade unions, with an reported affiliation of 200 units and 50,000 workers, were strong in Hyderabad city, Warangal, Gulbarga, Shahbad and Nanded.[27] The membership in registered trade unions increased from 12,000 in 1947 to 63,000 in 1949.[28] In fact the period immediately after the fall of the regime witnessed the greatest number of strikes organised by the Communists in aid of their peasant movement in parts of Telangana.[29]

To sum up, we can conclude that despite the general trend of decline, the industrial labour force in organised industry increased over time. These increases also reflect a subtle change in industry. But the labour force, to a considerable extent, was composed of small peasants and agricultural labours even in organised industry due to the very nature of industrialisation. Permanent labour, who were more or less exclusively dependent on industry for their sustenance, were confined to a small segment of organised industry, and it was in this segment that the organised activity of the workers emerged by the late 1930s.

At a different level of abstraction, we can make some observations on the changes in social relations. If, notionally, we define the proletariat as wage labourers who do not own any means of production and who have no option but to sell their labour, then we can conclude that such a distinct class emerged in Hyderabad state. The emerging working class was also involved in self-conscious political activity. In that sense, we can conclude that a working class, not only in itself but for itself, emerged in Hyderabad.

Notes

1. See Appendix. See also Indian Planning Commission, *Occupational Pattern of Indian Union, 1901–1951*, GOI, Delhi, 1951.
2. Census, 1901 and 1941. The data relates to 'actual workers' as

defined by the Census. The definition, however, was not the same in 1901 and 1941. The consequent problems make some difference to the actual numbers but not to the general trend, as we shall see later. Large-scale movements of population especially in urban areas, some territorial changes and the changes in definitions make it difficult for us to include 1951 data in the occupational structure.

3. Census 1911–1941. See also IS, pp. 7–8. Both in the 1911 Census and in the 1921 Census, a separate industrial census was included. But the detailed data could not be made use of as it was not always comparable with the data available from other sources for the later period.
4. FBIDAR, relevant years. The Hyderabad Factories Act, 1337 F came into force in 1930. A factory was defined as a unit that employs an average daily labour of 20 or more people [Clause 2(a)]. But exemptions and extensions of the clause would make it difficult for us to use the data more profitably. For instance, in the case of cotton-ginning and pressing factories, changes were made in the definition of a unit in 1931. CIDAR, 1340 F. We do not have details of all such exemptions.
5. SA, relevant years.
6. SA, relevant years. The 'year' adopted was not uniform for the entire period. In earlier years it was *Fasli* year while later it was the usual English financial year. In either case, the figures refer to average daily labour.
7. The seasonal factories, among those covered by the Factories Act, constituted 90 per cent in 1930–31 and 64 per cent in 1946–47. FBIDAR, relevant years.
8. That the wages in industry were higher than in agriculture is the inference one can draw from scattered references and data at different times. See, 'Report of Hyderabad Factory Commission', GOH, Hyderabad, 1922, p. 30; 'Report on Labour Census, 1344 F', GOH, Hyderabad, 1935, p. 29; and, S. Kesav Iyengar, *Rural Economic Enquiries in Hyderabad State, 1949–51*, GOH, Hyderabad, 1951, p. 556.
9. Census of Hyderabad, 1931, Part I, p. 64.
10. On the emergence of *mulki*, non-*mulki* categories in the state, see Section III, Chapter 7.
11. Industrial Census, 1911 and 1921.
12. Based on contemporary newspaper accounts and confidential records of Warangal Subedari, Ramakrishna Reddy reports that a significant

section of mining labour was from the United Provinces and also included evacuees from Burma in the 1940s. he attributes their presence to the discriminatory practice of the labour contractors. V. Ramakrishna Reddy, *Economic History of Hyderabad State: Warangal Suba 1911–1950*, Giani Publishing House, New Delhi, 1987, p. 481. Similarly, a number of workers in the tanneries in Warangal and Hyderabad were from Madras Presidency and belonged to the Muslim Labbies sect. Penesetti Madhav Rao, 'Industrial Development of Hyderabad', unpublished, Doctoral Dissertation, Nagpur University, Nagpur, 1956, pp. 122–23.

13. Census 1901 and 1941. See the section on women labour in the Appendix.
14. FBIDAR, relevant years.
15. GAR, 1304–1307 F.
16. GAR, 1321 F.
17. 'Report of the Hyderabad Factory Commission', 1922, op. cit. (note 8).
18. These included the Maternity Benefit Act (1940), The Workmens Compensation Act (1940), The Trade Disputes Order (1941), Payment of Wages Regulation (1942), etc. Under the original Factories Act, referred to above, only in Hyderabad city was an Inspectorate of Factories appointed to enforce these legislations. but in the new act (Hyderabad Factory Regulation 1353 F), passed in 1944, such inspectorates were envisaged for district centres also. But before they were set actually up, the all-India Act that came into force after the fall of the regime, replaced the 1944 Regulation. See, 'Report of the Conditions of Factory Labour in Hyderabad State' (Rege Committee), GOH, Hyderabad, 1949.
19. Ramakrishna Reddy, 1987, op. cit. (note 12), quoting from Confidential Records of Warangal Subedari, p. 481.
20. Christof von Furer-Haimendorf, *Tribal Hyderabad*, GOH, Hyderabad, 1945, p. 39.
21. This data is deduced from the details given in the 'Report on the Conditions of Factory Labour in Hyderabad State', op. cit. (note 18). Monthly wages have been converted into daily wages to maintain uniformity.
22. Sundarayya for instance, reported that the average wage of textile workers was Rs 10–15 per month. P. Sundarayya, *The Telangana Peoples Struggle and Its Lessons*, Communist Party of India (Marxist), Calcutta, 1972, p. 17. Similarly, Romesh Thapar reported that 80

per cent of the two lakh workers in the state received less than Rs 18 per month. Romesh Thapar, *Storm Over Hyderabad*, Kutub, Bombay, 1947, p. 117.

23. GAR, 1313 F.
24. SA, relevant years.
25. S.M. Caved Razvi, *hyderabad samstanamlo rajakiya chaithanyam: vidyarthi yuvajanula pathra*, (Telugu), Vishalandhra, Vijayawada, 1986, pp. 57–58.
26. The information on trade union activity given here is gleaned from different sources. These include Sundarayya, 1972, op. cit. (note 22), pp. 306–09; Razvi, 1986, cited above, pp. 57–60; and, the memoirs of Chandragupta Choudary and Gulam Hyder in Raj Bahadur Gowr et al., *The Glorious Telangana Armed Struggle*, Communist Party, New Delhi, 1973, pp. 130–32 and pp. 142–46.
27. Ramakrishna Reddy, 1987, op. cit. (note 12), quoting from AITUC files, p. 609.
28. Madhava Rao, 1956, op. cit. (note 12), p. 419.
29. In addition to a general strike in early 1950, seventeen major strikes involving 30,000 workers took place in 1949 alone, *Deccan Chronicle*, 16 June, 1949. See also HGBEA, No. 1–3, January–March 1950, p. 148.

APPENDIX 5-A

Labour: A Statistical Review

I. Occupational Structure

Data on the occupational structure, given in the decennial census, is an important source of information on the structure of the labour force. Unlike any other source it includes data on the artisan sector of industry. But the use of such data is beset with a number of problems. Changes in the definition of 'worker', along with changes in the occupational categories and their classification renders any comparative account over time difficult. Lacunae in enumeration further compound these difficulties. More importantly, in a predominantly agrarian society under transition, a significantly large number of people on the margins, would be in a permanent state of flux. The dynamics of such a phenomenon makes data collected on any finely defined occupational group at a static point in time, somewhat unreliable. Thus an analysis of long-term changes in the structure of the industrial labour force, based on census data, is not only difficult but can even be misleading.

In our analysis we have included only the labour engaged in what the census describes as preparation of material substances and not in their 'supply', i.e. industry but not trade. However, the 1901 census lumped them together. We have separated them in almost all cases, except in a few instances where it was not possible. Further, we have reclassified all census categories into the input-based groups adopted in our study. As a result some occupations have been shifted from their original orders and sub-orders to other categories. Thus oil-based industries now form part of agro-based industries-II and not 'chemical and analogous substances' as in the census. Similarly, a number of occupations listed under 'miscellaneous' in the census have been shifted to their respective categories. The following analysis should be read in the light of these adjustments and limitations.

Table 5.1 shows that the percentage of workers engaged in manufacturing industry generally declined over time, being lowest during the depression year, 1931. But this trend of decline was not uniform for all groups. In three of them, metal and engineering, forest-based and animal-based industries, the decline was continuous and secular. The decline of traditional smithies and tanneries affected these groups. In agro-based industries-I, the destruction of handlooms contributed to the decline. In particular, the conditions of production in cotton- producing Marathwada affected them badly. But there was a slight improvement in 1941, partly due to the war-time situation. In agro-based industries-II, the percentage of workers showed considerable fluctuation. Apart from the fluctuating conditions of agrarian production during the inter-war years, the development of many seasonal units in this group, like oil, rice and flour mills, seems to have contributed to the fluctuation.

A somewhat different picture will emerge if minerals and infrastructural industries are taken into account. Here there was no generalised trend of decline. On the contrary, in minerals, railways and other transport, the percentage of workers increased. The fact that the artisan sector was small or absent in these groups explains this phenomenon. The countervailing trends in these groups of industries explains the absence of any trend in decline in the grand total of manufacturing, mineral and infrastructural industries, where the proportion of labour increased from about 14 per cent in 1901 to 17 per cent in 1941.

If it is assumed that the data from the occupational census indicate the total labour force in manufacturing industry (excluding minerals and infrastructure) and the data on the labour force in organised industry, also given in the census, indicates the work force engaged in organised industry, then an estimate can be made of the labour force in organised industry. The proportion works out as 2.6 per cent in 1911, 3.6 per cent in 1921, 7.1 per cent in 1931 at the height of the depression and then the decline to 6.7 per cent in

1941. Given the number of limitations mentioned, the estimates can only be taken as approximations. But they do indicate the limited extent of organised industry.

Table 5.1
Occupational Structure: 1901–1941
(Percentage of total actual workers)

	1901	*1911*	*1921*	*1931*	*1941*
1. Agro-based Industries-I	3.99	3.84	3.36	2.97	4.42
2. Agro-based Industries-II	2.76	3.25	3.31	2.62	3.07
3. Metal and Engineering Industries	1.41	1.15	1.24	1.10	1.08
4. Forest-based Industries	1.39	1.06	1.32	0.84	0.77
5. Ceramics	1.40	1.57	1.57	0.92	1.18
6. Chemicals	0.01	0.01	0.02	0.02	0.03
7. Animal-based Industries	2.13	2.08	1.46	1.17	0.89
8. Others	0.27	0.60	0.90	0.70	0.55
Manufacturing Industry Total	13.37	13.55	13.20	10.36	11.99
9. Minerals	0.14	0.17	0.25	0.34	0.94
10. Railways	0.09	0.12	0.15	1.17	1.15
11. Other Transport	0.42	0.84	1.21	2.86	2.47
12. Power	-–	0.01	0.01	0.01	0.01
13. Communications	0.03	0.01	0.03	0.05	0.06
Grand Total of Industry	14.05	14.70	4.85	4.75	15.62
14. Agriculture and Allied	61.45	61.90	56.46	56.87	58.02
15. Trade and Services	7.52	8.04	9.45	11.52	9.30
16. Public Administration and Liberal Arts	7.28	4.56	5.45	3.88	5.02

Note: Actual workers were those who were 'principal earners' and those who follow the occupation were subsidiary earners. But in 1901, only agriculturalists among the subsidiary earners were included. In 1931 and 1941, 'total earners' with or without subsidiary were included. 'Agriculture and Allied' in case of 1901 includes the category called 'general labour'.
Source: Census, 1901–1941.

II. Labour Force in Organised Industry

The labour force in organised industry, contrary to the trends in the total industrial sector, increased over time. We have done a detailed analysis of the differential impact of changes in the labour force in organised industry for the period 1930–45, for which data was available on a systematic basis. The Annual Reports of CID (CIDAR) and Factories and Boilers Inspection Department (FBIDAR) give the factory-wise data for this period which were also reproduced in Statistical Abstracts (SA). Where data from one of the sources was not available, we have supplemented it with data from other sources. It should, however, be noted that the standard year adopted was not common for the entire period. For most cases it was the *Fasli* year while later, for some industries it was the usual British financial year. In either case the data relate to average daily labour employed. Similarly the definition of large industrial establishment also changed. Initially it included all units which employed an average daily labour of ten or more but in 1945 all units which employed daily labour of less than twenty were excluded. Thus by the initial definition, the data of the later period would be an underestimate. Since our attempt is to recapture and analyse the process of growth, these changes only strengthen our observations.

We have reclassified all factories according to the input-based divisions that we have adopted. Similar computations were made for each year in case of minerals and infrastructure, the data for which was available in Statistical Abstracts. On the basis of this reclassified data we have constructed an index for change in the labour force in organised industry with 1939–40 as the base year (see Table 5.5 at the end). The index forms the basis for the following regression analysis. The linear trends are fitted to the respective time series data.

Table 5.2 indicates that the average annual growth rate in the labour force was considerably higher in manufacturing industry proper (4.34) than in mineral and infrastructural industries (2.17). This was because in the latter two groups, the scale of operations, after reaching a certain level, could not absorb labour at the same pace as before. The last railway line, for instance, was laid in 1930. In coal mines, although a new mine was opened in 1936, at Kottagudem, the old one at Singareni, from which the name Singareni Collieries originates, was closed down in 1941. Recalling our observations on census data, we can note that minerals and infrastructure while maintaining a steady absorption of labour in comparison with the artisan sector, had a lower growth rate in labour compared to organised industry. As a result of the countervailing trend in these two groups, the annual percentage of increase in labour in the grand total of industry, minerals and infrastructure was lower (3.29) than that in manufacturing industry (4.34).

The labour force in chemical-based industries and metal and engineering industries increased at a substantially higher rate than the labour force in manufacturing industry. The growth rate reflects the structural change referred to earlier. Only in agro-based industries-I and ceramics, were the growth rates considerably lower (2.62 and 2.71 respectively) than the industry average. In these two groups, time as an explanatory variable for growth of labour force (R^2) was much lower than in other industries. The conditions of cotton production in Marathwada, the relatively lower investments from about the mid-1930s and the general decline in factories explain the phenomenon in the case of agro-based industries-I. In ceramics, the few modern industries that developed, like glass and cement, were highly capital-intensive. The relative stagnation in the labour-intensive brick kilns and stone quarries also explains the low rates of growth. In all other cases, the growth in number of units in small and medium scale industries explains the increases. In all cases the growth rates are statistically significant. Large industrial establishments that included production units in prisons and schools had, as can be seen from the table, a higher annual growth rate of labour (6.45) than those in manufacturing industry proper (4.34). Presumably students and prisoners increased at a faster rate than the labour force in organised industry.

Table 5.2
Growth of Labour Force in Organised Industry: 1930–45
(Base 1939–40)

	b	R^2	*t*
1. Agro-based Industries-I	2.62	0.25	2.15
2. Agro-based Industries-II	7.36	0.77	6.90
3. Metal and Engineering Industries	10.45	0.78	6.95
4. Forest-based Industries	7.04	0.54	4.04
5. Ceramics	2.71	0.12	1.39
6. Chemical-based Industries	17.94	0.80	7.55
7. Animal-based Industries	6.07	0.52	3.26
8. Others	6.69	0.47	2.98
Total Manufacturing Industry[a]	4.34	0.55	4.13
Large Industrial Establishments[b]	6.45	0.83	8.04
9. Minerals	3.74	0.71	5.60
10. Railways	0.64	0.32	3.30
11. Other Transport	11.24	0.96	16.80
12. Power	4.43	0.69	5.40
Total Minerals and Infrastructure	2.17	0.73	5.93
13. Grand Total of Industry, Minerals and Infrastructure	3.29	0.56	4.03

Notes: a. Units included were those employing an average daily labour of ten or more initially and twenty or more, later.
b. The total large industrial establishments also includes, in addition to all those covered in manufacturing industry, production units in prisons and schools.
Source: Index given in Table 5.5.

III. Structure of Industrial Labour Force

The same sources as above indicate the changes in the structure of the labour force in organised industry.

Table 5.3
Structure of Industrial Labour Force: 1930–45
(Percentage of total industrial labour)

	1930–31	*1944–45*
1. Agro-based Industries-I	67.82	44.78
2. Agro-based Industries-II	6.30	9.08
3. Metal and Engineering Industries	16.16	18.50
4. Forest-based Industries	3.09	7.77
5. Ceramics	3.48	14.36
6. Chemical-based Industries	0.94	2.06
7. Animal-based Industries	0.50	1.75
8. Others	1.71	1.70
Manufacturing Industry Total	52.73	62.87
9. Minerals	17.97	17.37
10. Infrastructure	29.30	19.76
	(100)	(100)

Source: SA, relevant years.

The labour force engaged in the manufacturing industry increased from 53 per cent to 63 per cent during this period evidently as a result of higher growth rates in the labour force that were analysed earlier. Within manufacturing industry, a structural change from agro-based industries, which declined from 68 per cent to 45 per cent, to others can be observed. Although labour in the second group of agro-based industries increased, the increase was only marginal. By the end of WW II, the labour force in metal and engineering, chemicals, ceramics and forest-based industries together constituted almost 43 per cent of the total. But the agro-based industries still retained their supremacy.

IV. Female Labour

The census data on occupational structure with all the attendant limitations mentioned earlier, provides detailed data on female labour in each occupational category. Cotton cleaning, sizing, spinning and weaving; garment and toiletry industries, manufacturing and refining of vegetable oils and food industries in agro-based industries; beedi and basket-making in forest-based industries; quarrying work and potteries in ceramics and tanneries were some of the notable industries where traditionally a female labour force was engaged in higher proportions in Hyderabad. The following table gives the proportion of female labour in each group of industries.

Table 5.4

Female Labour in Industry: 1901–1941
(Percentage in each category)

	1901	*1911*	*1921*	*1931*	*1941*
1. Agro-based Industries-I	35.09	38.00	36.79	30.61	35.74
2. Agro-based Industries-II	32.69	35.66	41.53	33.28	26.48
3. Metal and Engineering Industries	26.01	24.25	22.22	25.84	21.11
4. Forest-based Industries	26.54	25.62	28.59	24.91	33.58
5. Ceramics	28.97	30.87	44.24	30.66	30.08
6. Chemicals-based Industries	10.16	17.95	11.12	27.77	23.28
7. Animal-based Industries	24.31	28.90	20.88	17.70	18.44
8. Others	16.50	12.29	28.37	18.72	8.97
Manufacturing Industry Total	42.52	31.94	34.28	28.16	30.00
9. Minerals	47.46	22.22	30.38	18.01	38.58
10. Railways and other Transport	14.00	12.90	32.06	24.87	20.38
11. Power and Communications	0.01	0.05	3.90	0.53	2.70
12. Grand Total of Minerals, Infrastructure and Manufacturing Industry	12.51	4.49	5.03	3.97	4.75

Source: Census, 1901–1941.

Both in manufacturing industry and in the grand total of industry including minerals and infrastructure, the proportion of female labour declined quite sharply during this period of transition in industry. However, in agro-based, forest and chemical-based industries, the proportion increased to a significant extent. The decline was sharp in the metal and engineering industries, animal-based industries and minerals. An interesting insight into the decline of female labour can be obtained if this decline is compared with that in general industry given in Table 5.1. Except in forest-based industries (basket- making) and ceramics (potteries and quarry work), in almost all other cases the trends indicated by the above table correspond to the trends in the general industrial labour force (Table 5.1). The general decline, as noted earlier, was primarily due to the decline in artisan industry. Where the degree of change in technology (metal and engineering industry) or in nature of product (shoes and sandals) was more, the proportion of decline in female labour was sharper. Where the extent of such changes were less extensive, the decline was less, as in case of some agro-based industries. Where there was hardly any change in technology or product-mix, as in basket-weaving or quarry work or potteries, the proportion of female labour actually increased over time even when the total labour force in these groups declined. Thus in a sense the decline in the female labour force was determined, to a significant extent, by the degree of technological change in different groups of industries. However, the effects of migration, that followed the decline in artisan industry should also be noted. In general, it was only male labourers who migrated. Consequently the proportion of female labour increased.

As noted earlier, contrary to the general trend of decline, labour in organised industry increased over time. This increase was a reflection of structural change in organised industry. But here too the proportion f female labour declined over time. The proportion of female labour in the total factory labour covered under the Factories Act, according to the Annual Reports of Factories and Boilers Inspection Department, was 37 per cent in 1930–31, 32 per cent in 1935–36, 29 per cent in 1940–41 and 22 per cent in 1947–48. The restrictions imposed on the factory owners regarding the duration and timing of working hours for female labour under the Factories Act possibly contributed to this drastic fall in the proportion of female labour. This was because in the absence of

Table 5.5
Growth of Labour in Organised Industry: 1930–45
(1930–40 = 100)

Year	Agro-based-I	Agro-based-II	Metal and Engineering	Forest-based	Ceramics	Chemical-based	Animal-based	Others	Manufacturing Industry Total
1930–31	71	53	54	7	6	27	52	—	4
1931–32	79	38	54	7	10	35	—	42	5
1932–33	86	39	54	19	12	14	—	48	5
1933–34	82	72	81	29	12	36	7	46	6
1934–35	90	60	95	27	12	74	16	44	6
1935–36	90	73	92	38	12	106	—	35	6
1936–37	96	59	85	44	15	46	106	49	7
1937–38	100	62	105	116	102	50	67	83	9
1938–39	104	61	104	104	101	111	68	94	9
1939–40	100	100	100	100	100	100	100	100	100
1940–41	117	132	125	98	22	125	52	196	100
1941–42	47	98	115	45	14	246	96	—	5
1942–43	52	100	110	44	13	210	86	—	5
1943–44	128	123	154	41	51	210	105	—	10
1944–45	125	181	229	145	100	341	122	92	138
1945–47	NA	NA	NA	NA	NA	NA	NA	NA	NA
1947–48	144	153	268	152	18	269	NA	126	132

(*contd.*)

Table 5.5
(*Contd.*)

Year	*Mines*	*Railways*	*Other Transport*	*Power*	*Mineral and Infrastructural Industry*	*Grand Total*	*Large Industrial Establishments*	*Labour Covered by Factories Act*
1930–31	76	121	12	55	94	66	44	67
1931–32	76	110	11	45	88	66	46	55
1932–33	76	110	14	47	88	68	51	64
1933–34	80	114	18	41	92	72	61	69
1934–35	89	111	28	49	95	77	80	77
1935–36	80	106	36	67	90	76	97	78
1936–37	104	99	80	69	99	81	104	86
1937–38	95	98	93	75	96	97	85	93
1938–39	108	100	93	76	102	100	79	91
1939–40	100	100	100	100	100	100	100	100
1940–41	104	104	107	97	104	101	115	111
1941–42	109	108	120	896	109	74	105	129
1942–43	105	110	138	96	109	75	141	135
1943–44	102	110	135	95	108	107	143	140
1944–45	152	116	155	92	132	136	117	145
1945–47	NA	NA	NA	NA	NA	NA	NA	NA
1947–48	NA	NA	NA	NA	NA	NA	NA	156

Source: SA, relevant years, and, FBIDAR, Relevant years.

facilities for unfettered employment of female labour, usually at lower wages, the owners would opt for their retrenchment altogether. But the structural change referred to also involved change in the technological base of industry and should also be taken into consideration. Many of the new industries had a higher proportion of skilled labour. This also explains the gradual decline of the proportion of female labour. Thus the two most striking features of change in industry in Hyderabad during this period; the decline in artisan industry and the development of organised industry, both adversely affected female labour.

CHAPTER SIX

Appraisal

The industrial evolution of Hyderabad was limited by a number of factors. As the result of a decline in the artisan sector, the total labour force engaged in industry declined over time. Although organised industry did develop, its extent was very limited, with a labour force that was never more than 1,00,000 and as a proportion of the total industrial labour force it never exceeded seven per cent. Similarly, the total capital in the corporate sector never went beyond Rs 103 million, of which the mining and manufacturing sector was just Rs 50 million.

The indices of output for select commodities, also show very low growth rates. (See the series of tables in the Appendix). In fact, in a number of products, like cotton yarn, oil products, matches and glass, the growth rates even declined during the last phase. Only cigarettes, cement and sugar showed relatively high growth rates. Significantly all of them were export products to a considerable extent.

Thus the distinctive role played by the state in industrialisation could not, in the end, make any significant difference to the industrial backwardness of Hyderabad. Part of the failure can be traced to the specific limitations of state policy. We shall evaluate this policy with reference to cottage and small-scale industries and the financing of the corporate sector.

II

The general trend towards the decline of artisan industry both in Hyderabad and in India as a whole, was not particularly arrested by the policies pursued by the government. The most severely affected was the largest component, the handloom industry. The number of looms decreased from about 1,15,434 in 1921 to about 95,443 in 1941.[1] The drop was greater in cotton handlooms as compared with woollen and silk looms.[2] In the early 1930s, the Director-General of the Commerce and Industries Department noted that the decline of handlooms in Hyderabad was 'not so much from the effects of mill competition as from…handloom weavers in British India'.[3] Almost twenty years later, competition from handloom weavers in British India was noted as a contributory factor for their decline by Prof. Kesav Iyengar in his investigations.[4] The ITF-sponsored survey in the early 1930s identified the crux of the problem of the weavers as 'their indebtedness to local *sahukars* and yarn dealers'.[5] The department directly or through co-operatives provided financial help to improve the situation, as noted earlier. Yet reviewing almost two decades of cooperatives in 1937, the Co-operative Finance Enquiry Committee noted, ruefully, that 'co-operatives cannot be successful in this [handloom weaving] field'.[6] Similarly, a department publication at the end of WW II noted, reviewing the Department's efforts at financing, that 'cottage industries…could not much profit by it'.[7] In fact Iyengar noted that the Department itself was dependent on middlemen for the distribution of raw materials.[8] His case studies show a high incidence of debt among the weavers.[9]

Indebtedness affected not only handloom weavers but all other artisan workers also. Iyengar's case studies of the beedi industry, tanneries, toy and bangle-making and clay works—all show a high incidence of debt among artisans.[10] In that sense the efforts of the Department to provide financial support to cottage industries could not make any noticeable dent in the problem of indebtedness.

Among other factors that contributed to the deterioration of artisan industry was the shortage of raw materials. The efforts of the Department, through its outlets, could not augment supply. For instance, as against the normal demand of 6000 bales per month, the state was allocated 3865 bales and the actual supply was only about 1900 (32 per cent) bales in the late 1940s.[11] Consequent black marketing in yarn further increased indebtedness.[12] Similarly, a shortage of leather or its poor quality affected the tanneries.[13]

The structural change in industry that was referred to earlier, led to a direct decline in the demand for artisan industry. Handmade paper is a good illustration of this phenomenon. Before WW I there were about 200 workers engaged in this industry. Later the encouragement given by the government, especially by directing all the its departments to buy paper from the industry and give all wastage back, helped the industry. In the mid-1940s there were 150 families in seven centres engaged in the manufacture of handmade paper.[14] But as competition from mill-made paper from the state-financed Sirpur Mill increased, the government closed down its Emporium in Aurangabad, and in Kagazipura, the major centre, no more than 20 families were left by the late 1940s.[15]

In some cases, the efforts of the government to improve the situation of artisans were not sustained resulting in their collapse. Thus when a Jacquard Weaving Institute was set up at Aurangabad, the industry picked up. In the early 1930s there were around 2000 families engaged in this industry.[16] But once the Institute was closed and its place taken by an ITF-funded private company, the decline set in. By the late 1940s, there were only 200 families.[17] Carpet weavers suffered a similar fate when the famous Carpet Factory at Warangal was closed down with the number of weaving families going down from 50 to 20.[18]

Based on a number of field studies, Iyengar noted that indebtedness, lack of suitable technical support and market facilities, shortage of raw materials, closing down of government-owned units, emporia and other outlets, among other things were the causes of the decline in cottage industries.[19] The range of policy measures undertaken by the Department, including same innovative experiments, could not arrest the decline in artisan industry.

There were three consequences of the abject failure of government policies. Firstly, a number of independent artisans now became wage-earners.[20] The wages of even skilled artisans were much lower than those of unskilled labour in roads, railways, irrigation projects and factories.[21] Secondly, many artisans 'have been reduced to landless agricultural labourers'.[22] Thirdly, there was continuous and large-scale migration, especially to Bombay

Presidency.[23] The shift, which was generally only of males, also explains the predominance of women among artisan workers.[24]

One important factor that affected artisan industry but never received the attention of official surveys and publications was the nature of agrarian transition. This transition will be discussed in more detail later, but for the moment, an important feature in it should be noted. The commercialisation of agriculture intensified the feudal form of extraction of surplus from about the late 1920s or early 1930s. Consequently in *jagir* areas, which constituted more than a third of the total cultivated area, varieties of levies and taxes on the artisans and their products increased the burden on them.[25] In the Telangana region, the feudal extractions included *vetti pani*, a form of customary labour or service that all sections of the village were obliged to supply free to the landlords in both the *jagir* and *diwani* areas. This also included annual *nazaranas*, gifts at the time of special occasions like birth, marriage and death, supplying clothes or carrying them when relatives or officials visited them, supplying of cots, a particular job of weavers, and numerous other forms. Resistance to such services invited the punishment of lashing.[26] Due to this 'horrendous *vetti*, the weavers left their homes and migrated to the Bombay Presidency'.[27] Some attempts at organised resistance were also made from the late 1930s when the peasant movement developed in Telangana.[28]

In the face of what an official survey described as the 'death grip of the greedy *sowcars* or money lenders or yarn dealers'[29] over the artisans, the government attempted to provide relief in the form of alternative credit institutions. But these institutions never actually took root, as noted earlier. The reasons are not far to seek. In many cases the money lenders were either the landlords themselves or were closely aligned with them. Hyderabad State resolutely defended the landed gentry till the end. In the absence of any efforts to undermine their social power, their grip only tightened as demand conditions deteriorated for the artisans. As commercialisation intensified *vetti pani* and other such forms of extraction, artisans were squeezed by the social structure in the villages. Autonomous initiatives taken by the state in industry remained external to the dynamics of the oppression of the artisans.

III

Small-scale industry seems to have fared better as compared with the artisan sector. An overwhelming majority of 'large industrial establishments' which increased from 70 in 1901 to almost 1000 in 1948 consisted of small-scale units.[30] In Hyderabad they were defined as units with a capital of Rs 5000 or below.[31] Much of their growth was facilitated by the changes taking place in consumer products where local products replaced imports. These units included agro-processing units like cotton ginning and pressing units, decorticating, oil, rice and flour mills, motor and engineering workshops, metallic buttons, matches, shoes and sandals, wooden articles, biscuits and other food products and others. Except for agro-processing units, many of these were located in Hyderabad city. The little evidence there is regarding the sources of their finance, referred to earlier, indicates that capital for these units came from traders and moneylenders. In addition, the Department also financed them. Thus both on the supply side and on the demand side, small-scale industry had better prospects in the state. This explains their growth.

But growth in sheer numbers cannot be taken as an indicator of health, especially in the small-scale sector. In agro-processing units for instance, the mushrooming of the units itself restricted their performance. In number they remained the largest segment of industrial units in the state, growing from about 60 in 1901, to almost 700 units in 1948.[32] The actual working of these units in any season was subject to the conditions of production in agriculture, and in lean years many of them became redundant. In 1905, the increase in cotton ginning and pressing units became alarming enough for the owners to request the government to stop the further issue of licenses.[33] Later, by the 1930s, a 'considerable number of them remained closed every year'.[34] Similarly, small-scale units in chappals, sandals and shoes faced a crisis from the 1930s. Here a shortage of leather of suitable quality affected them as local tanneries found the export market more profitable.[35]

Since many of the small-scale units received financial support from the Department or ITF, the rate of recovery of loans can be taken as an indicator of their viability. Our computations on the basis of amounts recovered and outstanding, given in the Annual Reports of the Department (CIDAR) reveal that in the period 1920–34, the recovery was never more than ten per cent per annum. Later in 1934–35, it was about 25 per cent.[36]

To draw any conclusions regarding small-scale units, forty years later, is very difficult as the relevant data disappeared along with the units. But perhaps from our account here we can suggest that small-scale industries had a mixed performance, but certainly fared better than other sectors of industry.

IV

In the corporate sector, as already noted; state finance played a significant role. Here over-capitalisation was the single most striking feature of industry. Liberal finance, especially loans, led to a situation where the assets sunk in big companies had no relation to their returns. In some cases, the amounts of loans advanced exceeded the total paid-up value of their capital.[37] This situation was aggravated by the role of the ITF as the managing agent. Since it was not equipped for this function, it in turn, appointed private agencies to act on its behalf. It was here that corruption, speculation and inter-locking of funds originated which adversely affected the shareholders. Since in most cases the largest shareholder was the government, it became a victim of its own policies. The over-capitalisation was reflected in high average capital per company in the state.[38] Our analysis of capital intensity in the state also indicates this trend.[39]

Over-capitalisation was closely linked with the fact that the beneficiaries of government financing were the *jagirdar*-cum-civil servants. This also perhaps explains the inability of the regime to take any meaningful measures against the sinking of capital on such a large scale. That task was taken up by the military administration after 1948, when the abolition of the *jagirdar* system was under way.

The military administration took a position against further financial aid to industries.[40] It also sought to increase the role of private investment.[41] Kasturbhai Lalbhai, at the behest of the central government, investigated the ITF-financed industries in 1950. He noted the marginal role of managing agents, redundant labour and over-capitalisation as the main problems of these companies.[42] Eventually the ITF was merged with the state Industrial Finance Corporation in 1956.

Meanwhile, in the aftermath of the fall of the regime, a number of companies were closed down. In the financial year 1949–50, 32 out of the 90 companies in the mining and manufacturing sector, with a paid-up capital of Rs 19.19 lakhs were liquidated;[43] of the remaining companies, the new government opted for large-scale privatisation.[44] Thus Sirsilk, Sirpur Paper Mills, Allwyn Metals, Hyderabad Asbestos Cement were handed over to the Birlas. Notable among others that went into private hands were the Road Transport Service, Taj Glass Works, Osman Shahi Mills, Hyderabad Construction Company, Hyderabad Chemicals and Pharmaceuticals and others. In general, the change in government resulted in the drastic reduction of the role of the state in industry and the entry of big business houses and capitalists from other parts of India in a forceful way into Hyderabad industry.[45]

V

We can now identify certain features of the industrial development of Hyderabad. Although it would be tempting to make comparisons with industrial development in British India, the scale factor, variance in resource base and differential data base makes that difficult, if not positively misleading. We shall confine ourselves to some broad impressions. The most striking feature was that industry in Hyderabad, despite the distinctive role played by the state, was no less backward than industry in British India.

We should recall that in Hyderabad, state finance to industry made some difference to the constraints on industry. The state actively invested not only in social overhead capital but also in a variety of companies, especially in the modern sector. Yet the investments did not foster further investments. The explanation probably lies in political factors that inhibited the entry of external capital. But more importantly the overarching role of the state itself inhibited growth, because it prevented the emergence of autonomous capital capable of reproducing itself, on an expanding scale. Both trading-usury capital at lower levels and some agrarian surplus at higher levels did flow into industry. Yet neither of them attained a capacity to propel further industrial growth. They were mobilised by a favourable state policy but constrained by the social order. The unchanging agrarian social structure in which they were located was at the root of their immobility.

The incapacity of capital also explains the technological dependency. A favourable policy with an appropriate mix of technologies under differing systems of arrangements, was pursued by the state. Yet private investment could not make use of it to any significant extent.

In the case of labour, we can perhaps add that there were some notable distinctions. The supply of skilled labour was sought to be improved right from the time of Salar Jung when the civil engineering college was established. Despite subsequent ups and downs, by around the 1920s the government took the initiative to keep up the supply of skilled labour to industry. But in the absence of industrial expansion, just the efforts to impart training, at different levels, to labour, had no meaning. The share of labour, including skilled labour, in organised industry remained extremely low and somewhat uneven between different groups of industries.

The demand for industrial goods, especially consumer products, made notable progress in the state from about the 1920s. A cursory glance at external trade figures would reveal perceptible changes in industry after WW I.

At the outset we should note that external trade figures in the case of Hyderabad include trade with the rest of India as well. The volume of external trade increased from Rs 82 million to Rs 250 million by the end of WW I and reached a peak of Rs 800 million by the end of WW II.[46] From about the mid-1920s, as a result of the development of commercial crops, especially oilseeds, the balance of trade turned in favour of the state. It remained so till the end of WW II, a marginal exception being the depression period. The growth rate of exports was generally higher than that of imports (see Table 6.1).

Among imports, manufactured goods remained the dominant group throughout the period. They constituted about 50 per cent of total imports in 1912–21 and were around 58 per cent by the end of the period. However, in the later period it was not consumer products but machinery imports which increased.[47] This can be explained by the fact that the import of intermediate and capital goods was necessitated by the development of industry in the state. Manufactured goods which constituted only about 3 per cent of total exports in 1912–21, became over 30 per cent towards the end of the period (Table 6.2). Apart from coal, the major exports were cement, sugar, cigarettes, glass, and paper during the later period.

An overwhelming majority of industrial products served the domestic market. But this import substitution in consumer products, whatever its extent, has to be considered along with the far less restricted growth of intermediate and capital goods. In machines, machine tools and parts and other goods, the initiative taken by the ITF did make a difference to the situation from the early 1940s. But the capital goods sector itself remained a crucial constraint. Although in the last phase the government made some efforts to develop this sector, as in the case of the steel factory in the Godavari Valley Project, the plans did not materialise. In a sense this constraint was closely linked with the incapacity of capital noted earlier.

In the end, some perceptible changes notwithstanding, the domestic market remained very limited. In Hyderabad, unlike perhaps in British India, the industrial policy of the state could not be held responsible for this. It was the precapitalist social organisation that imposed the ultimate limits on the process of industrialisation. The nature of agrarian society in which a large majority of the population remained at subsistence level, restricted the demand for industrial products. Even the trends towards commercialisation of agriculture, as we shall see later, only intensified their oppression and reduced in the end, their consumption levels. On the other hand, the precapitalist forms of extraction of surplus remained the easier primary source of income for the agrarian rich. Whatever little of the agrarian surplus flowed into industry, it could never attain a self- propelling capacity. It was this kind of feudal social structure that in the ultimate analysis, became the constraint on industrial growth. State intervention in industry, somewhat isolated from its defence of the feudal social order, could not make any significant difference to the industrial backwardness of Hyderabad.

Notes

1. Census of Hyderabad, Part I, 1921 and 1941. See also IS, pp. 155, 192 and 215.
2. Ibid.
3. Director Abdy Collins in his foreword, P. Sahai, *Survey of Handlooms and Dyeing Industry*, GOH, Hyderabad, 1933, p. 1.
4. S. Kesav Iyengar, *Rural Economic Enquiries in the Hyderabad State, 1949–1951*, p. 474.
5. Sahai, 1933, op. cit. (note 3), pp. 12 and 72.
6. 'Report of the Hyderabad Co-operative Finance Enquiry Committee', GOH, Hyderabad, 1937, p. 50.
7. IS, p. 35.
8. Iyengar, 1951, op. cit. (note 4), p. 558.
9. The percentage of indebted weavers, for instance, was 47 in Kinhal, 67 in Maski and 60 in Armoor. Ibid., pp. 474, 477 and 514.
10. Ibid., pp. 474–558.
11. Ibid., p. 557.
12. For some reference to black marketing in yarn, see, V. Ramakrishna Reddy, *Economic History of Hyderabad State, Warangal Suba, 1911–1950*, Giani Publishing House, Delhi, 1987, p. 518.
13. Ibid., p. 508. See also Anwar Iqbal Qureshi, *Economic Development of Hyderabad, Vol. I, Rural Economy,* Orient Longman, Bombay, 1947, p. 83.
14. IS, pp. 263–65.
15. Iyengar, 1951, op. cit. (note 4), pp. 539–40.
16. Sahai, 1933, op. cit. (note 3).
17. Iyengar, 1951, op. cit. (note 4), p. 555. See also Penesetti Madhava Rao, 'Industrial Development of Hyderabad', unpublished Doctoral Dissertation, Nagpur University, Nagpur, 1956, p. 87.
18. Ibid., p. 545.
19. Ibid., p. 553.

20. The percentage of wage earners among weavers was 45 in Kinhal, 48 in Maski, 20 in Narayana Pet, 21 in Armoor and 55 in Jalna at the time of Iyengar's enquiries. Ibid., pp. 468–526.
21. Ibid., pp. 556. See also, Ramakrishna Reddy, 1987, op. cit. (note 12), pp. 526–27 and 'Report on Labour Census, 1344 F', GOH, Hyderabad, 1935, pp. 28–30.
22. Iyengar, 1951, op. cit. (note 4), p. 556.
23. Sahai, 1933, op. cit. (note 3), p. 13 for early 1930s and Iyengar, op. cit., pp. 468–556, for late 1940s.
24. The percentage of female artisan workers was 51 in Kinhal, 36 in Maski, 25 in Narayana Pet, 42 in Armoor in case of cotton handlooms, 50 in silk weaving at Armoor and 95 in beedi making at Nizamabad at the time of Iyengar's enquiries. Ibid., pp. 468, 481, 496, 501.
25. As many as 15 out of the listed 25 varieties of taxes in *jagir* areas were on artisans or their products, the most common being *adam-patti*, a tax levied on all groups of artisans. See, S. Kesav Iyengar, *A Review of Hyderabad Finance*, GOH, Hyderabad. But in the later period, since almost all official surveys were confined to *diwani* areas, there was not much information on artisans in *jagir* areas. For some reference, see Ramakrishna Reddy, 1987, op. cit. (note 12), p. 518.
26. For details of *vetti pani* among the weavers of Telangana, see *cheneta udyama pitamaha abhinandana grantham*, (Telugu), Sri Narsayya Pantulu Gari Shastipurti Utsava Sanghamu, Hyderabad, 1964, pp. 52–57.
27. Ibid., p. 52, translated from Telugu by the present author.
28. Along with the conferences of the Andhra Maha Sabha, which we shall refer to in Section III, a 'Nizam Padmasali Kastha Nivarana Sangham' (Nizam Padmasali Relief Association) was organised from about 1937. For details see, ibid., pp. 57–58. Padmasalis were the largest of the weaving castes in Telangana. Besides being weavers, they were also indigenous doctors in the villages.
29. Sahai, 1933, op. cit. (note 3), p. 72.
30. GAR, 1310 F, and FBIDAR 1357 F.
31. IS, p. 4.
32. GAR, 1311 F, p. 26.
33. GAR, 1313–1315 F, p. 26.
34. HBECR, p. 71. See also K. Sawhney, *Cotton Growing in Hyderabad State* (*Vol. I*), G. Claridge & Co., Bombay, 1936, pp. 35–36.

35. By 1945, fifteen of the thirty leather factories were closed down. See Madhava Rao, 1956, op. cit. (note 17), pp. 107. See also Ramakrishna Reddy, 1987, op. cit. (note 12), p. 508.
36. CIDAR, relevant years.
37. The loans advanced as a proportion of paid-up capital were, for instance, 76 per cent in the case of Sirpur Paper Mills, 110 per cent in the case of Sirsilk Ltd. and 200 per cent in the case of the Singareni Collieries. See M.F. Jussawala, 'Industrial Finance in the Former Hyderabad State, 1941–1956', unpublished Doctoral Dissertation, Department of Economics, Osmania University, Hyderabad.
38. According to the All India report on Joint Stock Companies, Hyderabad ranked second, after Gwalior in average capital per company. It was followed by Bombay and Indore. 'Report of the Joint Stock Companies in British India and the Native States', 1945–46, GOI, Delhi.
39. See Appendix.
40. Binod V. Rao, *Hyderabad Reborn: First Six Months of Freedom*, GOH, Hyderabad, 1949, p. 20.
41. For instance, the order prohibiting companies from raising capital without government sanction was amended to raise the exemption limit from Rs 1 lakh to Rs 5 lakhs. Ibid., p. 34.
42. HGBEA, June–July 1951.
43. HGBEA, December 1951.
44. The General Administration Reports (GAR), in 1948–56 refer, in a scattered fashion, to the handing over of these companies to private capitalists. The list given here is taken from these references and is not exhaustive.
45. It is interesting to note that during the Nizam's period it was the Tatas who maintained close relations with Hyderabad. But at the time of privatisation after the fall of the regime, the business house that benefited most was the Birlas, who entered Hyderabad practically as a camp follower of the Indian Army.
46. GAR, 1294 F, p. 241, GAR, 1322–1331 F, p. 148, and TS, 1356 F, p. 39.
47. The proportion of general machinery, for instance, in the total volume of imports, in value terms was 1.84 per cent in 1938–40, 2.25 per cent in 1940–45 and 4.72 per cent in 1945–50. TS, Relevant Years. See also SA, 1952–53, p. 72 and IS, p. 625.

APPENDIX 6-A

Statistical Tables

Table 6.1
External Trade: 1882–1950
(*O.S.* Rs Crores)

Period (Averages)	*Imports*	*Percentage Change Over Previous Period*	*Exports*	*Percentage Change Over Previous Period*
1882–1885	3.92	—	3.83	—
1885–1906	NA	—	NA	—
1906–11	7.05	—	8.28	—
1911–22	13.47	91	11.88	44
1922–25	20.22	50	17.47	47
1925–30	17.02	–16	17.92	3
1930–35	13.60	–20	12.35	–31
1935–40	15.01	10	15.24	23
1940–45	23.08	54	23.85	57
1945–50	47.19	105	32.19	35

Note: External trade also includes trade with the rest of India.
Sources: 1882–1930; GAR, Relevant Years.
1930–1950; TS, Relevant Years.

Table 6.2
Changing Composition of Trade: 1912–1951
(Percentage)

	Food Stuffs	*Raw Materials*	*Mfg. Goods*	*Others*
Imports:				
1912–21	9	7	50	34
1938–40	212	7	49	22
1945–47	16	17	58	9
1950–51	21	10	55	14

(*contd.*)

Table 6.2 (*Contd.*)

	Food Stuffs	*Raw Materials*	*Mfg. Goods*	*Others*
Exports:				
1912–21	8	73	3	16
1938–40	8	69	15	8
1945–47	11	56	30	3
1950–51	7	49	36	8

Notes: 1. The percentages given here are only approximations. In the absence of detailed information and uniformity of classification for the entire period, we have had to make some adjustments. In later years the data itself was given under these divisions (see for instance, 'Trade Statistics, 1356 F', Hyderabad, 1947, p. 397). But to maintain uniformity with earlier years we have reclassified the available detailed data according to the divisions we have adopted.

2. Railway articles and duty exempted goods have been excluded.

3. The percentages are based on the annual averages for each period.

Source: 1912–1921; GAR, 1322–1331 F, pp. 148–49.

1938–1951; TS, relevant years.

APPENDIX 6-B

Industrial Growth: A Statistical Review

In Hyderabad, data relating to aspects of industrialisation lacks uniformity and consistency. Data was not collected on a number of aspects, especially on the demand side, and where it was collected, this was not done on a regular basis. Considering that many units also received state finance, the returns submitted by these units, which form the basis of the official records, could also be unreliable. The private records of companies that survived were also not particularly useful. At the time when data was collected for this study, almost four decades after the fall of the regime, not more than fifteen companies in the corporate sector continued to exist. The change of ownership in many of them also resulted in loss of records. Consequently the data base of our analysis is imperfect, marked by doubtful veracity and yawning gaps.

For the first phase, 1875–1919, data was not available on many aspects. Just the number of large industrial establishments, along with their labour force in some cases, were given in the General Administration Reports (GAR) and data on railways and coal were the exceptions. For the second phase, 1919–1939, a range of data including those relating to corporate capital and output of some industries was available. But the most unfortunate part was the absence of data for the third phase, 1939–48, because, it was during this phase that industry took off. During WW II and the chaotic period that preceded the fall of the regime, data was either not collected or not published. Conditions of production were also badly affected, especially in 1946–48. Thus the data relating to the terminal year was either not available or shows an exceptional fall and this leads to certain kinds of problems in statistical analysis. We have attempted to circumvent the problem by taking different years as the terminal point for our analysis, subject to the trend under illustration and the availability of the data.

The currency used was the *Osmania Sicca* Rupee (*O.S.* Rs.) of the Hyderabad government. Where necessary, we have converted B.G. Rs. into *O.S.* Rs. at the official exchange rate, the problems related to which we have already referred to. In almost all cases, especially infrastructural industries, the data was given for the standard British financial year, from April to March. But we have clubbed it together with the data of the *Fasli* year, as it would not make any difference to our conclusions.

The selection of 1939–40 as the base year throughout the study, although arbitrary like any other base year, is prompted by two important considerations. Firstly, a relatively wider range of data was available for that year as compared with the earlier years when the data was imperfect. Secondly, and more importantly in our view, in an economy where development of organised industry was relatively recent, the selection of a base year should not be in the initial phase, because invariably, it results in an inflated picture of growth. The selection of a later year after some kind of take off, it is possible to counterargue, would result in deflation of the overall picture of growth. We believe that such a modest portrait of growth is a better reflection of reality where industrial growth was not very significant. The following statistical review should be read in the light of these considerations and limitations.

Composition of Industries

Table 6.4 gives the number of factories in each group as a percentage of the total number of factories, including both permanent and seasonal factories. For the third phase, we have taken two sets of figures with two different terminal years, for the reasons explained above.

Table 6.3
Composition of Industries: 1900–1952
(Percentage)

	1900–19	*1919–39*	*1939–48*	*1939–52*
1. Agro-based Industries-I	72	60	39	36
2. Agro-based Industries-II	24	29	39	41
3. Metal and Engineering Industries	—	5	7	8
4. Forest-based Industries	—	1.5	6	5
5. Ceramics	—	1.5	4	3
6. Chemical-based Industries	—	1.5	2	2
7. Animal-based Industries	—	1.5	2	2
8. Others	4	—	1	3

Notes: 1. Figures represent factories in each group as a percentage of total number of factories, and are averages for the period.
2. The category 'Others' does not consist of the same industries throughout.
3. Data based on the factory-wise list given in sources relates to large industrial establishments only.
4. The definition of a large industrial establishment originally included all units which employed an average daily labour of ten or more but from 1945 it excluded those that employed less than 20 average daily labour.
Sources: 1. 1900–1931; GAR, Relevant Years.
2. 1931–1945; SA, Relevant Years.
3. 1945–1952; GAR, Relevant Years, FBIDAR, 1357 F. And, 'Large Industrial Establishments in Hyderabad', GOH, Hyderabad, 1954.

Cotton products and other textiles, in the group agro-based industries-I, declined sharply from 72 per cent in the first phase to 36–39 per cent in the last phase. But the second group, agro-based industries-II increased over time from 24 per cent in the first phase to about 40 per cent in the third phase. They included seasonal units like rice, pulses and flour mills, oil products, cigarettes and food products. The overall proportion of agro-based industries declined over time from about 96 per cent to 77–78 per cent in the third phase. Their place was taken by metal and engineering industries and forest-based industries and to a lesser extent, by chemicals and ceramics. In many of these modern industries, fairly large-scale units, often a sole unit manufacturing a particular product, were established. The number of units in such cases was not a good indicator of the structural change that took place. The diversification of industry was more sharply reflected in other indicators.

Industrial Labour

The composition and growth of the labour force in organised industry have already been given in detail in Appendix 5-A. The following table gives a summary analysis of the growth of the labour force. Since detailed information was not available for the period, the first phase and part of second phase are not included.

Table 6.4
Growth of Labour Force: 1930–1948
(Base 1939–40 = 100)

	1930–39	*1939–45*	*1939–48*
1. Agro-based Industries-I	3.6	4.2	4.9
2. Agro-based Industries-II	0.8	13.5	5.9
3. Metal and Engineering Industries	5.6	20.0	18.7
4. Forest-based Industries	10.8	7.4	5.8
5. Ceramics	10.5	–0.1	–9.1
6. Chemical-based Industries	9.3	40.2	18.7
7. Animal-based Industries	1.7	3.7	NA
8. Others	6.5	–1.3	2.8
9. Total Manufacturing Industry	5.7	6.3	3.5
10. Factory Labour	3.9	6.0	NA

Notes for Table 6.4: 1. Figures represent average annual growth rates in each period.
2. Data relates only to the labour force in large industrial establishments.
3. Factory labour covers only those units covered by the Factories Act.
4. Based on an index constructed on the factory-wise data (see, Table 5.5, Appendix 5-A), given in the sources.
Sources: 1930–45; SA, relevant years.
1945–48; FBIDAR, relevant years.

Table 6.4 indicates that the labour force increased at a higher rate during the War period than during the preceding and the following phases. The growth rate in agro-based industries, especially in group I, was considerably lower than that in other industries. In metal and engineering industries and chemical-based industries and to a lesser extent, forest- based industries, it increased at a substantially higher rate after WW II. This was the period when a few large-scale factories in the corporate sector along with other units in buttons, motor and engineering workshops, matches, wooden articles, aerated water, etc. mushroomed in these industries. The only exception to the general trend was ceramics which had negative growth rates. The stagnation, or even decline for some years after WW II, in brick kilns and quarry work explains the negative growth rates. In general, the labour force in modern industries increased at a higher rate in the last phase. This trend has also been noted in our time series analysis for the entire period (Table 5.2, Appendix 5-A). The particularly high rates in the second phase confirm the structural change referred to earlier.

Corporate Capital

This has already been given in detail in Appendix 4-A. In particular, the chequered growth, in the initial phases, of industries in metal and engineering, chemical-based industries and ceramics, where the growth rates have no statistical significance should be noted. But it was those industries that attracted more capital after WW II. By the end of the war they constituted almost 25 per cent of the corporate capital in mining and manufacturing industries. As a result of the peculiar problems of analysis, the industry-wise and phase-wise growth rates in corporate capital would not be useful. We shall confine ourselves to some general features, based on the growth in the paid-up value of capital in the corporate sector (Table 4.2, Appendix 4-A).

In general, the growth rate of corporate capital was higher in metal and engineering and chemical-based industries and ceramics, than in agro-based industries during the third phase. However, taken altogether, it was not mining and manufacturing capital that had high growth rates but banking, trade and other services. In 1921–1939, the index of the mining and manufacturing sector shows some increase but in 1939–45, it remained more or less stagnant. In sharp contrast, during both phases, the capital in banking, trade and other services increased very sharply.

Capital Intensity

The Kasturbhai Lalbhai Committee which inquired into state-financed industries in 1950 after the fall of the regime, noted, among other things, overcapitalisation as one of the features of the companies in Hyderabad. One of the reasons for this was, as already indicated, the liberal granting of loans by the ITF. The amount of loans granted had no relation to either the paid-up capital or the scale and plant capacity of the companies.

Overcapitalisation is also reflected in the fact that Hyderabad had higher average capital per company. In 1935–36, for instance, the average capital per company in Hyderabad was Rs 13.73 lakhs while in the rest of India it was Rs 9.20 lakhs. Similarly, in 1940–41, it was Rs 9.20 lakhs in Hyderabad while it was Rs 4.70 lakhs in India according to a comparative account given in the Industrial Statistics of Hyderabad (IS, p. 78).

A more appropriate indicator of overcapitalisation is capital intensity, i.e., capital per unit output. But lack of complete and reliable data on both capital and output over the years makes it difficult to reach estimates for each industry. In addition, comparable data from other places, say British India, would be needed as a reference point, but this is not available. The particular problem in the case of Hyderabad is the absence of data on the loans advanced and debentures, year by year. We only have data on paid-up value of capital. Taking that as capital and output at constant prices (1939–40), we have arrived at Table 6.5. The data relates to all the six textile mills, and to one each of the cigarette, sugar, brick-making and coal companies. The cigarette manufacturing unit, which shows a relatively lower intensity of capital was managed by the Imperial Tobacco Company. Three of the textile mills and the rest of the companies were largely financed or owned or managed by the state.

Table 6.5
Capital Intensity: Select Industries

Industry	*Capital per Unit of Output*		
	1936–37	*1938–39*	*1944–45*
1. Textiles	1.919	1.078	1.073
2. Cigarettes	1.557	0.363	0.241
3. Sugar	—	5.710	3.379
4. Bricks	1.696	1.111	2.340
5. Coal	1.269	1.092	1.557

Note: Output in value terms with 1939–40 as the base year. Capital refers only to paid-up capital.
Source: SA, relevant years, and IS, pp. 167–68 (textiles), pp. 307 (coal), pp. 388–89 (bricks), pp. 433 (cigarettes) and pp. 575–76 (sugar).

Industrial Output

The output data was not available in many cases. Where available it was inconsistent and not particularly reliable. Any attempt to draw analytical inferences on the basis of such imperfect data would be misleading. Indices of growth for available products are given in the series of tables appended. In general, there was considerable growth of output in the second phase in the cigarette, oils, sugar, matches, cement and glass industries. But in the third phase, output in minerals, some cotton products, oil products, glass and matches declined.

Table 6.6
Industrial Output

Table 6.6-A
Infrastructure 1920–1945
(Base 1939–40 = 100)

Year	*Railways*	*Power*	*Year*	*Railways*	*Power*
1920–21	58	NA	1933–34	73	62
1921–22	57	NA	1934–35	76	65
1922–23	57	NA	1935–36	76	69
1923–24	59	NA	1936–37	83	80
1924–25	59	NA	1937–38	92	86
1925–26	60	NA	1938–39	95	91
1926–27	63	NA	**1939–40**	**100**	**100**
1927–28	61	NA	1940–41	100	115
1928–29	68	NA	1941–42	117	NA
1929–30	76	NA	1942–43	121	NA
1930–31	80	NA	1943–44	112	NA
1931–32	71	NA	1944–45	118	NA
1932–33	68	NA			

Note: Railway data relates to goods traffic carried in million tonnes and the power data relates to million KWH units generated.
Sources: 1920–1930; GAR, relevant years.
1930–1945; SA, relevant years.

Table 6.6-B
Mineral Output: 1920–1950
(Base 1939–40 = 100)

Year	*Coal*	*Marble*	*Limestone*
1920–21	57	NA	NA
1921–22	57	NA	NA
1922–23	53	NA	NA
1923–24	54	NA	153

(*contd.*)

Table 6.6-B: (*Contd.*)

Year	*Coal*	*Marble*	*Limestone*
1924–25	53	NA	151
1925–26	55	NA	NA
1926–27	52	NA	145
1927–28	58	NA	154
1928–29	61	NA	110
1929–30	67	NA	107
1930–31	67	NA	106
1931–32	62	NA	113
1932–33	64	NA	120
1933–34	62	NA	116
1934–35	63	NA	132
1935–36	60	82	106
1936–37	70	270	137
1937–38	89	242	196
1938–39	99	174	138
1939–40	**100**	**100**	**100**
1940–41	103	226	86
1941–42	107	54	120
1942–43	105	NP	119
1943–44	88	NP	109
1944–45	77	NP	91
1945–46	84	NP	NA
1946–47	NA	NP	NA
1947–48	96	NP	NA
1948–49	88	53	96
1949–50	90	43	96

Note: NA indicates non-availability of data, and NP indicates no production. Coal in thousand tonnes, marble in tonnes and limestone in lakh sq. ft.

Sources: 1920–30; GAR, relevant years.
1930–45; SA, relevant years.
1945–50; GAR, relevant years.

Table 6.6-C
Output of Agro-based Industries-I: 1921–1945
(Base 1939–40 = 100)

Year	*Cotton*			*Carpets*
	Bales Pressed	*Yarn*	*Woven Goods*	
1921–22	NA	18	13	NA
1922–23	NA	21	11	NA
1923–24	NA	21	8	NA
1924–25	NA	16	5	NA
1925–26	NA	20	12	NA
1926–27	NA	24	16	NA
1927–28	NA	27	22	NA
1928–29	NA	30	31	NA
1929–30	NA	32	30	NA
1930–31	NA	31	27	7
1931–32	42	35	32	NA
1932–33	68	40	37	120
1933–34	67	45	41	NA
1934–35	60	64	55	NA
1935–36	95	70	58	NA
1936–37	70	66	56	130
1937–38	94	79	70	NA
1938–39	60	96	92	100
1939–40	**100**	**100**	**100**	**100**
1940–41	120	93	100	167
1941–42	100	116	123	162
1942–43	67	117	130	NA
1943–44	70	107	118	NA
1944–45	66	97	108	433

Note: Bales in 400 lbs each, yarn and woven goods in lbs and carpets value in *O.S.* Rupees.
Sources: Cotton: 1921–30; GAR, relevant years.
1930–45; SA, relevant years.
Carpets: GAR, relevant years.
CIDAR, relevant years.

Table 6.6-D

Output of Agro-based Industries-II: 1921–1950

Year	*Alcohol*	*Power Alcohol*	*Cigarettes*	*Oil*	*Sugar*
1921–22	270	NP	NP	NA	NP
1922–23	257	NP	NP	NA	NP
1923–24	311	NP	NP	NA	NP
1924–25	344	NP	NP	NA	NP
1925–26	288	NP	NP	NA	NP
1926–27	278	NP	NP	NA	NP
1927–28	273	NP	NP	NA	NP
1928–29	284	NP	NP	NA	NP
1929–30	257	NP	NP	NA	NP
1930–31	198	NA	NA	NA	NP
1931–32	153	NA	NA	NA	NP
1932–33	158	NA	NA	NA	NP
1933–34	158	NA	NA	NA	NP
1934–35	148	NA	90	55	NP
1935–36	117	NA	87	68	NP
1936–37	167	NA	94	85	NP
1937–38	110	NA	89	106	NP
1938–39	90	NA	128	117	41
1939–40	**100**	**100**	**100**	**100**	**100**
1940–41	112	100	106	111	195
1941–42	133	100	122	78	161
1942–43	215	74	102	72	140
1943–44	198	113	162	51	167
1944–45	188	117	188	83	169
1945–46	NA	101	NA	NA	157
1946–47	NA	99	NA	NA	157
1947–48	NA	NA	NA	NA	182
1948–49	NA	NA	NA	NA	263
1949–50	NA	NA	NA	NA	189

Note: Alcohol in gallons, Power Alcohol in *O.S.* Rupees, Cigarettes in cases of 5 million cigarettes, Oil in lakh seers and Sugar in tonnes.

Source: 1921–30; GAR, relevant years.

1930–45; CIDAR, relevant years.

1945–50; HGBEA, June–July 1951, pp. 477–78 and CIDF. 88-207-106/1355 F 'Data Regarding Existing Industries'.

Table 6.6-E
Output of Ceramic Industries and Others: 1930–45
(Base 1939–40 = 100)

Year	*Cement*	*Glass*	*Hume Pipes*	*Bricks*	*Matches*
1930–31	87	NA	NA	NA	NA
1931–32	88	NA	NA	NA	NA
1932–33	74	NA	NA	NA	NA
1933–34	75	NA	NA	NA	72
1934–35	84	NA	232	80	115
1935–36	95	46	416	100	116
1936–37	93	70	244	120	134
1937–38	95	66	244	140	134
1938–39	83	97	284	180	134
1939–40	**100**	**100**	**100**	**100**	**100**
1940–41	98	97	444	240	84
1941–42	117	77	NA	NA	55
1942–43	121	38	361	NA	47
1943–44	110	37	NA	NA	40
1944–45	134	45	408	NA	35

Note: Cement in tonnes, Glass in maunds, Hume pipes in *O.S.* Rupees. Bricks in lakh bricks and Matches in gross boxes.
Source: SA; relevant years.
CIDF, 88-207-106/1355 F 'Data Regarding Existing Industries'.

SECTION III

State and Society: 1875–1948

CHAPTER SEVEN

Social Framework

The process of industrialisation that has been analysed took place during a period when Hyderabad State, along with the rest of India, saw significant economic and political change. The ultimate limits of industrialisation can only be explained in the larger social context of this transition and its character.

The population of Hyderabad which was 9.8 million in 1881, nearly doubled to become 18.7 million in 1951.[1] In general, the rate of growth of population in the state was higher than in India as a whole. But more importantly, the proportion of both the urban population and the working population engaged in industry was higher than all-India averages. Literacy, however, was conspicuously lower in Hyderabad.[2]

A year after the death of Salar Jung, in 1884, Mahbub Ali Khan became the eleventh ruler (sixth Nizam) of the state. The development of infrastructure and the advent of commercialisation in the agrarian economy took place under his regime. After his death in 1911, he was succeeded by his son Osman Ali Khan who continued till the Indian army action in 1948. The pioneering initiatives in industrial development took place during his reign.

The framework of unity and conflict that came to govern the relationship between the colonial power and the Hyderabad government by the late nineteenth century continued into the reigns of the last two Nizams, although there was a vast change in the situation. The complete subjugation of all the Indian states and the erection of a vast administrative apparatus in large parts of India consolidated Imperial control. There was no longer any need for the colonial power to periodically shape and reshape its powers and privileges and grant concessions to the princes. Internal territorial divisions between Indian states and British-administered provinces became stabilised. The growth of trade, now propelled by the commercialisation of agriculture and the penetration of capital, further strengthened the social base of the colonial regime. It was in this context that the colonial government increasingly assumed what Lord Minto referred to as a 'certain degree of the responsibility for the general soundness of their [native states] administration'.3 On matters of strategic importance, it did not brook any assertion of independence by the princely states. Thus in Hyderabad, the issue of the Berar provinces continued to remain in contention. Immediately after WW I, the issue came alive again. Tension between the two governments reached their peak in 1919–1925. The Residency sought to regulate the day-to-day administration of the state. The Resident not only used his power to select the President of the Executive Council (babe-hukumat) but also brought in British civil servants to head the police, revenue, commerce and industries departments. Eventually, in 1925, Viceroy Lord Reading firmly put down Hyderabad's claim on Berar. The final assertion made clear to the Nizam the meaning of paramountcy. The Berar issue was to come up time, again but this between the Indian nationalists and the Nizam.

Notwithstanding the consolidation of Imperial control over the Indian states, it would perhaps be facile to describe the latter as passive 'appendages' of colonial rule. The response of the Indian states to Imperial policy was marked by a greater degree of diversity and autonomy than has been hitherto acknowledged. Although questions of territoriality were settled, new dimensions considerably constrained the power of the colonial regime to assert its authority, leaving the Indian states some space for manoeuvre. The Anglo-German conflict in WW I compelled the British authorities to strengthen their relations with the princes. Later they were perceived as some sort of a counter-poise to nationalist forces. These pressures on the colonial government enabled the Indian states to manoeuvre and, in some cases acquire, some degree of autonomy.

The size and viability of the Indian states should also be taken into consideration. The usual treatment of all Indian states under the rubric of 'native India' obscures the heterogeneity and scale-factor within this part of colonial India. The status and the relations of bigger states vis-a-vis the colonial power were not the same as those of the numerous small states. In fact, the scale-factor influenced many measures initiated by the British. Thus in 1919–21, when the Chamber of Princes or *narendra mahal* as it was called, took shape the position taken by bigger states like Hyderabad, Mysore, Travancore, Udaipur etc., influenced the course of events. Later, it was only the smaller states that were included under States Agencies in different provinces. Similarly, the prolonged dispute over the status of princely states in the Government of India Bill (Act) was also marked by differences with the bigger states.

Hyderabad was the largest of the Indian states. Its total area exceeded the combined area of all the states grouped under 'Lesser States'. In fact, the total area of one of the otherwise bigger states like Travancore was less than the total *sarf-e-khas* area of Hyderabad. The implications of the size of the state to its political relations were that both in territory and revenue, the bigger states, like Hyderabad, enjoyed viability and strength. It should also be noted that Hyderabad was under Muslim rule, and there were not more than three Indian states under Muslim rule during the period. As the communal factor assumed importance in nationalist politics, the colonial power was compelled to take into consideration the fact that Hyderabad could have a special position in its strategy, so it acceded a number of concessions to the state. In fact this particular privilege of Hyderabad state was never lost on the nationalist force within Hyderabad, as we shall see later.

It should also be remembered that the ruling elite in Hyderabad was not the creation of the colonial power, as was the case in many other Indian states. Hyderabad was also unique in that it maintained its own currency, railways and communication. The size of its territory, the viability of its economy and the religion of its rulers enabled the state to enjoy a relative degree of autonomy. It was in this context that one can understand the growth of a powerful state apparatus and bureaucracy in Hyderabad that explains many policies of the state, including its industrial policy.

II

The departmentalisation of the administrative apparatus and a more rational redivision of the state initiated by Salar Jung continued in later years.[4] A number of new departments, like the Commerce and Industries Department, were set up and for each department an elaborate edifice was built. The introduction of a new budgetary system by Akbar Hydari in 1922 enabled the administration to take wide-ranging initiatives in various directions.[5] The introduction of an element of planning into the activities of each department and the creation of specially funded reserves marked the new budgetary system. This system was, till it broke down during WW II, the crucial element of modernisation. The expenditure on development services that included agriculture, industry and public works, as a proportion of total expenditure increased from about 7 per cent at the beginning of the century to almost 13 per cent in the later period. In the last years, however, due to the increase in expenditure on the military and police, its proportion came down. The increase in the proportion of expenditure on social services, like education, medical and public health services was also very significant (see Appendix Table 7.1). On the revenue side, the proportion of land revenue declined sharply from 50 per cent in 1900–1901 to about 16 per cent by the end of the period. Its place was taken by a more elastic state excise (see Table 7.2). On the whole, the growing fiscal strength of the state served as the most important backdrop for administrative modernisation.

Fiscal strength coupled with departmentalisation facilitated the emergence of the bureaucracy as an important entity and this explains many paradoxes and complexities of Hyderabad under the Nizams. It was the bureaucrats who formulated and executed, without any constraint, the policy on practically every important matter. Interference from the Residency was confined only to periods of crisis, as happened in 1920–22. The Nizam, especially Osman Ali Khan, was indifferent to the day-to-day affairs of the state. But his seal of approval, based on his choice and judgement of the personnel selected for key posts, was crucial for every measure undertaken by the bureaucrats. This seal gave a finality to the authority of the civil servants. If their power and legitimacy originated from their position in the bureaucracy, their background strengthened it in the given feudal environment. Parentage, creed together with heritage, status in the social hierarchy and the extent of land owned and controlled, were the elements that made them the choice of the ruler. In fact they were the instruments through which 'the feudal aristocracy maintained and defended its base'.[6]

The first generation of civil servants recruited by Salar Jung, were almost all alumni of the Aligarh Muslim University. Even in the later period, Aligarh University remained the route to the upper echelons of civil service in Hyderabad, now along with Madras University. Trained in British India, in a more liberal atmosphere, these civil servants sought to rival British India in administrative modernisation. A few British officials serving, or retired, who were engaged by the Hyderabad state helped this process.[7]

It was the first generation of these Aligarh alumni and their control over the state apparatus that gave birth to the *mulki*, non-*mulki* conflict. This conflict between domiciles and outsiders later, after the establishment of Osmania University in 1918, diffused into the educational arena.[8] The tensions between the two sections of the elite as they developed became the basis for some kind of Deccani nationalism.[9] Although the operative content of these two categories, *mulki* and non-*mulki* changed, the conflict served as the basis of the policy of preferential treatment for domiciles that influenced public policy as for instance, in industry.[10]

The modernisation of the bureaucracy and its autonomous role in Hyderabad, which was often obscured by the resistance to any demand for political modernisation, was a crucial factor that explains many features of transition in the state. That is not to suggest that the bureaucracy enjoyed freedom from the framework of the larger interrelations of power that governed society. It opted for a non confrontational policy with the colonial power and the feudal aristocracy. In fact, as a social group which came from traditional aristocratic families and was trained in the culture of colonial administration, the bureaucracy had no need to seek freedom from the ruling powers. It was not merely a representative of the ruling class, but often the ruling class itself. But within the given framework, as a social apparatus, it showed an awareness of its collective responsibility. Its evolution from the time of Salar Jung had given it the strength and autonomy to initiate policy measures which had farreaching implications. It was thus able to lay the foundations of the infrastructure, develop educational facilities and provide a social organisational framework for economic transition. This development, at one level, further perpetuated colonial domination, especially in trade. On the other hand it paved the way for the development of industry and commercial agriculture. In fact, the changes in the agrarian economy illustrate the character of the transition that was brought about by the state. For, even while leading to the commercialisation of agriculture, it perpetuated the social power of the traditional ruling class in the village economy.

III

The penetration of the market economy on a wider scale can be considered the most significant change in the agrarian economy during the period under review. Reforms undertaken by Salar Jung, in particular the establishment of administrative control over large parts of the state and the shift in the basis of revenue from the village to the individual in *diwani* areas, introduction of cash payment of revenue, the spread of cash payment under tenancy during the later period, increase in demand for food grains and other raw materials and finally export trade, were some of the factors that led the peasants to produce more for the market on an expanding scale. These developments were accompanied by the growth of the credit market and helped by the development of transport. As the external demand for cash crops like cotton and oilseeds grew, the agrarian economy underwent fundamental changes. Cotton had long been well-established in Marathwada but its commercial importance grew from about the late nineteenth century. Later, new areas in Adilabad, Telangana, were brought under cotton cultivation. Although over time its commercial importance declined in relative terms, even in the 1930s, over 60 per cent of cotton outturn was being exported.[11] Oilseed cultivation was prevalent in Telangana in the nineteenth century but its importance grew phenomenally from the 1930s.[12] The penetration of these high profile cash crops resulted in the incorporation of the Hyderabad economy into the world market.

The development of commercial cropping was helped by state policies, especially in relation to technology. Towards the latter half of the period, the government financed large-scale canal irrigation. The total irrigated area increased from 0.8 million acres in 1922 to almost 1.7 million acres by 1945.[13] Within the irrigated area the proportion of canal irrigation increased. However, net irrigated area as a proportion of net sown area was never more than six per cent.[14] The government also made a concerted attempt to introduce improved varieties of seeds in all major crops. The attempt appears to have been most successful in cotton and sugarcane.[15]

The growth of a market economy led to an increase in the area under cultivation. This was around 15.26 million acres in 1921–22, 26.87 million acres in 1925–26 and reached an all-time high of 30.00 million acres during the depression year, 1932–33.[16] Our index (Table 7.3 Appendix) shows that almost until 1934–35, the net sown area went on increasing. Much of the increase was made possible by bringing fallow land and grazing land under cultivation, especially for cash crops. The growth declined during the later period, but this could be due to deliberate understatement of figures by the landlords to evade controls and regulations during WW II.

The cropping pattern also changed over time (Table 7.4 Appendix). The area under foodgrains declined from 75 per cent in 1920–22 to around 68 per cent in 1949–50. Within foodgrains, bajra and maize declined as rice gained. In non-food crops there was a decisive shift towards oilseeds whose proportion increased from about 9 per cent in 1920–22 to almost 20 per cent in 1949–50, groundnut being the most striking gainer.

The indices of the area under cultivation of principal crops reveal interesting features of the agrarian change (Table 7.3, Appendix). The export-oriented crops like groundnut and castor show consistently high increases throughout the period, with sugarcane being the only other crop that kept pace. This was facilitated by the extension of canal irrigation under the Nizam Sagar Canal and the establishment of the large-scale sugar factory. Among other oilseeds, sesamum did not show any particularly significant growth and was in fact marginally on the decline. This was also the case with cotton. Tobacco which was otherwise flourishing in India declined sharply. This could be explained by the fact that the local varieties of tobacco, like *zarda, jawari, bushnare, sulipetty*, were not suitable for the manufacture of cigarettes. Among food crops, jawar increased consistently but modestly till almost the end of WW II, while growth rates of the area under rice fluctuated violently.

Output trends were more or less in tune with trends in acreage, with groundnut, castor and sugarcane showing higher growth rates (Table 7.5 Appendix). Cotton consistently declined. Sesamum declined upto 1935–36 but made improvements during the later period. Among food grains, jawar, which showed much less fluctuation, declined till the war but improved later on, as rice shortage became acute. Rice showed violent fluctuations since it was dependent on the rains. The available data on yield, subject to methods of estimation, shows neither consistency nor uniformity.[18]

The changes in the agrarian economy as reflected in changes in pattern and trends in output indicate the growth of the commercialisation of agriculture. But any analytical inferences on the agrarian transition, on the basis of this data, must be drawn with caution. At the outset one should note the imperfections in data. The absence of uniformity in coverage and lack of reliable data on movement of prices even in such important commercial crops as groundnut, are formidable problems. We are in no position to state to what extent the changes noted above are due to mere limitations in data and to what extent they indicate real changes.

With all these limitations, we have made an analysis of price-acreage-output relations (see Appendix 7-B). Our analysis reveals the role of non-price factors in conditioning the price responses of producers. These non-price factors were essentially located in the feudal social structure. In fact, the feudal forms of extraction of surplus appears to have been intensified by the process of commercialisation.

In any case, we should note that the process of commercialisation was extremely uneven. This unevenness was evident between the regions of Marathwada, Karnatic and Telangana and also within a region. Agro-climatic conditions and crop variations partly explain the unevenness. But even the same crop with similar agro-climatic conditions did not seem to have generated similar social effects. Groundnut, a crop that otherwise serves as an illustration of the process of commercialisation, for instance, did not generate the same effects in Raichur, Karnatic which topped in its cultivation and in Telangana districts where *jagirdars, deshmukhs* and other big landlords were dominant.[19] Similarly within Telangana, in the region north of the river Godavari in Adilabad, where there were no *jagirdars*, the conditions were radically different despite the introduction of cotton.[20] Thus, there was unevenness in the penetration of the commodity economy both in extent and quality.[21] Capital, instead of remoulding social organisation in its image, only accentuated the precapitalist forms of surplus extraction. Thus bondage, customary services, tenancy, indebtedness, and land alienation were all intensified by the growth of commoditisation. But their genesis lies not in commercialisation itself but in the social organisation where traditional landowning classes, to the end, were defended by the state. There were some notable instances of some landlords even financing industrial capital as noted earlier, but this could not make any difference to social relations in agriculture.

The most striking feature of agrarian relations during this period was the complete defeat of the objectives of the reforms undertaken by Salar Jung. Remember that in 1881 *diwani* tenures constituted about 87 per cent of the total area while non-*diwani* tenures declined to about 54 per cent.[22] But by 1912–13, *diwani* tenures declined to about 54 per cent.[23] Towards the end, just before the abolition of *jagirs* and the take over of *sarf-e-khas*, the *diwani* areas became about 64 per cent.[24] The total area remaining the same, the decline was also in absolute terms, with *diwani* areas declining to about 37 per cent. It should be noted that the distinction between *jagir* and *diwani* tenures was not merely a juridicial one made for the purposes of revenue administration but there were social and political differences rooted in the history of the evolution of these classes as noted earlier. The reemergence of *jagirs*, was thus the reemergence of that traditional social power which Salar Jung sought to regulate.

A part of the non-*diwani* tenures, about 8–10 per cent, were crown lands, *sarf-e-khas*. But all the rest were *jagirdars* who controlled over 30 per cent of the areas.[25] They included *samsthanams* in addition to the variety of *jagirs* referred to earlier. In many of these areas even till the end, survey and settlement were not undertaken as the relevant part of Hyderabad Land Revenue Act had a proviso for their exemption. In these areas, all cultivators were treated as tenants and had to pay a wide range of taxes and cesses. The revenue collected was about 25–50 per cent more than that in *diwani* areas. Remissions, *taccavi* loans and such other governmental measures never reached the peasants of the *jagir* areas. The *jagirs* were, as Ali Mohammad Khusro aptly put it, 'states within the state'.[26] Although there were some apparent similarities in some legal and quasi-legal categories, like *shikmidars* and *asami shikmidars*, the law itself did not reach them.[27]

Even in *diwani* areas the situation was not particularly different because there is evidence that non-*diwani* tenures within the *diwani* areas increased over time. Earlier *watans*, *agraharams*, *sdarbasta* and *ijaras* and other such grants were made under easy terms. There were a considerable number of *ijaras*, where easy terms were granted to bring new areas under cultivation during the earlier part of the period under review. Further grants were discontinued in 1909. But they reappeared in a different form when colonisers were granted such assignments on easy terms, especially in the northern parts of Telangana.[28] The holders of all these kinds of tenures were invariably officials or landlords of considerable wealth and power. We do not have data to estimate the extent of these non- *diwani* tenures in *diwani* areas but it appears to have been significant. In the *diwani* proper where the state was supposed to have a direct relationship with the *pattadar*, intermediaries emerged over time. They were, unlike the *jagirdars*, more directly related to the production process but like *jagirdars* very powerful. The notorious *deshmukhs* of Telangana belonged to the category of big landlords who 'exercised a good bit of real sovereignty subordinating every person and every process to the supreme purpose of his (their) maximum net income'.[29] It was the emergence of this type of powerful landlords that was responsible for the degeneration of the *diwani* tenures. The Hyderabad Land Commission described some of the features of these *diwani* areas as 'increase in the number of tenancies, the passing of land and its concentration to a large extent in the hands of non- cultivating classes, deterioration of agriculture and the excessive competition among the tenants for land, leading to growth of rents', etc.[30]

Thus, from the time of the reforms of Salar Jung to the end of the regime of the Nizam, *jagir* areas increased and non-*diwani* degenerated into a type of *jagirdari.* This larger social process was the framework within which commercialisation took place and was in fact intensified by it.[31] Feudal social power was thus the ultimate limiting factor of commercialisation and its social effects. This social power was the foundation of the state in Hyderabad. The initiatives that the state took in other areas of public policy, like industry, only led to the further strengthening of the feudal social base of its power. The resolute opposition to any political change in the form of governance was located in the attempt to retain and strengthen the power that this landed gentry held in society. The contradictions generated by this kind of intensification of the social power of the feudal classes, in parts of Telangana, were directly responsible for the biggest political challenge faced by the regime—the rise of the communists.

Notes

1. Census, 1881–1951. There wee some marginal territorial changes in 1951.
2. In 1941, for instance, the proportion of urban population was 13.4 per cent in Hyderabad while it was 13.0 per cent in the rest of India. Working population dependent on industry was 12.9 per cent in Hyderabad while it was 10.2 per cent in India and literacy was 6.8 per cent in Hyderabad while it was 9.5 per cent in India. Census, 1941.
3. Lord Minto quoted in 'Report of Indian States Committee' GOI, Delhi, 1929, p. 19.

4. At the time of the last major redivision of the state, in 1905, there were 15 districts, 98 taluqs and 14200 villages, GAR, 1313–15 F, pp. 2–3.
5. For an account of Akbar Hydari's fiscal reforms see, B.K. Narayan, *Financial and Fiscal Policy of Hyderabad State (1900–1956)*, GOAP, Hyderabad, 1973, Chapter IV, pp. 21–28. See also, S. Kesav Iyengar, 'Working of the Departmentalisation Scheme of Finance in Hyderabad During 18 Years', *Indian Journal of Economics*, July 1942, pp. 24–25.
6. Shamim Aleem, *Personal Management in a Princely State*, Gitanjali Publishers, New Delhi, 1985, p. 101.
7. For personal details about some of the English civil servants in Hyderabad, see Zahir Ahmed, *Life's Yesterdays: Glimpses of Sir Nizamat Jung and His Times*, Thacker, Bombay, 1945, Parts II and III, pp. 210–12, 227–30 and 237–39.
8. See Karen Isaken Leonard, 'Hyderabad: The *Mulki*–non-*Mulki* Conflict' in Robin Jeffrey (ed.), *People, Princes and Paramount Power: Society and Politics in Indian Princely States*, Oxford University Press, Delhi, 1978.
9. For some reflections on Deccani nationalism see the pamphlet published by Nizam's Subjects League, Syed Abid Hussain, *Whither Hyderabad?*, Madras, 1935, pp. 58–70. For an analytical critique of the idea of Deccani nationalism, see Karen Isaken Leonard, 'The Deccani Synthesis in Old Hyderabad: A Historiographic Essay', *Pakistan Historical Society Journal*, 21, 1973, pp. 205–18.
10. The all-pervasive nature of the preferential treatment was reflected in the fact that even soliciting by non-*mulki* prostitutes was prohibited, by the Hyderabad *Mulki* Prostitutes and Dancing Girls Act, 1350 F.
11. The proportion of cotton lint exported out of the total outturn of lint, was 62 per cent in 1935–40 and 61 per cent in 1940–45, 18, pp. 134–35.
12. The proportion of castor exported seems to have declined, from about 83 per cent in 1928–29 to about 62 per cent by 1940, IS, p. 528. But the proportion of groundnut exported increased from about 12 per cent in 1930–31 to 45 per cent in 1935–36, IS, p. 520.
13. Anwar Iqbal Qureshi, *Economic Development of Hyderabad: Vol. I, Rural Economy*, Orient Longman, Bombay, 1947, p. 93.
14. The data on irrigation, especially for the earlier period, is unreliable. Figures given by Qureshi (ibid., pp. 93–96) do not tally with some

of those given in SA, 1952–53, p. 22. In fact, in Qureshi's estimates for 1930, the total area under canals, tanks and wells, even after excluding irrigation from other sources, exceeds the total gross area irrigated (Qureshi, op. cit., pp. 93–96). The data available for the later period, 1939–50, given in SA, 1952–53, p. 22 appears to be more reliable. Our observations on the proportion of the net irrigated area are based on this source.

15. In 1947–48, the area under improved seeds was 39 per cent in sugarcane, 33 per cent in cotton, 13 per cent in groundnut, 7 per cent in paddy and less than one per cent in jawar and wheat. S. Kesav Iyengar, *Economic Enquiries in Hyderabad State; 1949–51*, GOH, Hyderabad, 1951, p. 207. For earlier efforts in case of cotton, see Census of Hyderabad, Part I, 1921, pp. 281–82.
16. 1921–22, GAR, 1321–1330 F. 1925–33; AS, relevant years. Agrarian statistics in Hyderabad, however, are not particularly reliable. The data from *jagir* areas was not regularly included. Sometimes the uncovered area could even be 20–25 per cent of the total cultivated area.
17. A number of sources point out these inaccuracies in the data. See, SA, 1952–53, p. 20. Census, 1951, Hyderabad Report, Part I, p. 37 and 'The Report of the Agrarian Reforms Committee', GOH, Hyderabad, 1949, p. 201.
18. For variations in yield data see, Iyengar, 1951, op. cit. (note 15), p. 290. Groundnut seems to have been the only crop which had a significant improvement in yield.
19. The difference between Raichur and the Telangana districts in almost all aspects, can be noticed in Iyengar's enquiries cited above.
20. See Christof von Furer Haimendorff, *Tribal Hyderabad*, GOH, Hyderabad, 1945.
21. An interesting feature in this context is the extent of monetisation. Khusro noting the similarities in this respect between *jagir* areas and *diwani* areas, indicates the limited extent of monetisation, for 1948–49, in *diwani* areas. Of the total income of the cultivating classes, cash income constituted only 33.5 per cent. The percentage was about 40.7 per cent for all occupations. A.M. Khusro, *The Economic and Social Effects of* Jagirdari *Abolition and Land Reforms*, Osmania University, Hyderabad, 1958, p. 100.
22. Moulavi Chirag Ali, *Hyderabad Under Salar Jung, Vol. I*, Bernard Quaritch, London, 1881, p. 71. See also Chapter 2, above.
23. GAR, 1322–1331 F, p. 82.

24. Khusro, 1958, op. cit. (note 21), pp. 5 and 9. These proportions differ, marginally, from those given by Iyengar, 1951, op. cit. (note 15), p. 20.
25. Iyengar, 1951, ibid., p. 20.
26. Khusro, 1958, op. cit. (note 21), p. 1.
27. Most observations on the effect of commercialisation in *jagir* areas are spun off from the data generated by surveys and reports on *diwani* areas. We do not feel that this is a correct method because of the fundamental distinctions between these two types referred to earlier.
28. Christof von Furer Haimendorff, 1945, op. cit. (note 20) for details of colonisation in the tribal areas of Adilabad. See also V. Ramakrishna Reddy, *Economic History of Hyderabad State: Warangal Suba, 1911–1950*, Giani Publishing House, Delhi, 1987, p. 121.
29. Iyengar, 1931, Vol. 3, Warangal District, p. 61.
30. 'Reports of the Hyderabad Land Commission', GOH, Hyderabad, 1954, quoted in Khusro, 1958, op. cit. (note 21), p. 19.
31. The process of commercialisation is a subject of conflicting interpretation among scholars engaged in the study of the Communist movement in Telangana. The basis of the debate was the commercialisation in a few districts of Telangana, since the depression. A good part of the debate also takes into consideration the period after the fall of the regime, 1948–51, when *jagirs* were abolished and *sarf-e-khas* lands were taken over. Hence a detailed response to the debate falls outside the scope of the present work. One line of interpretation, in essence, suggests that commercialisation generated sharp differentiation among the peasantry, leading to a polarisation between rich peasants and agricultural labour, as contending classes. (Inukonda Tirumali, 'Aspects of Agrarian Relations in Telangana: 1928–1948', unpublished M.Phil Dissertation, Centre for Historical Studies, Jawaharlal Nehru University, New Delhi, 1979 and Barry Pavier, *The Telangana Movement: 1944–51*, Vikas, New Delhi, 1981). In sharp disagreement with this interpretation, K. Balagopal suggests that commercialisation played no significant role in the agrarian crisis in Telangana. (K. Balagopal, 'Telangana Movement Revisited', *Economic and Political Weekly*, Vol. XVIII, No. 18, 30 April 1983, pp. 709–12.) It may be noted that the implications of our argument disagree with both.

APPENDIX 7-A

Statistical Tables

Table 7.1

Patterns in Public Expenditure: 1900–1948
(Percentages)

Year	*General Administration*	*Military & Police*	*Development Services*	*Social Services*	*Others*
1900–01	4.41	21.22	7.00	3.16	64.21
1910–11	5.91	21.47	12.01	4.51	56.10
1920–21	4.70	18.38	13.83	4.70	58.39
1930–31	5.37	16.77	12.57	12.66	52.63
1940–41	6.20	14.50	10.26	13.87	55.17
1947–48	6.48	26.30	8.48	12.34	46.40

Notes: 1. This excludes expenditure on capital outlay, most of which was on railways during the initial period and irrigation and electricity schemes, during the later period.
2. Development Services include agriculture, industry, public works and others.
3. Social Services include education, medical and Public Health.
Source: Compiled from 'Financial Statistics, 1301–1359 F', GOH, Hyderabad, 1950.

Table 7.2

Patterns in Revenue Receipts: 1900–1948
(Percentages)

Year	*Land Revenue*	*State Excise*	*Customs*	*Others*
1900–01	49.57	4.32	NA	46.11
1910–11	49.53	16.30	NA	34.17
1920–21	31.87	22.19	18.43	27.51

(*contd.*)

Table 7.2 (*Contd.*)

Year	*Land Revenue*	*State Excise*	*Customs*	*Others*
1930–31	39.42	20.86	12.72	27.00
1940–41	30.32	18.00	11.97	39.71
1947–48	16.28	28.43	9.55	45.74

Source: Compiled from, 'Financial Statistics, 1300–1359 F', GOH, Hyderabad, 1950.

Table 7.3
Acreage by Crop: Index of Growth: 1925–1950
(Base 1927–28 = 100)

Year	*Rice*	*Jawar*	*Sugarcane*	*Sessaum*	*Castor*	*Groundnut*	*Cotton*	*Tobacco*	*Net Sown Area*
1926–27	94.1	99.6	130.0	92.7	100.7	68.0	97.8	118.2	100.6
1927–28	**100.0**	**100.0**	**100.0**	**100.0**	**100.0**	**100.0**	**100.0**	**100.0**	**100.0**
1928–29	98.7	103.0	89.1	103.6	99.5	121.8	102.4	88.7	102.6
1929–30	88.6	106.5	102.6	103.2	104.6	136.1	101.6	84.8	106.4
1930–31	92.9	107.7	112.5	95.2	115.6	144.7	98.1	78.1	109.6
1931–32	112.9	109.0	115.8	97.0	126.8	179.4	98.7	76.7	110.8
1932–33	138.2	106.1	128.6	96.4	129.1	227.5	99.4	72.7	109.4
1933–34	141.6	103.9	144.6	96.5	125.5	240.5	94.4	71.5	108.7
1934–35	144.2	101.7	164.4	99.6	125.3	236.3	95.3	70.1	107.6
1935–36	137.3	103.8	177.6	94.3	124.9	214.1	92.4	70.4	107.0
1936–37	128.2	102.3	155.9	96.6	111.3	247.1	96.7	66.8	104.5
1937–38	129.4	103.5	126.9	89.4	109.6	286.3	94.8	66.5	101.9
1938–39	122.4	107.5	111.8	88.8	102.0	348.4	98.9	69.4	102.5
1939–40	135.9	111.5	130.9	84.6	115.4	385.0	102.3	73.2	104.8
1940–41	123.3	113.4	145.1	90.8	119.8	377.1	103.0	71.7	103.8

(*contd.*)

Table 7.3: (*Contd.*)

Year	*Rice*	*Jawar*	*Sugarcane*	*Sessaum*	*Castor*	*Groundnut*	*Cotton*	*Tobacco*	*Net Sown Area*
1941–42	132.3	111.3	142.1	91.8	123.6	371.6	97.4	63.1	101.4
1942–43	136.6	110.4	157.7	102.0	126.2	451.0	98.9	60.2	101.4
1943–44	157.5	108.5	175.9	105.2	119.0	526.9	84.1	48.2	101.7
1944–45	167.2	99.3	212.5	111.7	122.2	565.4	75.3	57.6	99.8
1945–46	161.1	39.8	246.7	116.0	120.6	519.0	58.2	45.5	95.1
1946–47	161.3	78.8	315.5	125.2	122.7	429.3	57.7	43.3	91.9
1947–48	154.2	73.5	335.9	128.0	119.4	412.4	57.2	26.5	88.5
1948–49	159.9	72.7	309.8	125.9	123.4	355.9	57.0	27.5	88.0
1949–50	152.2	76.6	269.2	117.2	125.8	330.5	61.7	29.2	88.3

Note: The indices are based on three year moving averages.

Source: AS, relevant years and SA, relevant years.

Table 7.4
Cropping Pattern 1920–1950
(Percentages)

Crops	*1920–22*	*1939–40*	*1949–50*
Jawar	39.09	36.60	27.46
Bajra	9.44	5.70	3.84
Wheat	2.02	4.10	1.60
Rice	2.70	3.40	5.79
Gram	2.70	3.30	4.29
Maize	4.04	2.00	1.44
Other food crops	15.01	13.40	23.30
Food Crops (Sub-total)	75.00	68.50	67.72
Groundnut	0.27	6.90	6.75
Castor	4.18	2.40	3.65
Sesamum	2.40	1.90	2.88
Linseed	0.10	1.80	2.27
Other Oil Seeds	1.95	—	3.39
Oil Seeds (Sub-total)	8.90	13.00	18.84
Cotton	10.86	13.10	9.24
Other non-food crops	5.24	6.30	4.00
Non-Food Crops (Sub-total)	25.00	32.40	32.08

Source: 1920–22, GAR, 1322–1331 F.
1939–40 and 1949–50: AS, relevant years.

Table 7.5
Index of Agricultural Output: 1925–1950
(Base 1927–28 = 100)

Year	*Rice*	*Jawar*	*Sugarcane*	*Sesamum*	*Castor*	*Groundnut*	*Cotton*	*Tobacco*
1926–27	102	92	NA	96	118	59	106	NA
1927–28	100	100	NA	100	100	100	100	100
1928–29	96	107	NA	113	86	139	86	106
1929–30	78	103	NA	112	88	255	65	119
1930–31	104	93	NA	99	107	386	50	133
1931–32	92	92	100	96	128	609	54	149
1932–33	112	89	112	86	144	791	60	143
1933–34	108	89	127	84	132	801	58	143
1934–35	113	84	139	84	129	772	59	138
1935–36	118	95	167	99	131	751	58	149
1936–37	120	103	190	118	125	971	63	150
1937–38	129	110	134	112	133	1219	60	157
1938–39	119	113	116	109	119	1440	63	167
1939–40	135	127	143	105	143	1564	65	184
1940–41	113	134	153	118	143	1454	66	173

(contd.)

Table 7.5: (*Contd.*)

Year	*Rice*	*Jawar*	*Sugarcane*	*Sesamum*	*Castor*	*Groundnut*	*Cotton*	*Tobacco*
1941–42	132	136	151	130	171	1542	63	145
1942–43	133	120	157	137	166	1941	61	122
1943–44	148	108	168	134	155	2210	50	99
1944–45	146	85	201	133	132	2248	40	118
1945–46	151	76	220	136	114	1848	29	88
1946–47	152	67	303	152	117	1675	29	82
1947–48	140	61	316	151	114	1344	29	45
1948–49	125	59	311	150	137	1230	29	51

Note: The indices are based on three year moving averages.

Source: Compiled and computed from AS, relevant years, SA, relevant years.

APPENDIX 7-B

Commercialisation of Agriculture

The commercialisation of agriculture in Hyderabad has generated considerable literature. In particular, scholars working on Telangana are engaged in what can be described as a polemical debate over the implications of the process for class relations. In the light of this debate, the details of which need not detain us here,[1] we must note some departure points of our review here. As far as possible we have attempted to qualify our statements with a proviso regarding the particular limitations of the primary data. These relate mainly to the unreliability of the data, especially from the *jagir* areas and to the limitations of data on price movements. It is necessary to state the qualifications explicitly, because, very often as it circulates in academic research, primary data acquires an autonomy if not sanctity, of its own and the original small print that qualifies it is almost forgotten, as has happened in the case of data on groundnut prices in Hyderabad. We should also note that precapitalist forms of extracting surplus cannot always be captured by quantifiable indicators. This is especially the case when dealing with a process of intensification over time. But very often, the absence of quantifiable indicators is presumed to indicate the absence of the phenomenon itself. To counter this methodological fallacy, we have referred to the perceptions and responses of people as reflected in the literature of the Communist movement in Telangana.

I

After the integration of the agrarian economy into the world market, movements of prices influenced the acreage and output of agricultural commodities. A detailed analysis of price movements, however, has to factor in a number of inconsistencies in the available data. For the period 1890–1920, prices of rice, wheat and jawar are available but not of cotton whose importance in Marathwada became significant during this time. For 1921–44, data on wholesale commodity prices of almost all but not all major crops is available. It is not available for the most important crop, groundnut. The data on prices of groundnut was collected in Hyderabad only from 1934. For the earlier period Anwar Iqbal Qureshi, to circumvent the problem, had taken the ruling prices of Bombay Port from where most of the crop was exported. But his data, for 1928–34, was converted from B.G. Rs to *O.S.* Rs at the official exchange rate.[2] If the official exchange rate was not a true indicator of the rate in general, as noted earlier, it was more so in the case of export-oriented agricultural commodities. For the period 1941–48, data on average prices in select regulated markets is available but is not exactly comparable with the earlier set of data. The following should be read keeping these limitations in mind.

For the earlier period 1890–1904, Qureshi observed that the fluctuations in the price of rice, wheat and jawar were essentially governed by domestic factors.[3] But thereafter, market forces outside the state came to have a decisive influence on the prices in the state. This was particularly true during and after WW I. Famines also aggravated the situation. The price of rice went up by 106 per cent, wheat by 123 per cent and jawar by 160 per cent in 1914–21.[4] In that sense the linkages between the world market and Hyderabad agriculture can be traced to the period before WW I and it was located in food grains.[5] However, it was during this period that the commercial importance of cotton in Marathwada became significant, but price data is not available.

After peaking in 1921, prices declined modestly till the Great Depression began in 1929 but the trend was not uniform. Prices of oilseeds even rose a bit while foodgrain prices in general declined. The decline was sharpest in the case of jawar (Table 7.7).

During the depression, Qureshi's index shows that prices of all commodities declined from 77 to 47 in the period from 1929 to 1934.[6] The decline was sharper in oilseeds than in foodgrains with groundnut showing the largest fall. But from about 1934–35, prices began to improve. The partial recovery, which was also followed by a brief recession was sharper in oilseeds than in foodgrains.

WW II affected the movement of prices in Hyderabad only after it reached East Asia in 1942. All prices showed sharp increases in

1942–43 and in fact reached, for the first time, the pre-depression level. The separate index of average prices in the regulated markets brings out this phenomenon more clearly, than the earlier index (Table 7.8). Foodgrain prices in particular, reached extreme heights. Towards the end of the regime, the anarchy in the state and the economic warfare between the Hyderabad government and the Indian government contributed to the rise in prices.[7] In 1947–48, prices reached an all-time high in all commodities.

We can now examine the inter-relationship between the movement of prices, acreage and output, for some select commodities. We have divided the periods, following the general trend in prices, into pre-depression, depression, recovery and war periods. The demarcating point for the war period was taken as 1942, for reasons explained above. In each case, the terminal year of the earlier phase is taken as the base year of the next phase to bring fluctuations into sharp focus. In the case of prices, the change is the difference between the first year and the terminal year, and thus does not indicate the fluctuations within the period. In the cases of both acreage and output, the growth rates are compound growth rates for the period, based on a three-year moving average of actual figures. The same trends can also be established on the basis of the indices of prices, acreage and output that were referred to earlier.

Table 7.6
Prices, Acreage and Output: Select Commodities 1926–1945

	1926–30	*1929–35*	*1934–42*	*1941–45*
Rice:				
Price	–7	–38	21	54
Acreage	–1	10	–2	5
Output	–5	7	3	2
Jawar:				
Price	–5	–41	7	95
Acreage	1	–1	2	–2
Output	2	–4	10	–9

(*contd.*)

Table 7.6 (*Contd.*)

	1926–30	*1929–35*	*1934–42*	*1941–45*
Cotton:				
Price	–10	–21	14	95
Acreage	1	–1	1	–5
Output	–9	–2	1	–9
Groundnut:				
Price	NA	–41	NA	94
Acreage	15	12	9	9
Output	34	25	15	1
Castor:				
Price	–23	–36	13	143
Acreage	1	4	–1	–1
Output	–6	8	6	–5
Sesamum:				
Price	–14	–35	–2	112
Acreage	2	–1	–1	4
Output	3	–6	9	1

Notes for Table 7.6: 1. All prices, except groundnut, are wholesale commodity prices and the change indicated here is based on the index with the base year 1927 = 100. See Table 7.7.

2. In the case of sesamum in the last period, the prices of the last year were not included due to non-availability.

3. Groundnut prices for 1929–34 are based on an index with base year 1928. The prices of 1941–45 taken were not the same as earlier but average prices in regulated markets with base year 1938–39 (Table 7.8). The data is included here only as representing general trends and is not strictly comparable with the earlier period, 1929–35.

4. Compound growth rates of output and acreage given here are based on three-year moving averages.

Source: Prices—Table 7.7 and 7.8.

Acreage and output—Computed from AS, relevant years and SA, relevant years. See also Tables 7.3 and 7.5 in Appendix 7-A.

The most striking feature in the table is that there is no unique relationship between movements of prices and growth rates in acreage and output either across crops or across periods. During the pre-depression period, rice acreage and output declined as prices declined while the reverse is true of jawar. The same inverse relationship can be seen in the case of sesamum while the reverse is true of castor. During the depression period, in general, the fall in prices resulted in an increase in area and output. The sharpest fall in prices accompanied by the sharpest fall in acreage and output was in groundnut. But this general trend was not true of jawar and sesamum. In the post-depression period, the recovery of prices did not result in an increase in area and output even to the extent the fall in prices seems to have achieved in the depression period, in the case of rice. The growth rate of acreage was actually negative. In jawar and cotton there was a positive relationship between prices and acreage and output, although the extent was vastly different. Oileeds, castor and sesamum had a negative growth rate in acreage while output rates were positive. In the WW II period, the spectacular increase in prices only had a positive effect on the growth rates of rice, groundnut and sesamum. But the increases in acreage and output were very marginal as compared with the increase in prices. In cotton, jawar and castor, the increase in prices led to negative growth rates both in area and output. In general, the acreage and output of cotton, with marginal exceptions, had negative growth rates throughout the period, irrespective of price movements.

Some of the factors contributing to these responses were the indirect effects of price movements. For instance, the relative factor prices and the differential ratio for different crops influenced the changes in acreage and output. Thus, where the cost of cultivation was appreciably less, as for example, jawar, the cultivators preferred the crop, and for jawar, unlike groundnut, the relative factor prices and the prices of output of substitute goods like coarse grain also played a role.[9] Other factors that influenced price movements had to do with the nature of the crop. Rice for instance, being more dependent on rain, was significantly influenced by climatic conditions.[10]

Price movements, as explanations for changing growth rates of acreage and output serve as necessary but not sufficient variables.

Table 7.7
Index of Agricultural Prices: 1921–1944
(Base 1927 = 100)

Year	*Rice*	*Wheat*	*Jawar*	*Castor*	*Linseed*	*Sesamum*	*Cotton*	*Groundnut*
1921	114	124	179	111	100	124	125	—
1922	100	136	123	121	114	104	117	—
1923	98	112	127	117	108	101	104	—
1924	97	104	95	127	97	98	109	—
1925	100	95	100	120	104	101	11	—
1926	93	96	89	117	101	96	107	—
1927	**100**	**100**	**100**	**100**	**100**	**100**	**100**	—
1928	99	100	102	96	91	95	108	100
1929	86	86	95	94	87	82	96	79
1930	81	80	93	97	90	79	90	62
1931	74	67	55	79	74	56	75	100
1932	50	49	54	68	47	53	86	61
1933	50	49	54	70	49	54	84	32
1934	48	49	54	58	48	47	75	38
1935	55	47	68	61	49	64	86	61
1936	53	45	61	66	52	65	86	67
1937	56	62	66	78	56	64	91	—
1938	57	64	63	73	57	58	84	—
1939	57	56	75	71	55	54	81	—
1940	66	63	80	90	67	64	98	—
1941	69	65	68	71	58	45	89	—
1942	82	77	80	109	65	91	123	—
1943	121	145	150	203	133	157	191	—
1944	123	152	163	214	137	NA	184	—

Notes: 1. For groundnut, the base year is 1928.
2. All prices, except groundnut, are wholesale commodity prices in the state.
3. The base year was chosen as 1927, to maintain uniformity with acreage and output. The base year chosen by the sources, 1921, was a famine year.
4. For groundnut, the data for 1928–34 was based on Bombay Port prices. For later years, it was the wholesale commodity prices in the state.

Source: A.I. Qureshi, *Economic Development of Hyderabad, Vol. I, Rural Economy*, Orient Longman, Bombay, 1947, pp. 248–269.

Table 7.8
Agricultural Prices: 1941–1948

Year	*Rice*	*Wheat*	*Jawar*	*Castor*	*Sesamum*	*Groundnut*	*Cotton*
1938–39	100	100	100	100	100	100	100
1939–41	NA	NA	NA	NA	NA	NA	NA
1941–42	83	122	100	133	106	83	155
1942–43	100	217	155	308	237	184	323
1943–44	133	239	244	341	265	208	385
1944–45	118	278	211	291	305	177	338
1945–46	168	282	233	341	400	280	438
1946–47	NA	183	211	517	459	330	492
1947–48	264	585	400	525	218	354	508

Note: The prices, unlike earlier prices, are average prices in select regulated markets of the state.
Source: Appendix 'E', 'Report of the Agrarian Reform Committee', GOH, Hyderabad, 1949.

In fact, any attempt to analyse the agrarian transition with the focus more or less exclusively on price movements can be misleading. What is important is to take into consideration the set of non-price factors that modified the influence of price movements.

II

The nature of the political economy into which the commodity market penetrated serves as the origin of the non-price factors. The intensification of the profit motive of the landlords, in addition to the plunder, only accentuated the social power they held over both peasants and labourers. In such a context every fall in the real income of the peasants forced them to work more in order to maintain themselves over and above the demands of the landlords. Thus during the depression period, acreage and output increased due to the 'desire of the cultivator to make good the loss of his income from the fall in prices by producing a larger quantity than before'.[11] Where such augmentation could not be sufficient, when the value of the crop was relatively low as in the cases of jawar and sesamum, the inverse relationship was true. Even in the post-depression period when prices recovered, it did not make any difference to the peasant cultivators. Their needs obliged them to sell when the prices were low, in the harvesting season and buy when they were high. The control of landlords, moneylenders and traders over the peasantry neutralised much of the effect of the price recovery. During the WW II period, two new dimensions aggravated the situation. Firstly, the widespread food shortages hit the peasantry badly. Secondly, the efforts of the government to regulate the proportion of food crops to non-food crops and the collection of grain under the levy system also increased the pressure on the peasantry. Thus it was not price movements *per se* but the varying, often conflicting, responses to them by different classes of people that become important for analysing change. In other words, the focus should be on the context of commercialisation in the given social structure.

The growth of the market economy was one of the factors that led to an increase in the area under cultivation as landlords grabbed more and more land in order to cultivate profitable cash crops. We shall see later that this was not the sole cause of land- grabbing. But the increase led to an increase in demand for cultivators and labourers. As a consequence tenancy increased.

The spread of tenancy was particularly marked in *diwani* tenures. In non-*diwani* areas, for all practical purposes, all cultivators were treated as tenants, especially in smaller *jāgirs*.[12] It was in *diwani* areas that both the increase in the net sown area and changing crop patterns contributed to the increasing need for tenant cultivators. The proportion of tenants to total cultivators was, according to the 1931 census, about 32 per cent. By 1937–38, the Tenancy Committee, based on a survey of 48 villages, put the figure at 36 per cent. And in 1945, Qureshi estimated the proportion of tenants to be about 45 per cent.[13] Similarly *shikmi pattadars* (protected tenants) as a proportion of total *pattadars* increased from about 12 per cent in 1926 to 21 per cent in 1940.[14] The data, it should be noted, does not give a clear picture of a significant part of tenants *viz.* part-tenants. Given the restricted base of the surveys and the nature of their limitations, it is difficult to make many generalisations on the basis of these quantitative estimates. Suffice it to say that tenancy spread after the advent of commercialisation.

More than the spread of tenancy, it was the conditions of tenancy that revealed the consequences of the growth in the market economy. As production for market increased, along with its attendant uncertainties, especially the depression, more and more tenants were engaged without any form of protection. The half-hearted attempts made by the state to protect tenants further aggravated their insecurity. The proportion of *asami shikmidars* (tenants-at-will) among tenants, in the surveyed villages of 1929–1930, was about 76 per cent and by the time of the second inquiry, in 1949–51, it had become 78 per cent.[15] Even more dramatically, the proportion of landless tenants increased sharply from about 32 per cent to 47 per cent during the same period.[16] Landless tenants, significantly, included *bhagelas*.[17] *Bhagela*, along with *vetti* (often confused with *vettipani*, as we shall see later) were forms of bondage that were prevalent in the Telangana region of the state. Here labourers, in order to clear debts, incurred or inherited, became bonded to the landlord. Some of them served as farm servants (*jeetagadu*), attached to particular landlords for generations.

With commercialisation and a fall in real income, coupled with deteriorating tenancy conditions, indebtedness increased. By the late 1920s, as a result of the development of an export market for some commodities, a hierarchical structure in the credit market acquired control over the agrarian economy. At the apex were Bombay merchants and joint-stock banks who effectively converted independent dealers of agricultural commodities into their commission agents.[18] Smaller local merchants and in some cases, landlords, were next in the hierarchy. At the village level there were professional moneylenders, Marwaris in Marathwada and Komatis in Telangana. But as the conditions of the peasantry deteriorated it was not the professional moneylenders but landlords-cum-moneylenders who grew in importance. Marathas in Marathwada, Lingayats in Karnatic and Reddys (possibly some Velamas also) in Telangana were part of these 'cultivating classes' that sucked the peasantry into a spiral of debt. In 1949–51, Iyengar estimated that of the total debt in the surveyed villages, 38 per cent was due to these 'cultivating families' while it was 31 per cent in the case of professional money lenders.[19]

In 1937, the government conducted an inquiry into indebtedness. This inquiry, covering 312 sample villages in four districts was, like Iyengar's enquiries, confined to *diwani* areas. It concluded that every acre of land, on an average, had a burden of roughly about six times the revenue assessment.[20] That average also included absentee landlords, constituting 48 per cent of *pattadars* who were free from debt.[21] The average annual interest was estimated to be around 18 per cent but Qureshi suggests that this was an underestimate and puts it around 35 per cent.[22] Similar trends can also be noted from Iyengar's investigations. According to the peasants in the surveyed villages, the total amount of their debt increased by 63 per cent in 1931–39 and by 83 per cent in 1939–50.[23]

But these estimates of indebtedness could not have captured the real magnitude of the problem. Almost all the official and semi-official surveys during the period, which serve as source materials, were confined to *diwani* areas. Even within these areas, the government-sponsored survey in 1937 was confined only to *pattadars*. Iyengar's surveys indicate that crop and personal security and not land served as the important basis of the credit market indicating the extent of indebtedness among those who did not legally own land.[24] Among small peasants and labourers, who had no property worth the name, land or crop, to offer as security, credit requirements accentuated their bondage. Most of the increasing proportion of landless tenants, including *bhagelas*, fall into this category. In addition, Kabuliwalas, Rohillas and Arabs dominated the underworld of the credit market where the annual interest ranged from 75 to 150 per cent.[25]

The indebtedness of the peasantry also contributed to the alienation of land. In 1929–30, in the surveyed villages of four districts, almost 15 per cent of land under cultivation had changed hands during the preceding 25 years.[26] In 1937, in the villages surveyed by the Committee on Indebtedness, the percentage was about 10.4 per cent[27] and in the 1949–51 survey, it was 7 per cent.[28] There is a reason for this ostensible decline. Land alienation through formal debt was not the major mode of land-grabbing by landlords. Manipulation of land records, forcible occupation under various pretexts such as non-payment of tax, refusal to do *vettipani* (customary free service) default on loans and other things played a far more significant role, especially in Telangana.[29] The alienation of land and its concentration in the hands of landlords was not merely for cultivation of cash crops but also to extract rents, grazing rent in case of grazing land and to accumulate marginally cultivable land in order to prevent the landless from acquiring land.

Commercialisation also seems to have accentuated forms of extraction that were peculiar to the region like *vetti pani* (or *vetti chakiri*). Under this customary form prevalent in Telangana, all the toiling classes, from rich peasants to labourers and artisans had to supply either service or products free of charge to the landlord. There was no limit on the extent and the concessions on which such free service was expected from the villagers.[30] Among many such customary practices was provision for *adabapas*, a sort of concubine to be presented to the landlord at the time of marriage. The landlords were also arbitrators of justice on all aspects related to the personal and social lives of people. The fines levied as punishments were exhorbitant and were a major source of aggrandizement for landlords.

In such a context the conditions of the lowest strata of peasantry, small peasants and labourers, were particularly oppressive. Neither the category called 'agricultural labour', nor their number, proportion and wage levels are particularly useful in understanding their conditions of life and labour.[31] This strata included small peasants who worked as wage labourers, women of peasant families who worked as labourers while their men worked on their own land, attached labour, bonded labour and *bhagelas* referred to earlier, some of whom were also tenants and some worked as labourers on the lands of rich peasants. But one should note that the rich peasants' ability to engage labourers was subject to the overall control of the landlords. It is difficult to suggest that they were 'free labourers' considering the absolute social power of the landlords.

In this context it is worthwhile to note some interesting features of the peasant movement in Telangana. The movement highlighted the issue of feudal forms of extraction. These included bonded labour, customary services and extractions, fines and payments, forceful occupation of land, and other issues. Significantly, the areas in which the movement and these issues became important were those that had been subjected to intense commercialisation during the preceding decades, mostly Nalgonda and Warangal districts in Telangana. It was these two districts that witnessed a militant mass peasant movement. Outlying areas, in Mahbubnagar, Adilabad and Medak districts, which were not firmly integrated into the larger market economy remained, by and large, outside the influence of the peasant movement.

The absence of a determinate or unique relationship between movements of prices and changes in acreage and output, their differential impact on different classes of people, the extent to which they were governed by the specific characteristics of social organisation, the intensification of feudal forms of extracting surplus reflected in particular in the peasant revolt against them —would all indicate the nature and limitations of the process of commercialisation of agriculture in Hyderabad.

Notes

1. See note 31, in the main text, Chapter 7.
2. Anwar Iqbal Qureshi, *Economic Development of Hyderabad: Vol. I, Rural Economy*, Orient Longman, Bombay, 1947, p. 263.
3. Ibid., pp. 244–45.
4. Ibid., p. 246.
5. Ibid., pp. 244–46.
6. Ibid., p. 255.
7. During the last year both governments seem to have imposed restrictions on the movement of goods. For Hyderabad's version see, 'Hyderabad's Relations with the Dominion of India', GOH,

Hyderabad, 1948, pp. 32–44. For the Indian side 'White Paper on Hyderabad', GOI, Delhi, 1948.

8. Qureshi, 1947, op. cit. (note 2), p. 257.
9. Ibid., p. 257.
10. Ibid., p. 257.
11. Ibid., p. 257.
12. 'Report of the Tenancy Inquiry Committee', GOH, Hyderabad, 1940, pp. 10–15.
13. All figures from Qureshi, 1947, op. cit. (note 2), p. 133.
14. Ibid., p. 63.
15. S. Kesav Iyengar, *Economic Investigations in Hyderabad State: 1929–30, Vol. I (General Survey)*, GOH, Hyderabad, 1931, p. 20 and S. Kesav Iyengar, *Economic Enquiries in Hyderabad State: 1949–51*, GOH, Hyderabad, 1951, p. 55. Iyengar's first enquiry was confined to 56 villages spread over six districts while the second enquiry covered 118 villages in almost all districts. Only four villages were common to both surveys. The first survey was confined only to *diwani* villages. The comparative account from both these surveys, thus cannot be taken as precise quantitative estimates, on any aspect.
16. Iyengar, 1931, op. cit. (note 15), pp. 20–21 and Iyengar, 1951, op. cit. (note 15), pp. 55.
17. Iyengar, 1931, p. 20.
18. This account is based on 'Hyderabad Ranking Enquiry Committee Report', GOH, Hyderabad, 1931. See also Appendix 4-A above.
19. Iyengar, 1951, op. cit. (note 15), p. 412. It may be noted here that a survey conducted in 1952 in Osmanabad indicates that 54 per cent of the credit advanced to cultivators was by agricultiralist moneylenders. 'All India Rural Credit Survey: District Monograph: Osmanabad', Reserve Bank of India, Bombay, 1957, p. 40.
20. S.M. Bharucha, *Agricultural Indebtedness in H.E.H. The Nizam's Dominions*, GOH, Hyderabad, 1937, p. 9.
21. Ibid, pp. 7–9. We should note however that estimates of indebtedness of landlords absent from a village in a village-based survey cannot be accurate.
22. Qureshi, 1947, op. cit. (note 2), p. 158.
23. Iyengar, 1951, op. cit. (note 15), p. 436.
24. Ibid., pp. 422–428 and Iyengar, 1931, op. cit. (note 15), pp. 29–31.
25. Bharucha, 1937, op. cit. (note 20), p. 45.

26. Combined total of dry, wet and garden land. Figures rounded off in acres. Iyengar, 1931, op. cit. (note 15), pp. 11 and 18.
27. Bharucha, 1937, op. cit. (note 20), p. 7.
28. Iyengar, 1951, op. cit. (note 15), p. 116.
29. Puchhalapalli Sundarayya gives numerous instances of this type. P. Sundarayya, *Telangana People's Struggle and its Lessons*, Communist Party of India (Marxist), Calcutta, 1972. In particular, see pp. 9–16. Also see Ch. Rajeshweara Rao et al. *buswamya vidhanam raddu ki rythula virochita tirugubatu* (Telugu), Andhra Pradesh Communist Samiti, Vijayawada.
30. Ibid., pp. 12–14. See also Devulapalli Venkateswara Rao and Baddam Yella Reddy, *neti hydarabadu—mana kartavyam*, (Telugu), Prajasakti, Bezawada (Vijayawada), 1944.
31. Iyengar, for instance, notes that landless agricultural labour families as a proportion of the total increased from 1929–30 to 1937 but declined sharply in 1949–51. (Iyengar, 1951, op cit., note 15, p. 218). Tenants were included in his category but not in the labour census of the government (Report on Labour Census, 1344 F, GOH, Hyderabad, p. 23). On wages see Qureshi, 1947, op. cit. (note 2), p. 67, and, Iyengar, 1951, op. cit. (note 15), pp. 210–11. For the general conditions of agricultural labour and poor peasants, see Sundarayya, 1972, op. cit. (note 27), pp. 507–20.

CHAPTER EIGHT

Crisis and Collapse

In Hyderabad, the autocratic political structure, based on the feudal social organisation, remained impervious to changes from both above and below. The growth of commercial agriculture and the development of industry unleashed forces that became a potential threat to the traditional ruling powers. The development of organised industry gave rise to a working class whose organised movement put direct pressure on the state and indirectly helped the birth of a peasant movement. The intensification of feudal forms of extraction as a result of commercialisation, led to a peasant movement that eventually posed an armed challenge to state power. In the face of a crisis, the state became more and more defensive of its autocratic political character. But around the same time, pressure also began to build from above as the colonial administration was forced to respond to the nationalist movement. The colonial state acquiesced in the demand for popular sovereignty, albeit in bits and pieces, by the mid-1930s. Its echo in Hyderabad was strongly resisted by the Nizam.

Although the state apparatus was able to lay the foundation for the social and organisational framework of the economy, it nevertheless remained committed to the assiduously built relationship between bureaucracy and autocracy, which was historically located in the Mughal period. Subsequent modernisation, since the time of Salar Jung, did not fundamentally disturb this relationship. This arrangement also served the colonial power by providing a firm foundation for its rule. It was in this rather paradoxical context that the crisis in polity began to emerge in the state.

II

The turning point in the growth of political consciousness in Hyderabad was the emergence of the demand for constitutional reforms with the formation of the Hyderabad Political Reforms Association in 1921.[1] Independently, at around the same time, linguistic-nationalist groups began to emerge. The first such association was the Andhra Jana Sabha of the Telugus, formed in 1922. The Telugus constituted almost 48 per cent of the state's population, the Marathis around 24 per cent and the Kannadigas 10 per cent.[2] These associations had their origin in the cultural and linguistic aspirations of the urban intelligentia. But they were also influenced by the nationalistic struggle that was by then acquiring a mass base in British India. By the 1930s these groups and associations became important forums of public opinion against the autocratic rule of the Nizam. The government responded with restrictions on political and social activities in the state.[3] But these groups grew in strength and number. The Andhra Jana Sabha acquired a wider base, and became the Andhra Maha Sabha in 1930. The Maharashtra Parishad took shape by 1936 and the Karnataka Parishad by 1937.[4] It was these provincial associations that strengthened the State Congress Party, which in turn helped them to grow.[5] The major focus of this nascent political consciousness was the political form of the government, especially regarding constitutional reforms and civil rights.

But the state resolutely opposed any meaningful changes in the form of government. Whatever measures it took were primarily defensive and weak responses to developments taking place in British India. Thus the Montagu-Chemsford reforms led to the formation of *babe-hukumat*, a nominal Executive Council, in 1921. The British Resident played a prominent role in the formation and control of the council in the earlier years. Similarly, after the promulgation of the Government of India Act in 1935, the Hyderabad government initiated some reforms. A committee headed by Aravamudu Iyengar was appointed to suggest changes in the constitutional form of the government. But its recommendations were never carried out. The form of the government remained in the apt description of the committee—'pure autocracy...carried through the *diwan*'.[6] It was in this context that the famous *satyagraha* took place in 1938, demanding change in the form of government.

But, in the face of rising democratic consciousness, the regime gradually adopted an aggressively Islamic character. The Deccani nationalist sentiments referred to earlier could not emerge as a force in the political arena. The slogan 'Long live the royal Embodiment of Deccani Nationalism'[7] gave way to the slogan 'Long live the Royal Embodiment of Muslim Sovereignty in the Deccan'.[8] Osman Ali Khan's reference to Hyderabad as the 'Last symbol of the Muslims' sums up the self-image that the regime actively propagated.[9]

In an all-pervading communal environment, helped by the polarisation that was taking place in British India, democratic consciousness gradually became entwined with communal forces in Hyderabad. Hindu communal organisations, to a large extent backed by the state, became rivals in generating communal strife. The Arya Samaj, especially in Marathwada, the Hindu Maha Sabha and the Hindu Civil Liberties Union as well as the Ittehadul Muslimeen and Anjuman-e-Tabligh-ul-Islam grew in strength. By the late 1930s communal strife assumed significant proportions in Raichur, Bidar and Gulbarga in Karnatic, Aurangabad and Nanded in Marathwada and Mehabubnagar in Telangana and Hyderabad city where, for the first time, riots broke out in 1938.[10] Originating in this period, communal strife continues till today in some of these areas.[11] The Ittehadul Muslimeen, especially after the death of its legendary founder Bahadur Yar Jung and the emergence of the Razakars, became a sort of private army of the state.[12] On the other side, the nationalist movement became 'a movement of the majority community against the tyranny and religious domination of the fanatical Muslims' as a contemporary observer described it.[13] The provincial associations too were drawn into the vortex of communal politics.

The only exception was the Andhra Maha Sabha which the Communists steered in the direction of the oppressed peasantry.

The Communist Party had established its organisational roots in Hyderabad by the late 1930s.[14] It was under its influence that the issues of the peasantry came to the fore in the Andhra Maha Sabha.[15] Thus, over time it was able to forge a broad alliance against *jagirdars, deshmukhs* and other big landlords in Telangana. In fact, the struggle against big landowners was opposed by sections of the Andhra Maha Sabha as they argued that it would divide the movement against the Nizam.[16] Eventually the Andhra Maha Sabha split in 1944 with the majority siding with the Communists. Within two years, by 1946, the movement had developed into an armed peasant struggle. Over time in a large number of villages the Communist Party was able to establish alternative centres of political power at the village level.[17] Although it was only confined to less than a third of Telangana, largely the Nalgonda and Warangal districts, it became a powerful force that threatened the regime.

Meanwhile, as the British prepared to leave India, the conflict between Hyderabad and the nationalists acquired significance. The Nizam, claiming a special status, once again raised the issue of paramountcy as it applied to Hyderabad and the question of the status of Berar.[18] After Independence, refusing accession, Hyderabad declared its own independence and even maintained some kind of relationship with Pakistan.[19] Initially the Indian government entered into a Standstill Agreement in November 1947, but the conflict continued. The Congress Party organised the people against the regime.[20] The Communists intensified their struggle in Telangana. The Razakars indulged in widespread anti-social violence. The prolonged negotiations between the two governments did not yield any results.[21] The nobility, as a class could not take a coherent and united position in the conflict.[22] Class struggle and communal violence added to the general atmosphere of anarchy in the state.[23] The widespread strike organised by the trade unions and the economic warfare between the two governments forced Hyderabad to spend large sums of money on defence, making the economy of the state deteriorate further.[24] Eventually the Indian Army entered the state in September, 1948.

III

The military action, always referred to as Police Action for some inexplicable reason, led to the collapse of the regime in less than four days. Codenamed 'Operation Polo', it was to become independent India's first army intervention in a civilian conflict, because the military stayed on to suppress the communist movement.[25]

As the collapse became imminent a good number of Hyderabad Muslims emigrated to Pakistan, including industrialists Moin Nawaz Jung and Mir Laik Ali.[26] Fear of reprisals appears to have been the motivating factor. There are no available estimates of the magnitude of emigration from Hyderabad to Pakistan, but it seems to have been significant. The Government of India itself deported non-*mulki* Arabs, belonging to the abandoned troops of the Nizam, to the Western Protectorate.[27] With the military action, the military governor became the chief administrator of the state and the deposed Nizam became the *Rajpramukh*. Later, in December 1949, the military administration handed over charge to a civilian official. Finally, in March 1950, an interim administrative system was set up and Hyderabad became a part B state of the Indian Union.

The interim administration took a number of measures that paved the way for the integration of the Hyderabad economy with the rest of India. In legal and administrative matters the state was brought on par with the rest of the country with Indian laws and legislation replacing Hyderabad Regulations. A number of formal and informal committees were appointed on matters related to the economy: Gulzari Lal Nanda and R.K. Patil on agrarian reforms,[28] Kasturbhai Lalbhai on state-owned or aided industries,[29] the Rege Committee on industrial labour,[30] Vijayalaxmi Pandit on cottage industries,[31] and T.T. Krishnamachari on finance,[32] were notable among these committees. As a result of some of the recommendations of the individuals and committees, the *Osmania Sicca* Rupee was abolished,[34] *jagirs* were abolished, *sarf-e-khas* was taken over, and some industries were handed over to private industrialists.[35]

In 1956, after the linguistic reorganisation of states, Hyderabad

Karnatic became part of Karnataka, Marathwada became part of what is now called Maharashtra and Telangana became part of Andhra Pradesh.

Notes

1. See, *The Freedom Struggle in Hyderabad, Vol. IV (1921–47)*, Andhra Pradesh Committee for the Compilation of History of Freedom Struggle in Andhra Pradesh, 1966. Achyut Khode (ed.), *The People's Movement in Hyderabad*, no publisher, Nanded, 1947, and Varanasi Venkatanarayana Sastry, *hyderabadu prajala swatantra poratan* (Telugu), Desi Kavita Mandali, Bezawada Vijayawada, 1947.
2. Based on 1931 and 1941 census.
3. The infamous *gasti* no. 53 that prohibited public meetings was part of these restrictions, which led to political conferences on Hyderabad being held outside the state for a number of years. See, *Freedom Struggle in Hyderabad*, op. cit. (note 1), pp. 58–78.
4. For the origin and growth of the Andhra Maha Sabha, see Mandumula Narasimgarao, *ebhai samstarala hyderabadu* (Telugu), Narasimgarao Smaraka Samiti, Hyderabad, 1977, and, Madapati Hanumantha Rao, *telanganalo andhrabhyudayam* (Telugu), Andhra Chandrika Granthamala, Hyderabad, 1949.
   For Maharashtra Parishad, see Khanderao Kulkarni, *hyderabadu ajnata charitra putalu* (Telugu), Navbharati, Hyderabad, 1979.. For a brief account of all three associations, see Khode, 1947, op. cit. (note 1).
5. Internal discussions and intermittent bans by the government led to a situation where the State Congress existed only 'symbolically' according to its leader Swami Ramananda Thiratha. (Swami Ramananda Thiratha, *Memoirs of the Hyderabad Freedom Struggle*, Popular Prakashan, Bombay, 1967, p. 138.) Thiratha gives an account of the mutually strengthening relations between the provincial associations and the State Congress.
6. 'Report of the Reforms Committee', GOH, Hyderabad, 1938, p. 5.
7. The slogan was given by the Nizam's Subjects League, See Abid Hasan, *Whither Hyderabad?*, Madras, 1935.
8. The slogan of the Ittehadul Muslimeen. Muslims constituted about 12 per cent of the population in the state, with the largest concentration being in Hyderabad city.

9. In a couplet, Osman Ali Khan lamented *saltine-surf sub huguye nazar-e-aijal, Osman, muslaman-e-kateri sultanate se hai nishan baqi* (All the kings are dead Osman, they realm remains the last symbol of Muslims). See, Gulam Hyder, 'Anti-Nizam Struggle: Participation of Muslims'. In Rajbahadur Gowr, et al., *Glorious Telengana Armed Struggle,* Communist Party, New Delhi, 1973, p. 173. See also Muneer Ahmed Khan, 'Muslim Politics in Hyderabad', unpublished Doctoral Dissertation, Department of Political Science, Osmania University, Hyderabad, 1980.
10. For details about the riots in Dhulpet, Hyderabad in 1938, see GAR, 1348 F. See also Tiratha, 1967, op. cit. (note 5), p. 76.
11. When material for this book was being collected in 1984, Hyderabad city was under curfew while at the time this report was written in 1988, Aurangabad was under curfew, due to communal disturbances.
12. Muneer Ahmed Khan, 1980, op. cit. (note 9).
13. Lanka Sundaram, *Hyderabad, Our Diseased Limb*, Sarvodaya Sahitya Parishad, Delhi, 1948, p. 17.
14. Not many details are available about the precise origin of the Communist Party organisation in Hyderabad prior to its influence in the Andhra Maha Sabha. It appears, contrary to popular belief, to have originated from the urban middle-class, some of whom were already associated with the burgeoning working class movement. The Comrades Association, as they were known, played a significant role as a conduit for the Communist Party to eventually spread its influence into rural areas. For some scattered details, see S.M. Javed Razvi, *hyderabadu samstanamlo rajakiya chaitanyam, 1938–56—vidyarthi yuvajanula patra* (Telugu), Vishalandra, Vijayawada, 1985. Gulam Hyder's essay in Rajbahadur Gowr, et al., 1973, op. cit. (note 9), pp. 140–46 and Pavier's interview with D.V. Rao in Barry Pavier, *The Telangana Movement, 1944–51*, Vikas, New Delhi, 1981, pp. 80–82.
15. For the evolution of the agrarian demands of the Andhra Maha Sabha, see Ch. Rajeswara Rao et al., *Buswamaya vidhanam radduki rytula virochita tirugubatu* (Telugu), Andhra Pradesh Communist Samiti, Vijayawada, 1973.
16. See Narasimgarao, 1977, op. cit. (note 4). See also Ravi Narayana Reddy, *veera telangana: na anubhavalu-jnapakalu* (Telugu), Andhra Pradesh Communist Samiti, Vijayawada, 1972. Latter day critics were to argue that the alliance was too broad and should have excluded rich peasantry. See, Pavier, 1981, op. cit. (note 14).

17. The basic work on the history of the Communist struggle in Telangana remains Sundarayya's monumental work. Pucchalapalli Sundarayya, *Telangana People's Struggle and its Lessons*, Communist Party of India (Marxist), Calcutta, 1972.
18. For the stand of the Hyderabad government, see 'Hyderabad Relations with the Dominion of India', GOH, Hyderabad, 1948 and for the Indian Government's position, 'White Paper on Hyderabad', GOI, Delhi, 1948.
19. The Nizam's government was reported to have transferred Rs 40 million to Pakistan. Binod U. Rao, *Hyderabad Reborn, First Six Months of Freedom*, GOH, Hyderabad, 1949, pp. 19–20.
20. *The Hyderabad Problem: The Next Step*, the Hyderabad Struggle Committee, Socialist Party, Bombay, 1948.
21. Interestingly, all three members of the negotiating team in this phase Moin Nawaz Jung, Pingali Venkatrama Reddy and Abdur Rehman were industrialist civil servants or ministers.
22. In fact, Muhammad Ali Jinnah was reported to have described them as 'a handful of effete nobility', quoted in K.M. Munshi, *The End of an Era*, Bharatiya Vidya Bhavan, Bombay, 1957, p. 235.
23. For an account of the situation during the least days of the regime, see Fareed Mirza, *Pre and Post Police Action Days in the Erstwhile Hyderabad State*, no publisher, Hyderabad, 1976. See also Zahir Ahmed, *Dusk and Dawn in Village India*, Praeger, New York, 1965.
24. For references to this economic warfare, see William Paton Barton, 'Crisis in Hyderabad', *National Review*, 131, 1948, pp. 25–28. See also note 18 above. In the last year, 1947–48, the government was reported to have spent Rs 118.40 million on the military and the police. Binod U. Rao, 1949, op. cit. (note 19), p. 68
25. The threat from the Communists as foreseen by the Indian government appears, in retrospect to have been a bit exaggerated. But there was an impression, as the editor fo the army archives on the operation noted that 'the Communists would have been the future rulers of Hyderabad if the government of India had not intervened'. S.N. Prasad, *Operation Polo: The Police Action in Hyderabad, 1948*, Historical Section, Ministry of Defence, GOI, New Delhi, 1972, p. 9. For similar impressions among the political leadership, see Durga Das (ed.), *Sardar Patel's Correspondence*, Vol. 7. For army operations against the Communist movement, see Sundarayya, 1972, op. cit. (note 17), pp. 195–205. See also Tiratha, 1967, op. cit. (note 5), pp. 214–28.

26. Laik Ali escaped dramatically from the custody of the Indian government. For details, see Taya Zinkin, *Reporting India*, Chatto and Windus, London, 1962, pp. 69–70. See also Mir Laik Ali, *Tragedy of Hyderabad*, Pakistan Cooperative Book Society, Karachi, 1962 and Moin Nawaz Jung, *Hyderabad Under Military Occupation*, Karwan-i-Adab, Karachi, 1951.
27. Binod U. Rao, 1949, op. cit. (note 19), p. 213.
28. Tiratha, 1967, op. cit. (note 59), p. 213.
29. HGBEA, Vol. III, No. 12, December 1950.
30. 'Report on the Conditions of Factory Labour in Hyderabad State', GOH, Hyderabad, 1950.
31. Binod U. Rao, 1949, op. cit. (note 19), p. 35.
32. HGBEA, Vol. III, Nos. 1–3, January–March 1950, p. 140.
33. In fact the demonetization of the *Osmania Sicca* Rupee led to widespread disturbances in Hyderabad city, GAR, 1952–53.
34. For matters related to industry, see Chapter 6 above. For details of other sectors of the economy, see GAR of the period 1948–56 and issues of *Hyderabad Government Bulletin of Economic Affairs* (HGBEA).

CHAPTER NINE

Conclusion

'The Country that is more developed industrially only shows, to the less developed, the image of its own future'.

— Karl Marx, *Capital I*

Industrialisation is, for a backward country, its idea of its future. In particular, the role of the state has gradually assumed importance in the process of industrial development. Thus, for many less-developed countries, progress has become synomymous with the role of the state in industrialisation. These images of progress are now part of the official discourse on development. Our account of industrialisation in Asaf Jahi Hyderabad disputes the assumptions of such a discourse.

In Hyderabad, the agrarian surplus generated by a feudal social structure did not get mobilised for industrial development despite state intervention. As in any feudal social order, wealth invariably centred around land. The ownership of land also conferred social prominence and unfettered power over vast masses of people. In such a context, who could have assumed the leadership of a dynamic industry? Not the subordinate brokers and bankers of colonial trade who would find keeping idle cash more profitable than any investments, nor the landlords or money lenders who, because of colonial trade, would find land and agrarian trade more profitable than industrial investment. Thus it was the state, through a combination of civil servants and *jagirdars* that assumed the leading role in industrial development.

The role played by the state in Hyderabad should not be

underestimated even though it remained limited in its significance. In many respects it anticipated the features of the policies that later came to be identified with the postcolonial state, and its idea of development. The civil servant-*jagirdar* social group was ideally suited to serve as an instrument of these policies. If their background as *jagirdars* gave them the strength to pursue a course of development, their function as civil servants shaped its policies, and as in any elitist approach to economic development, the elite bureaucracy grew in importance. It was this small group, tied by caste, religion, social status and kinship that managed to advance a programme of industrial development. At an informal level, their working was very much 'akin to the working of a joint stock company where collective security enhanced individual initiative' as a perceptive scholar described a similar kind of a situation in eighteenth century Prussia.[1] But this group was part of a feudal ethos that was ideologically incapable of what is often referred to as entrepreneurship. If anything, the civil servants-*jagirdars* were the antithesis of a Schumpeter entrepreneur. The abject failure, at a managerial level, of Hyderabad companies, despite more favourable circumstances as compared with Indian companies in British India, is eloquent testimony to the feudal ethos.

This business climate was derived from the feudal social order and the political structure based on it. In the context of a resolute defence of the old order what appears to be a modernist approach loses its meaning. Thus the process of industrialisation in a feudal social order loses its progressive connotations. The bourgeoisie, to the extent that they can emerge as an independent social group becomes complementary, rather than antagonistic, to the feudal lords. In fact, both materially and ideologically, they are organically linked with each other. In a different context, the early nineteenth century classical political economist, Marx said of Malthus that he 'wants bourgeois production in so far as it is not revolutionary, in so far as it not a historical force, but materially creates a broader and more convenient material basis for the old society.'[2] Perhaps there is no better description of the industrial programme of the state in Hyderabad. The constraints on industrial growth in that sense were located not in state policy but in the 'old society'. The forces unleashed by the imperial economy had no potential to propel larger social transformation, because maintaining the 'old society' was in the political as well as economic interest of the empire. Hyderabad state or sections of its bureaucracy had recurring tensions with the colonial power. But these skirmishes cannot be deemed anti-imperialist in their character. In fact, anti-imperialism in a social framework which maintains colonial domination through a feudal social base, has no meaning unless it is also simultaneously anti-feudal.

Thus, in a sense the particular social structure becomes the ultimate constraint on industrial growth whatever the favourable factors, because social structure gets reflected in the relations of power between groups and classes in society. But very often the social structure is confused with a set of input-output relations. It is now widely believed for instance, that changes in technology or market structure can by themselves, *autonomously*, bring changes in the social structure. Such an approach denies the adaptability and resilience of the relations of power and hence also the role of politics.

If it is possible to reach one general conclusion from our above account, it is that in the context of given power-relations, industrialisation has no historical significance to social development. In such circumstances, industrialisation represents the future only in its form, but in its essence it signifies the continuation of a past, as the peasants of Telangana must have realised, as they faced the armed might of the state both before and after the fall of the regime. In an extended sense the question, from the viewpoint of the oppressed people, is not what is development but what happens to the development process in a society where the power relations that subjugate them remain essentially the same. I regret the relevance of this conclusion to postcolonial India.

Notes

1. Herbert Kisch, *Prussian Mercantilism and the Rise of the Krefeld Silk Industry: Variations upon an Eighteenth Century Theme*, The American Philosophical Society, Philadelphia, 1968, p. 21.
2. Karl Marx, *Theories of Surplus Value*, Part III, Progress Publishers, Moscow, 1971, p. 52.

Bibliography

I. Note on Sources

The primary sources for this work are essentially government publications. In addition to the bias and limitations that are common to all official publications, in the case of Hyderabad the availability of material is an acute problem. In many cases, even where material was published, it was not traceable in the Archives or anywhere else. The sources listed below, however, are available at the Andhra Pradesh State Archives, Hyderabad. A few of the sources are available in Hyderabad at the Interim Repository of Andhra Pradesh State Archives, Secretariat, Library of the Salar Jung Museum, State Central Library, Nizamat Jung Memorial Library, Library of the Institute of Economics and Library of Osmania University.

1. General Administration Reports (GAR): Officially called *The Report on the Administration of H.E.H The Nizam's Dominions*, the GARs are a prolific source of information on various aspects of the economy and society in Hyderabad. Although, generally, they were annual reports, sometimes, the reports of a few years were combined into one volume. No reports were published in 1889–1892 or in 1942–48. Otherwise the reports were published and are available.
2. Statistical Abstracts (SA): Initially, in 1911–1931, decennial Abstracts were published. Later, they were published annually as *Agricultural, Industrial and Trade Statistics* upto 1934 and as the *Statistical Year Book* later on. Sometimes, as in 1941–45, combined issues were published. No issues are available for 1945–49.
3. Agricultural Statistics (AS): Statistics relating to agriculture were published regularly from about 1926. They were published, in different volumes, as *Notes and Estimates of Area and Yield of Crops in Hyderabad.* Both for the earlier period and for the years for which

the AS are not available, we have used the data available in SA and GAR. The Government of India's 'Indian Agricultural Statistics', also included Hyderabad state in later years.

4. Trade Statistics (TS): Separate trade statistics are available for the period 1932–1948. We have supplemented the data from GAR and SA for other years.
5. Industrial Statistics (IS): There were only two volumes covering the periods, 1935–40 and 1940–45, respectively. However we were only able to locate the later volume. The reference to IS in the present work is only to this volume. Hence no mention of the year.
6. CID Publications: The Commerce and Industries Department was set up in 1918. Matters relating to the Industries Department, prior to that period, were under the Revenue Department, some of whose material is available in the Interim Repository of State Archives. The Commerce and Industries Department published annual reports, sometimes bringing out combined issues. Officially called *The Report of the Administration of Commerce and Industries Department of H.E.H The Nizam's Government*, the reports were published more or less regularly, except during the WW II period. These reports are referred to as CIDAR, in our text.

   In addition, the Department published a series of bulletins on various industries. these include the ITF-sponsored surveys. We have consulted about twenty such bulletins or survey reports. They are listed under individual authors below.

   The transfer list of the State Archives, or the Index of Commerce and Industries Department Files lists about 3000 files both in Urdu and English (CIDF). We have referred to them with the index number of the Transfer List which includes the year along with the title of the file, if there was a title.
7. Factories and Boilers Inspection Department's Annual Reports (FBIDAR): The Annual *Report on the Administration of Factories and Boilers Inspection Department of H.E.H The Nizam's Government*, are available for the period 1931–1948, again with the exception of the WW II years.
8. The Hyderabad Companies Act Annual Reports (HCCAR): Although the Act was passed in 1910, the Annual *Report on the Administration of Hyderabad Companies Act of H.E.H The Nizam's Dominions* was published only, it appears, from 1920. We were able to locate only a few Reports. As in other cases, we have supplemented the data with figures given in the SA.

II. Official Publications

A. Hyderabad

A-I: Collective

1. A Preliminary Note on the Iron Ore Resources in the Hyderabad State, 1940.
2. The Chronology of Modern Hyderabad, 1720–1890, Central Records Office, 1954.
3. First Five Year Plan, 1946.
4. Financial Statistics (1301–1359 F), 1951.
5. Hyderabad Banking Enquiry Committeee Report (HBECR), 1931.
6. Hyderabad Relations with the Dominion of India, 1948.
7. Industrial Trust Fund Secretariat, 1929–1949, ITF, 1950.
8. Papers Pertaining to the Proposal of the Federal Finance Committee, 1932.
9. Post-War Planning Incorporating the First Five Year Plan (First Draft), 1944.
10. Prospectus of Cottage Industries Institute, 1938.
11. Report of the Agrarian Reforms Committee, 1949.
12. Report on the Conditions of Factory Labour in Hyderabad State (Rege Committee), 1949.
13. Report of the Hyderabad Co-operative Finance Enquiry Committee, 1937.
14. Report of the Hyderabad Factory Commission, 1922.
15. Report of the Hyderabad Land Commission, 1956.
16. Report on Labour Census, 1935 and 1940.
17. Report of the Reforms Committee (Aravamudu Iyengar Committee), 1938.
18. Report of the Tenancy Enquiry Committee, 1940.
19. Report on the Working of Co-operatives in H.E.H. The Nizam's Dominions, Various Issues.

A-II: Individual Authors

1. Bharucha, S.M. *Agricultural Indebtedness in H.E.H. The Nizam's Dominions, 1937.*

2. Bilgrami, S.H. — *History of the Operations of H.H. The Nizam's Education Department of Last Thirty Years, Together with a Detailed Report and Returns for 1883–84–85, 1886.*
3. Furer Haimendorf, C. von — *Tribal Hyderabad*, 1945.
4. Guthrie, A. — *Report on the Hides and Leather Industries Survey in Hyderabad State, CID*, 1931.
5. Hasan, K.H. — Report on the Working of the Industrial Laboratory, CID, 1929.
6. Inuganti, N.N. — *The Manufacture of Glue, CID*, 1924.
7. Iyengar, S.K. — *Economic Investigations in Hyderabad State, 1929–30 (5 Vols.), 1931.*
8. ——— — *Rural Economic Enquiries in Hyderabad State: 1949–51, 1951.*
9. ——— — *A Review of Hyderabad Finance, 1951.*
10. Karan Bahadur, R.R. — *Industries in Malwala Estate, 1941*
11. Khan, Y.H. (ed.) — *Farmans and sanads of Deccan Sultans (1408–1687)*, State Archives, 1980.
12. Mirza Khurshid — *A brief Outline of the Geographical history of Hyderabad State with Special reference to its Mineral Resources*, 1943.
13. Mohammad, Gulam — Report on Economic Civil Service.
14. Mohammad Gulam Ali — *Handicrafts Industries in H.E.H. The Nizam's Dominions* (1346 F) 1937.
15. Munn, Leonard — *The Geology and Economic Minerals of H.H. The Nizam's Dominions*, 1915.
16. Palmer, George — Report on the Operations of H.H. The Nizam's Public Works and Allied Department (1277–1293 F), 1885.
17. Pillai, N.K.P. — Report on Silk Industries, CID, 1930.
18. Raman, C.V. et al. — Report on the Working of Industrial Laboratory, CID, 1934.
19. Rao, Binod U. — *Hyderabad Reborn: First Six Months of Freedom, 1949.*

20. Sahai, P. — Survey of Handlooms and Dyeing Industries, CID, 1933.
21. Sen, M.K. and Talwarkar, T.W. — Report on the Prospects of Glass indutry in the State, CID, 1932.
22. Slaughter, E.W. — *Godavari Industrial and Agricultural Development Plan, 1944.*
23. Srivatsav, K.C. — Report on the Prospects of Sugar Factory in the Nizam Canal Area, CID, 1934.
24. Taraporewala, K.B. — Report on the Proposed Establishment of a Central Bank of Hyderabad (confidential), 1947.
25. Temple, Richard — Report on the Administration of the Government of H.H. The Nizam in Deccan, 1868.
26. Visweswarayya, M. et al. — City Improvement Schemes, CID, 1930.
27. Wakefield, W.A. — *A Note on Industrial Potentialities of Hyderabad, 1917.*
28. Yuill, A.F. — Report on the Vegetable Oil Industries in Hyderabad State, CID, 1930.

Journals

Ilm-o-Amal, Journal devoted to industrial activities, in Urdu. Seems to have had a brief life in 1927–1930.

Numaish, Journal devoted to industrial activities, in Urdu. Ceased publication after a few issues in 1930–31.

Mulki Industries, Monthly published, by Industrial Exhibition society with the help of CID, irregularly in 1934–1940.

Hyderabad Government Bulletin of Economic Affairs (*HGBEA*), Published in the period 1947–1955.

B: Government of India, Calcutta/Delhi

B-II: Collective

1. All India Rural Credit Survey, District Monograph; Osmanabad, Reserve Bank of India, Bombay, 1957.
2. Census, 1881–1951.

3. Occupational Pattern of Indian Union, 1901–1951, Planning Commission, 1951.
4. Report of the Indian States Committee, 1929.
5. Report on the Joint Stock Companies in British India and Indian states, Various Issues.
6. White Paper on Hyderabad, 1948.
7. White Paper on the Indian States, 1952.

B-II: Individual Authors

1. Crawford, J.A. *Precis of Correspondence Regarding Railways in Native States*, Foreign Department Press, Calcutta, 1884.
2. Mehadi Khan, Mirza Imperial Gazetteer of India, Provincial Series, Hyderabad State, Calcutta, 1909.
3. Prasad, S.N. *Operation Polo: The Police Action in Hyderabad—1948*, Historical Section, Ministry of Defence, 1972.

C. Secondary Sources

C-I: General

1. Bagchi, A.K. *Private Investment in India: 1990–1939* (1972), Orient Longman, New Delhi (Reprint), 1980.
2. Balkrishna, R. *Industrial Development of Mysore*, Bangalore, 1940.
3. Chattopadhyay, R. 'An Early British Government Initiative in the Genesis of Indian Planning', *Economic and Political Weekly*, Vol. XXII, No. 5, 31 January 1987, pp. 19–29.
4. Das, Durga (ed.) Sardar Patel's Correspondence (Vol. 7).
5. Gadgil, D.R. *The Industrial Evolution of India in Recent Times: 1860–1939* (Fifth Edition), Oxford University Press, Delhi, 1972.
6. Jeffrey, Robin (ed.) *People, Princes and Paramount Power: Society and Politics in Indian Princely States*, Oxford, Delhi, 1978.

7. Kaye, J.W. — *Life of Charles Metcalfe* (2 Vols), Smith and Elder, London, 1858.
8. Kisch, Herbert — *Prussian Mercantilism and the Rise of the Krefeld Silk Industry: Variations upon an Eighteenth Century Theme,* The American Philosophical Society, Philadelphia, 1968.
9. Kumar, Dharma (ed.) — *Cambridge Economic History of India, Vol. 2, 1757–1970,* Orient Longman, Delhi, 1982.
10. Mahadevan, Raman — 'Some Aspects of Pattern of Industrial Investment and Entrepreneurship in Travancore During the 1930s and the 1940s', Paper presented at the seminar on 'South Indian Economy, 1914–1945'. Centre for Development Studies, Trivandrum, April, 1988.
11. Marx, Karl — *Capital, Vol. I,* Progress Publishers, Moscow, 1970.
12. Morris, D. Morris — *Private Investment in the Indian Sub-Continent: 1900–1939*; some Methodological Considerations, Modern Asian Studies, Vol. 8, No. 4, October, 1974.
13. ——— — 'The Growth of Large Scale Industry' in Dharma Kumar (ed.), *Cambridge Economic History of India, Vol. 2, 1982,* pp. 553–676.
14. Raychaudhuri, T. — *Jan Company in Coromandel, 1650–1690: A Study in the Inter-Relations of European Commerce and Traditional Economics,* S. Grave, The Hague, 1962.
15. Raychaudhuri, T. and Irfan, Habib (ed.) — *Cambridge Economic History of India, Vol. I, 1200–1750,* Orient Longman, Delhi, 1984.
16. Ray, R.K. — *Industrialisation in India: Growth and Conflict in the Private Corporate Sector, 1914–47,* Oxford, Delhi, 1982.
17. Sen, S.P. (ed.) — *Historical Biography in Indian Literature,* Institute of Historical Studies, Calcutta, 1979.

18. Shyam, Radhe — *Life and Times of Malik Amber*, Motilal Banarasi Das, Delhi, 1968.

19. Tharakam, P.K.M. — 'An Enquiry into the Historical Isaac, T.M.T. Roots of Industrial Backwardness of Kerala—A Study of Travancore Region'. Paper presented at the Seminar on 'Industrialisation of States in India', Department of Economics, University of Hyderabad, August 1987.

20. Tomlinson, B.R. — *The Political Economy of the Raj, 1914–1947: The Economics of Decolonisation in India*, Macmillan, London, 1979.

C-II: Hyderabad

1. Ahmed Khan, Muneer — Muslim Politics in Hyderabad, Unpublished Doctoral Dissertation, Department of Political Science, Osmania University, Hyderabad, 1980.

2. Ahmed, Zahir — *Life's Yesterdays: Glimpses of Sir Nizamat Jung and His Times*, Thackar, Bombay, 1945.

3. ——— — *Dusk and Dawn in Village India*, Praeger, New York, 1965.

4. Aleem, Shamim — *Personnel Management in a Princely State*, Gitanjali Publishers, New Delhi, 1985.

5. Balagopal, K. — 'Telangana Movement Revisited', *Economic* and Political Weekly, Vol. XVIII, No. 18, 30 April 1983, pp. 708–712.

6. Barton, P.W. — Crisis in Hyderabad, *National Review*, 131, 1948, pp. 25–28.

7. Bawa, V.K. — *The Nizam Between Mughals and British; Hyderabad Under Salar Jung I*, S. Chand & Co., New Delhi, 1986.

8. Bilgrami, S.H. and C. Willmott — *Historical and Descriptive Sketch of H.H. The Nizam's Dominions (2 Vols.)*, Times of India Press, Bombay, 1883.

9. Brahma, D.K. — 'Sugar Production in Hyderabad', *HGBEA*, Hyderabad, June–July, 1951.

10. Briggs, H.G. — *The Nizam, His History and Relations with the British Government (2 Vols) 1861*, Reprint, Manas Publications, Delhi, 1985.

11. Campbell, C.A. — *Glimpses of the Nizam's Dominions,* C.B. Burrow, London, 1898.

12. Chari, Govindaraja — Role of the State of Hyderabad in the Uprising of 1857, Unpublished Doctoral Dissertation, Department of History, Andhra University, Waltair, 1972.

13. Chaturvedi, B.M. — *Descriptive Atlas of Hyderabad*, Indian Press, Allahabad, 1956.

14. Chirag Ali, M. — *Hyderabad Under Salar Jung (4 Vols)*, Bernard Quaritch, London, 1885.

15. Chowdary, N.G. — *British Relations with Hyderabad (1798–1843),* University of Calcutta, Calcutta, 1964.

16. Futehally, Zeenuth — *Zora*, Bombay, 1951.

17. Fathulla Khan, M. — *A History of Administrative Reforms in Hyderabad State*, New Hyderabad Press, Secundarabad, 1935.

18. Fukuzawa, H. — 'Agrarian Relations and Land Revenue: Medieval Deccan and Maharashtra' in Raychaudhuri and Habib (ed.), *Cambridge Economic History of India, Vol. I, 1200–1750,* Orient Longman, Delhi, 1984.

19. Furer Haimendorf, C. von — *Tribal Hyderabad*, 1945.

20. Gowr, Rajbahadur, et al. — *The Glorious Telangana Armed Struggle,* Communist Party, New Delh, 1973.

21. Hammed, S.A. — 'Industrial Pattern of Telangana: A Geographical Analysis', *The Indian Geographical Journal*, Vol. XXXVI, No. 2, April–June, 1962, pp. 45–54.

22. Hamumantha Rao, M. *telanganalo andhrabhyudayam* (Telugu), Andhra Chandrika Granthmala, Hyderabad, 1949.

23. Hasan, Abid Syed *Whither Hyderabad?*, Nizam's Subjects League, Madras, 1935.

24. Hussain, S.B. 'Hand-made Paper Industry in H.E.H. The Nizam's Dominions in the 18th and 19th Centuries', First Deccan History Congress Proceedings, Hyderabad, 1945, pp. 350–52.

25. Iyengar, S.K. Central Banking in Hyderabad, *Economic Journal*, 53, 1945, pp. 274–80.

26. -do- Working of the Departmentalisation Scheme of Finance in Hyderabad During 18 years, *Indian Journal of Economics*, July, 1942, pp. 24–25.

27. Jussawala, M.F. Industrial Finance in the Former Hyderabad State, 1941–1956, Unpublished Doctoral Dissertation, Department of Economics, Osmania University, Hyderabad, 1961.

28. Khan, Y.H. *The First Nizam: Life and Times of Nizamul Mulk Asaf Jah I*, Asia Publishing House, Bombay, 1963.

29. Khode, Achyut (ed.) *The People's Movement in Hyderabad*, no publisher, Nanded, 1947.

30. Khusro, A.M. *The Economic and Social Effects of Jagirdari Abolition and Land Reforms*, Osmania University, Hyderabad, 1958.

31. Kulkarni, K. *hyderabadu ajanata charitra putalu* (Telugu), Navbharathi, Hyderabad, 1979.

32. Laik Ali, Mir *Tragedy of Hyderabad*, Pakistan Cooperative Book Society, Karachi, 1962.

33. Latif, Bilkees *Her India: The Fragrance of Forgotten Years*, Arnold Heinemann, Delhi, 1984.

34. Leonard, K.I. 'The Deccani Synthesis in Old Hyderabad: A Historiographic Essay', *Pakistan Historical Society Journal*, 21, 1973, pp. 205–18.

35. K.I. Leonard — 'Hyderabad: The *Mulki*–non-*Mulki* Conflict', in Jeffrey (ed.), 1978.

36. ——— — *Social History of An Indian Caste: The Kayasthas of Hyderabad*, University of California Press, Berkeley, 1978.

37. Lyton, H.R. and Rajan, M. — *The Days of the Beloved: Life and Times of Mehbub Ali Pasha*, University of California Press, Berkeley, 1974.

38. Madhava Rao, P. — Industrial Development of Hyderabad, Unpublished Doctoral Dissertation, Nagpur University, Nagpur, 1956.

39. Madhava Rao, P. Sethu — *Eighteenth Century Deccan*, Popular Prakashan, Bombay, 1963.

40. Mehadi Ali, M.S. — *Hyderabad Affairs (12 Vols.)*, Times of India Press, Bombay, 1886.

41. Mirza, Fareed — *Pre and Post Police Action Days in the Erstwhile Hyderabad State*, no publisher, Hyderabad, 1976.

42. Munshi, K.M. — *End of an Era*, Bharatiya Vidya Bhavan, Bombay, 1957.

43. Muttalib, M.A. — *The Administration of Justice Under the Nizams, 1724–1947*, Unpublished Doctoral Dissertation, Department of Political Science, Osmania University, Hyderabad, 1957.

44. Nagraj, A. — *Nationalised Road Transport in Hyderabad State (1932–1956)*, Unpublished Doctoral Dissertation, Department of Economics, Osmania University, Hyderabad, 1967.

45. Narayan, B.K. — *Agricultural Development in Hyderabad State, 1900–1956*, Kesav Prakashan, Secunderabad, 1960.

46. ——— — *A Survey of Industries in Telangana*, Kesav Prakashan, Secunderabad, 1962.

47. ——— — *Finances and Fiscal Policy of Hyderabad State (1900–1956)*, Government of Andhra Pradesh, Hyderabad, 1973.

48. Narsimgarao, M. *ebhai samstarala hyderabadu* (Telugu), Narsimgarao Smarak Samiti, Hyderabad, 1977.

49. Narayana Reddy, R. *veera telangana: anubhavalu - inapakalu* (Telugu), Andhra Communist Samiti, Vijayawada, 1972.

50. Nawaj Jung, Moin *Hyderabad Under Military Occupation*, Karwan-i-Adab, Karachi, 1951.

51. Nayeem, M.A. *Mughal Administration of Deccan Under Nizamul Mulk Asaf Jah (1720–48)*, Jaico, Bombay, 1985.

52. Neogy, Ajit 'British Role in the Selection of Nizam's *Diwan* in Nineteenth Century', *Quarterly Review of Historical Studies*, Vol. XI, No. 3, 1972.

53. Pavier, Barry *The Telangana Movement, 1944–51*, Vikas, New Delhi, 1981.

54. Pershad, Satguru *farkundah bunyad hyderabad* (Urdu), Hyderabad, 1964.

55. Prasad, Rajendra *The Asaf Jahis of Hyderabad: Their Rise and Decline*, Vikas, New Delhi, 1984.

56. Qureshi, A.I. Note on the Financial System of Hyderabad, *Indian Journal of Economics*, April 1940, pp. 668–77.

57. ——— A Planned Economy for Hyderabad, *Indian Journal of Economics*, July 1940, pp. 83–100.

58. ——— *Economic Development of Hyderabad State, Vol. I (Rural Economy)*, Orient Longman, Bombay, 1947.

59. Rahman Khan, M.A. *My Life and Experiences*, Hyderabad, 1951.

60. Rajeswara Rao, Ch. et al. *buswamya vidhanam radduki rytula virochita tirugubatu* (Telugu), Andhra Communist Samiti, Vijayawada, 1973.

61. Ramakrishna Reddy, V. *Economic History of Hyderabad State, Warangal Suba, 1911–1950*, Giani Publishing House, New Delhi, 1987.

62. Rao, D.V. et al. — *neti hyderabadu-mana kartavyam* (Telugu), Prajasakthi, Bezawada (Vijayawada), 1944.

63. Ray, Bharati — 'Salar Jung, Berar and the British', *Calcutta Historical Journal*, 2, July–December 1977, pp. 102–113

64. -do- — 'The Genesis of Railway Development in Hyderabad State: A Case Study of Nineteenth Century British Imperialism', *Indian Economic and Social Historical Review*, Vol. XXI, No. 1, 1984, pp. 45–69.

65. Razvi, S.M.J. — *hyderabadu samstanamlo rajakiya chaitanyam, vidyarthi yuvajanula patra*, 1939–1956 (Telugu), Vishalandhra, Vijayawada, 1986.

66. Regani, Sarojini — *Nizam-British Relations, 1724–1857*, Book Lovers, Hyderabad, 1963.

67. -do- — 'The Appointment of *Diwans* in Hyderabad State (1803–1887)', *Andhra Historical Research Society Journal*, Vol. XXV, 1960, pp. 11–18.

68. Richards, J.F. — *Mughal Administration in Golconda*, Oxford University Press, London, 1975.

69. Sastry, V.V. — *hyderabad prajala swatantra poratam* (Telugu), Desi Kavita Mandali, Bezwada (Vijayawada), 1947.

70. Sathyanarayana, K. — *andhrula sanskriti-charitra* (Telugu), Hyderabad Book Trust, Hyderabad, 1982.

71. Sawhney, K. — *Cotton Growing in Hyderabad State (Vol. I)*, G. Claridge & Co., Bombay, 1936.

72. Sherwani, H.K. — *History of the Qutub Shahi Dynasty*, Munshiram Manoharlal, New Delhi, 1974.

73. Smith, W.C. — 'Hyderabad—A Muslim Tragedy', *The Middle East Journal*, 4 (1950), pp. 27–51.

74. Sundaram, Lanka — *Hyderabad, Our Diseased Limb*, Sarvodaya Sahitya Parishad, Delhi, 1948.

75. Sundarayya, P — *The Telangana People's Struggle and Its Lessons*, Communist Party of India (Marxist), Calcutta, 1972.

76. Talpallikar, M.B. — Life and Labour of Women Workers in Bellampalli Mines, *Indian Journal of Social Work*, 9 (1948), pp. 208–17.

77. Thapar, Romesh — *Storm Over Hyderabad*, Kutub, Bombay, 1947.

78. Tiratha, S.R. — *Memoirs of the Hyderabad Freedom Struggle*, Popular Prakashan, Bombay, 1967.

79. Tirumali, I. — Aspects of Agrarian Relations in Telangana, 1928–1948, Unpublished M.Phil Dissertation, Centre for Historical Studies, Jawaharlal Nehru University, New Delhi, 1979.

80. Tyabji, B. — Memoirs of an Egotist, (Vol. I, 1907–1956), Roli Books, New Delhi, 1988.

81. Vithal Rao, M. — *Bustn-i-Asafia* (Vol. I), (Urdu), Hyderabad, 1909.

82. Yar Jung, Ahsan — *Manufacture of Steel in H.H. The Nizam's Dominions by the Direct process*, Nizam Silver Jubilee Press, Hyderabad, 1943.

83. Yazdani, Ghulam — *Bidar: Its History and Monuments*, Oxford University Press, London, 1947.

84. Yazdani, Zubaida — *Hyderabad During the Residency of Henry Russel, 1811–1820: A Case Study of the Subsidiary Alliance System*, University Press, Oxford, London, 1976.

85. Wadiar, M. Laxmi — The Impact of Nizam Sugar Factory on Bodhan Taluq, Unpublished M.A. Thesis, Department of Economics, Osmania University, Hyderabad, 1963.

86. Zinkin, Taya — *Reporting India*, Chatto and Windus, London, 1962.

C-III: Organisations and Collectives

1. All India Industrial Exhibition Society — *Industries in Hyderabad*, Hyderabad, 1950.
2. Andhra Pradesh State Committee for the Compilation of the History of Freedom Movement in Hyderabad — *Freedom Struggle in Hyderabad (IV Vols.)*, Hyderabad, 1956–1966.
3. Guntaka Narasayya Pantulugari Shastipurti Utsava Sangam — *cheneta udyama pitạmaha abhinandana grantham* (Telugu), Hyderabad, 1964.
4. Hyderabad Struggle Committee, Socialist Party — *The Hyderabad Problem: The Next Step*, Bombay, 1948.

Glossary

Adabapa	Concubine
Adalat-e-fauzdari	Basic critical courts of judicature since the reforms in 1864.
Adam-patti	A tax levied on all groups of artisans in *jagir* areas.
Agraharam	Village or part of a village granted to Brahmins and held either as rent-free or at reduced rates of assessment.
Babe Hukumat	Executive Council, formed in 1921 with power of overall administration of the state.
Bhagela	Serf, or bonded labour. Generally prevalent in Telangana.
Chaudari	Trader or head of the traders.
Dadani	Advance contract system under which cash or raw materials were advanced to local traders or artisans in return for the supply of manufactured goods in a stipulated time at prefixed rates. Introduced into the Deccan by Dutch traders.
Daftar-i-diwani	Office of the revenue administration, prior to the reforms undertaken by Salar Jung.
Daftar-i-mal	Office of accounts, prior to the reforms.
Daftardar	Heads of these two offices. Usually hereditary occupants.
Dar-ul-insha	Office of official correspondence.
Dar-ul-jahad	Land of war. Aurangazeb's description of Hyderabad.

Deshi	Native, as in Deshi literature. Distinct from Sanskrit based *marga* literary tradition.
Deshmukh	Hereditary officer exercising revenue authority who over time became landowner.
Deshpande	Principal revenue officer of the district who over time became landowner, like the *Deshmukhs*.
Diwan	Prime Minister.
Diwani	Office of the *diwan*. In land tenure, *diweani* territories were those under the direct change of the *diwan*.
Farman	Order or mandate. A royal grant or charter. Golden *farman* granted to European traders permitted them to trade anywhere in the state.
Farman-e-mubarak	Government order.
Fauz-e-baiquda	Irregular Troops of the Nizam State.
Gasti	Regulation.
Hali Sicca	Literally 'current coin'. This coinage was introduced by Salar Jung in 1857. It was valued at about 15 per cent less than the British Indian government Rupee. It was replaced by *Osmania Sicca* in 1912.
Ijara	The system of revenue farming prevalent during the Qutub Shahi period. Later it came to mean the system whereby lands were granted on easy terms.
Inam	Grants of land, for the support of religious leaders or institutions or for other charitable purposes, usually rent-free and in hereditary and perpetual occupation.
Jagir	A tenure introduced by the Mughals in the Deccan by which the revenues of a given tract of land were made over to a servant of the state.
– tankahi mahalat	The *jagirs* granted in lieu of debts or advances made to the state. They became prevalent in late eighteenth century Hyderabad.
Jagirdar	The holder of a *jagir*.
Jeetagadu	Attached farm servant.

Khalisa	Lands under the direct administration of the state. The term was in use during the Qutub Shahi period.
Kunta	Pond.
Madad-i-ma'ash	Same as *inam* grants, in vogue during the Qutub Shahi period.
Mahajan	Trader and moneylender.
Mamul	Customary payment that peasants were/are obliged to pay to the landlord on various occasions.
Mansab	Office, dignity or rank conferred by the king. When introduced in Hyderabad by the Mughals, it carried an obligation to furnish troops. But later the obligation was not customary.
Mansabdar	The holder of a *mansab*, usually *jagirdar*.
Maqta	Stipulated tenure.
Mirasidar	Grantee of the right to collect revenue on a hereditary basis during the Qutub Shahi period.
Mulki	Domicile of the state. A social category whose connotations changed over time. Legally it included a citizen who had resided in Hyderabad state for fifteen years or had been in state government service continuously for at least 12 years.
– *Gair Mulki*	Non-*mulki*.
Muqasadar	Person assigned land, either rent-free or at lower rates, on conditional service, during the Qutub Shahi period.
Naib	Local Chieftain or leader.
Narendra Mandal	Chamber of Princes.
Nazar-pahani	Glance survey. Introduced in the Deccan by Malik Amber.
Nazrana	Gift.
Nizam-ul-mulk	Regulator of the Realm. The title given by the Mughal ruler to his chief representative in Hyderabad.
Osmania Sicca Rupee	The currency of Hyderabad State, valued at about 17 per cent less than B.G. Rupee.

Paighah	Household troops or guards of the Nizam. The *paighah* nobles in the state inter-married with the Nizam's family and acquired considerable power in the state.
Paibaqi	Unassigned lands.
Paishkash	Tribute
Paragana	Similar to a district, in the earlier administrative structure.
Pattadar	Holder of a legal tenure.
Poktadar	Moneychanger.
Rahdari	Transit duties levied on merchandise passing through the respective territories, by the *jagirdars* or the state.
Raja	Usually the king. In Hyderabad the title signified that the holder belonged to the ruling family of one of the five *samsthanams*.
Rajpramukh	Governor of a Part B state, in postcolonial India.
Sahukar	Trader and moneylender.
Samsthanam	A small tendatory state.
Sarbasta	The system of farming out land on a contract basis during the Asaf Jahi period.
Sarf-e-khas	Literally privy purse. Land or revenue assigned to the king for his personal expenditure. Successive measures to reform the revenue system including those by Salar Jung left these territories untouched.
Shikmidar	Protected tenant
– Asami Shikmidar	Tenant-at-will.
Shia	The sect of Muslims who maintain that Hazarat Ali was the only legitimate successor of the holy prophet and reject other *khalifas*. The Qutub Shahi's were Shias.
Sunni	The sect of Muslims who acknowledge all the first four *khalifas* as the rightful successors of the holy prophet. The Asaf Jahis were Sunnis.

Ta-ah-hud	The system of auctioning revenue collection rights to the highest bidder. It came into prominence during the late eighteenth century.
– *Tahuddar*	The holder of the bid.
Takdama	The practice by which peasants were forced to pay a portion of revenue in advance, under threat of eviction.
Taluqdar	Originally revenue collector and general administrator for a taluq. Later also became *jagirdar*.
Tarafdar	Governor of a province.
Ulema	Religious head in Islam.
Vetti	Compulsory labour, or bonded labour.
vettipani	Customary service which all classes of people in the village were (and are) obliged to provide the landlord.
Watandar	Originally holders of official tenure.
Zakat	A tax on merchandise prevalent from the Qutub Shahi period.
Zarida	Official Gazette.

Index

A

administration
  reform of, 28, 145, 146
  see also agrarian revenue collection, civil service, Salar Jung, tenurial system
agrarian
  change, 148–9;
  reforms, 182;
  revenue system, 3, 5, 13, 25–9
  transition, factors in, 170
  economy and world market, 148, 164–5
  see also agriculture, agro-based industries, cash crops, tenurial system
agriculture,
  commercialisation of, 170–5;
  output, 162–3
  prices, 169, 170
agro-based industries, 64–6, 130
  capital, 69, 81, 82;
    changes in, 86;
    growth of, 83, 84–5;
  labour in, 93, 104, 106, 107;
    female labour in, 109;
    growth of labour, 111, 131;
    structure of, 108;
  output, 137–8;
  state aid to, 88–9
Ali Khan, Nizam, 4,
    treaties with British, 4–5, 10
Aligarh Muslim University, 147
  see also civil services
All Hyderabad Trade Union Congress (AHTUC), 98
Alladin, 73
Andhra Bank, 89
Andhra Maha Sabha, 1930, 179–81
animal-based industries, 130
  labour in, 104, 107;
    females among, 109;
    growth of labour, 111, 131;
    structure of labour, 108
Anjuman-e-Tabligh-ul-Islam, 180
armament industry, 9, 20
artisan industry,
  decline in, 102–12, 114;
    reason, 115–7;
  labour in, 93;
  state assistance to, 43–4
Arya Samaj, 180
Asaf Jah dynasty, 4,
Asaf Jah IV, Nizam, 23;
Asaf Jah V, Nizam, 23
Ashan Yar Jung Bahadur, 73, 180

B

Babu Khan, 73
banking and trade, 69–70, 89–92;
capital in, 81, 82,
growth of, 83, 84–5;
changes in, 93
see also moneylenders
Berar, states of, 5, 144, 181
bidriware, 19, 20
biscuit manufacturing, 65
Bohras, 11
British Raj, *see* colonial power, colonial traders, English

C

calendar workers union, 97
capital intensity, 133–4 see industry
carpet manufacture, 17, 43
location, 18
cash crops, export of, 148–9 *see also* cotton
castor, 149, 159–60, 161, 167, 168, 169, 170
cement industry, 66–7
ceramic industries, 66–7, 130
capital, 81, 82
changes in, 86;
growth of, 83, 84–5,
state and, 88
labour, 104,
females among, 109;
growth 106, 107, 111, 131;
output, 139
Central Bank of India, 89
chemical-based industries, 67, 130
capital, 81, 82;
changes in, 86;
growth of, 83, 84–5;
labour in, 93, 104
female, 109;
growth, 106, 107, 111, 131;
structure, 108
cigarette manufacturing, 65 *see* tobacco
civil service, 29–30, 145;
and industry, 73–4, 187–8;
modernisation of, 146–8
see also fendal social system
class struggle, 181 *see also* communists, peasant movement in Telengana, tenurial system
coal mining, 39–40, 63–4
colonial
power and Hyderabad State, 12–3, 143–4;
Traders, 3, 10, 11
Commerce and Industries Department
initiates, 41–2
commercial banks, 90;
crops, 5, 40
commercialisation of agriculture, 170–5
process of, 150–1
Committee on Indebtedness, 1937, 174
committees on economy, 182
commodity markets, 161–70
communal
strife, 11, 180
violence, 181
communalism, 180
communist 180–1
movement in Telengana, 153, 164 *see* peasant movement in Telengana
Party, 181;
trade unions, 98
Congress Party, 179, 181
Constitutional reforms, 179
cooperative Bank, 90
cooperatives, 44
corporate sector, 37, 68–9

capital,
changes in, 86
distribution, 81,
growth, 83–5, 132–3
state financial aid, 45, 87–9, 119–20
cottage Industries,
state assistance to, 43
cotton, 5, 40, 64, 150, 159–60, 161, 165, 167, 168, 169, 170;
commercial importance of 148;
industry, 40, 64–5
credit market,
growth, 148;
structure, 172
see also Banking and Trade
crops, acreage, 159–60
cropping patterns, 161
changes in, 149
currency, 91 *see* Osmania Sikka currency

D

development services, 27, 157–8
diamond mining, 9, 18
location, 19
domestic market, 122–3
Dutch traders, 10

E

education, 147,
establishment and growth, 28
elite in Hyderabad state, 12–3, 145–8;
see civil service, jagirdars, landlords
engineering workshop, 37, 40
English traders, 4, 10 *see also* colonial power
exchange rate, 165
external trade, 121, 127

F

Factories Act, 1930,
provisions and enforcement, 96
and female labour, 110, 113
factory labour 131 *see also* labour, industries
famine, 165
female labour,
industrial, 95–6, 108–110, 113
see also labour
feudal social system
implications of, 7–8
and industrialisation, 187–9
see also jagirdars, tenurial system
First Five Year Plan of Hyderabad State, 50
fiscal policy, 45–6, 146, 182
food crops, 161 *see also* crops
food shortages during WW II, 171
see WW I and WW II
forest-based industries, 66, 82, 130;
labour in, 103, 104;
females, 109;
growth, 107, 111, 131;
structure, 108
French traders, 2, 10 *see also* colonial traders

G

general administration, 157–8 *see also* administration, reform of, Salar Jung
Giri, V. Venkata, 97

Girni Kamgar Union (Textile workers union), 97, *see also* Trade Unions
gold mining, 64
Government of India Act, 1935, 179
Great Depression, effect on prices, 165, 168
groundnut crop, 149, 159–60, 161, 164, 165, 167, 169, 170

H

Handloom industry, 43
 decline in, 115–6
Hindu Civil Liberties Union, 180
Hindu Maha Sabha, 180
Hindu Communalism, 180
Hydari, Akbar, 73
Hyderabad City, importance as trading centre, 21
Hyderabad Political Reforms Association, 1921, 179
Hyderabad state, 3–5
 Bank, 89, 80;
  functions, 90;
 origins, 3–4,
 profile, 59–60, 182
 size and viability, 5, 143–5

I

Imperial Bank of India, 89 *see also* banking and trade
imports into Hyderabad state, 122, 127
industrial
 areas, 45
 capital, sources of, 69–70
  private investment, 70–2;
  state financing, 70;
 establishments, 40;
 laboratory (1917),
  aims of, 44;
  research by, 44–5
 labour, 93–4
  composition, 95;
  occupational structure, 102–5;
  recruitment of, 96;
  wages, 96, 97
  working conditions, 96
  see also labour
industrial output, 134–9;
 policy, 47
 Trust Fund (ITF) (1929), 116, 120;
  aims, 41, 42, 45;
  as source of capital to industry, 70
industrialisation,
 different from British India, 50–4
 evolution, 30–1;
 phases, 37–8
  first, 39–40;
  second, 41–7;
  third, 48–50;
 social framework, 143–5
industrialists
  indigenous, 72–3;
 from British India, 71
industries,
 composition of, 129–31;
 development of, 21;
 list, 19–20;
 location district-wise, 61–2;
 ownership of, 79
industry,
 development of, 148;
 indigenous, 17–8;
 in Hyderabad, 60;
  India, 60;
  Pakistan, 60;
 state finance to, 120–1;
 state policy on, 37;
 structural changes in, 48–9

Indian Army intervention, 181, 182
infrastructure,
development of, 29–30;
industries, 63;
labour in, 93, 103, 105
females, 109;
growth, 107, 112;
structure, 108
output, 135
interim administration, 182
iron and steel industry, 18–9
location, 19
irrigation works, 28, 40, 149
Ittehadual Muslimeen, 180
Iyengar, Aravamudu, 179
Iyengar, Kesav, 115, 116

J

jagirdars, 6,
and industry, 72–4, 187–8
jagirs, 164
abolition of, 182
see also tenurial system
jawar crop, 5, 150, 159–60, 161, 165, 167, 168, 169, 170 see also crops
judicial structure, 28

K

Karnataka, 183
Karnataka Parishad (1937), 179
Khojas, 11
Khusro, A. Mohammad, 152
Komatis, 172
Krishnamachari, T.T., 182

L

labour, 40, 170,
composition,
skilled, 95
unskilled, 95
in industrial sector, 47
occupational structure, 102–5
see also female labour, industries
Laik Ali, 73, 182
Lalbhai, Kasturbhai, 120, 182
Lalbhai Kasturbhai Committee, 133
land
alienation, 179–80
grants, types of, 5–6
revenue collection, 6–8
see also tenurial system
landlords, 170–5;
power of, 152–3
see also jagirdars,
leather industry, 20, 67
levy system, 171, *see* tenurial system
linguistic reorganisation of states, 182–3

M

Maharashtra Parishad (1936), 179
Mahbub Ali Khan, 143
Maimoons, 11
Malik Amber, 6
manufacturing industry,
labour in, 105, 109;
growth of, 106, 107, 111, 112, 131
Marathwada, 172, 183
Marwaris, 11, 90, 172
Marx, Karl, 188
Mazdoor Sevak Sangh, 98
metal and engineering industries, 66, 130
capital, 81, 82
changes in, 86;
growth of, 83, 84–5;

state and to, 88;
labour, 103, 104, 109;
growth, 106, 107, 111, 131,
structure, 108
migrant labour, 95
see also labour
militants and police, 157–8
mills, setting up of, 40
minerals, 63–4;
labour force, 93, 103, 104, 105, 109;
growth, 106, 107, 112;
output, 135–6;
structure, 108
mining and manufacturing companies,
capital, 81, 82;
changes in, 86;
growth, 83, 84–5;
state and, 88–9;
labour, 112
Moin Nawaz Jung, 73, 182
moneylenders, 90–1, 171, 172 *see* credit structure
Montagu-Chelmsford Reforms, 179
Mughal Empire, 3, 6
mulki-non-mulki conflict, 147
Muslim communalism, 180

N

Nanda, Gulzarilal, 182
nationalist movement
and Hyderabad state, 178, 179, 181
nobility, 181 *see* feudal social system, Paigah nobles
Northern Circars, 6, 9

O

oilseeds crop, 5, 65, 148–9, 161, 165, 168, 169
organised industry,
labour force in, 105–7;
growth of 111–2
see also labour, industries
Osman Ali Khan, Nizam, 143, 146, 180
Osmania Sikka currency, 27, 40, 91–2;
abolition of, 182
Osmania University, 147
over capitalisation, 133–4

P

Paigah nobles, 23
origins, 6
Pakistan, 181
emigration to, 181
Pandit Vijayalaxmi, 182
Parsis, 11
Pahl, R.K., 182
peasant movement in Telengana, 98, 175, 189
peasants
cultivators, 170–1;
oppression of, 180;
and tenancy, 171–3
see also landlords, moneylenders, tenurial system
police, 28
political instability in Hyderabad state, 11, 178, 179
Post Office Savings Bank, 90
power industry, 63
labour in, 107, 109,
growth, 112;
output, 135
private investment in industry, 74–5
privatisation of industry, 120
public expenditure, 26, 157–8
Public Works Department, 27–8

Q

Qureshi, Anwar Iqbal, 165, 171
Qutub Shahi dynasty, 3

R

rack-renting, 173–4
Razakars, 181
Reddy, P.V. Rama, 73
Rege Committee on Industrialisation, 182
railways, 37, 39, 40, 47, 63
  establishment of, 27
  labour in, 104, 106, 109,
    growth, 107, 112;
    output, 135
Railway Workers Union, 97
revenue system,
  reform of, 148
rice crop, 5, 159–60, 161, 165, 166, 168, 169, 170
  mills, 40, 65
  rural indebtedness, 172–4 *see also* landlords, moneylenders, tenurial system

S

Salar Jung, 8, 12, 38, 143, 148, 151;
  background, 23;
  infrastructural measures, 39
  personality of, 24–5
  relations with
    aristocracy, 23, 24;
    British, 24, 31
    Nizams Asaf Jah IV and Asaf Jah V, 23–4;
  social restructuring by, 25–8
Salar Jung III, 73
Secunderabad, 4
sesamum crop, 159–60, 161, 167, 168, 169, 170
shipbuilding, 9
  location, 19
small-scale industries, 118–9
  loans to, 42–3, 60–1
social organisation,
  restructuring of, 25–30;
social services, 157–8
social unrest, 11
Standstill Agreement (1947), 181
state,
  revenue, increase in, 26;
  role in industrialisation, 187–8
state-planned economic development, 49–50, 146
strikes, 97–98 *see also* Trade Unions
Subsidiary Alliance, 4, 12
sugarcane crop, 65, 149, 159–60

T

tariff policy, 46–7
Tata group, 71
Tayabjee, Comar, 73
Telengana, 5, 20, 40, 148, 149, 151, 152, 153, 164, 172, 174, 181, 183
Tenancy Committee (1937–8), 171
tenurial system, 5–7, 151–3, 171–4
textiles, 9, 17, 37, 65
  location, 18
  see also handloom
tobacco, 150, 159–60 *see* cigarette
trade, 9–11, 17–21
  mechanism, 26–9
trading communities, 11
trade unions, 97, 181
transport, development of, 148
tribal insurrections, 11–12

V

village-based industry, 17 *see* artisan
Visweswarayya, M., 45

W

wage labour, 98 *see* labour
Wahabi movement, 11
wheat 5, 161, 165, 169, 170 see crops
women workers *see* Female labour
working class, 93–8
WW I and W W II, effect on prices, 52-3, 65–6

Z

Zahid Hussain, 73